Black Mesa

From the Fields to the Garden: The Life of Stitch Duran

Jacob "Stitch"Duran

Zac Robinson

Black Mesa Publishing
Florida

Black Mesa Publishing
Florida
www.blackmesabooks.com

Contents

From the Fields to the Garden: The Life of Stitch Duran

Introduction

BY BAS RUTTEN
SEPTEMBER 2010

I HAVE SEEN JACOB, AKA STITCH, work on fighters, in and out corners, a long time before I met him. Carlos Santana, I always thought that Stitch looked like him. Not the other way around, that would make him older, and I couldn't do that to him in this little "praise" I am writing. Praise I say because that's what pops up in my mind right away, its simple, when you meet Stitch, you like him, he's that guy that everybody likes.

The first time that I had more then just a "hello, how are you doing?" with Stitch, was, I believe, in Japan at the Pride Fighting Championships back in 2000, and since then we have been friends.

Because of the jetlag, everybody from the U.S. would be up early in Japan, so breakfast in the "Tokyo Hilton" was always a happening. All fighters, doctors, trainers, referees, commentators, managers, fighters, etc., would have breakfast in one room and I would always end up sitting at the same table as Stitch. Man, those times were awesome, ask any person who was there at the time and they will tell you the same, "Breakfast at the Tokyo Hilton was the best!" Books could have been written from the stories told there, and Stitch always had great ones, because lets face it, the boxing, Thai Boxing and MMA scene is an interesting one, and he has been in it for a long time!

Of course I have seen him at work on fighters hands and cuts, and I dare you to find ONE guy who doesn't think that he's the best at what he's doing. It's very simple—he's the multiple, zillion time, best cut man and hand wrapper in the business. And because, in this profession, age actually makes you even better, I don't see anybody taking that title away from him.

Godspeed Stitch, and party on!

Prologue

FORREST GRIFFIN BRINGS A FOLDING CHAIR OVER, flips it around backwards, and lowers his 6'3" and 205 pound frame into it. I grab my own chair and pull my gauze, tape, and scissors from my bag

Griffin places his arm on the back of the chair. I adjust my glasses. "You want the knock out wrap or the tap out wrap?" I ask.

A sideways grin flashes on Griffin's face. "Give me the knock out."

With that I go to work. First with the gauze. I start on the top and work my way to the outside, one, two, three times around. Slowly a solid cast forms around Griffin's hand. With each wrap, he knows he is that much closer. His tiny bit of equipment is being formed in front of his eyes and I can see he is thankful that I am the one who is giving him his tools.

Griffin, normally quite the jokester, isn't really in the mood. The fight is running through his head. He's seeing it unfold. Soon he will be in the Octagon with Mauricio "Shogun" Rua. The Pride FC great is making his UFC debut. With a 16-2 record and crushing wins over guys like Quinton Jackson and Alistair Overeem, Shogun is as dangerous as they come.

The right hand is done. Griffin flexes and nods his approval. The process begins again on the left. Another cast of tape forms and I pack it around the hand, more flexing and another nod of approval from Griffin.

The quiet, calm part of my job is complete. We stand and Griffin gives me a hug. "You know I'll take care of you like you're a son," I say.

Another sideways grin. "I know Stitch, thanks."

Octagon at UFC 76

Mauricio "Shogun" Rua peels off his shirt and shoes. I stand a couple steps away and watch as Leon Tabbs applies Vaseline to Shogun's brow. The fighter works his jaw open and closed, a physical sign of the anticipation of combat. Shogun climbs the steps. He circles the Octagon and the lights go out.

The music changes and the lights come back on. Forrest Griffin makes his way cageside. The hair on my arms stands. No matter how many times I've done this, the energy still gets me. Mike Goldberg talks of Forrest's pro debut, a decision loss to Dan Severn, and I begin applying the Vaseline. Griffin stands face stoic as I wipe his left brow, then the right. I then work to the cheeks and nose and finally indicate that I am done. Forrest gets a final check from the referee and joins Shogun in the Octagon.

I head to my seat just outside of the cage and plop down next to fellow cutman Don House and Dana White Sr. We watch the back and forth action and I keep an eye on Griffin's face. Round one passes, Forrest sheds no blood.

In round two, Shogun is in Griffin's guard. Griffin defends well, but with 3:46 remaining Shogun drops a sharp elbow between Forrest's eyes. A river of red appears and I get ready for action. I can tell that this cut is a bad one. With a little less than two minutes in the round Goldberg talks to Rogan about the blood running into Forrest's eye.

I'm prepared. I know that the fight might now be in my hands.

The horn sounds and I meet Griffin before he reaches his stool. I apply pressure with the right hand and guide Forrest with the left. He sits down and I go to work.

I pull the cloth away and see that it's a lightning bolt cut. The skin is split from just above the inside corner of Griffin's right eye and it zigzags to the center of his forehead. It looks terrible, but only I know how deep it is. I also know that Griffin will see my reaction. I have to remain confident, steady, and fast.

The camera shot squeezes between my hands and the world sees the extent of the cut. The crowd groans. Joe Rogan and Mike Goldberg groan as well. Goldberg compliments me by calling me the best.

The world looks on and I do my best to show that Goldberg's compliment is spot on. With my left hand I hold a cotton swab soaked in Adrenaline 1-1000 to the wound. The vessel constrictor works to decrease the blood flow. At the same time I use my right hand to mold Avitene, the coagulant is sticky like cotton candy and I form it to fit the gash. Forrest tilts his head down. "Don't move I need to work on you," I say.

Griffin stays still and I remove the swab and quickly press the Avitene into the trench. The coagulant fills the wound perfectly and I work it into place. The Vaseline and Adrenaline 1-1000 mix is smoothed over the cut and everyone is ushered out of the Octagon. Just less than one minute of furious work. Now we will watch to see if it holds.

The third and final round begins and Forrest is still in the fight. I return to my seat next to Don House and Dana White Sr. and they watch the action. One minute passes, Shogun is in Griffin's guard and the gash is not bleeding. Another minute goes by and Griffin sweeps Shogun rolling into an Omaplata. Almost everyone forgets about the gaping wound because it has not begun bleeding again. House hits me on the shoulder. "It's still not bleeding," he says.

I nod, but don't respond. I don't want to jinx it. Another minute goes by, Griffin is in Shogun's half guard and this time it is Dana White Sr., "Still no blood!"

Now I breathe a little easier. Even if the cut begins to bleed, Griffin will be able to deal with it for the final two minutes.

Shogun is exhausted. He turtles up giving up his back. Griffin pounds away, delivers knees to the body, only a minute remains. I hear Griffin's cornermen, Randy Couture and Mike Pyle, scream for him to posture up as he works for the mount. Again Shogun gives up his back and this time Griffin gets the hooks in. Only a half minute remains. The cut, still dry, is not an issue.

Griffin flattens out Shogun. Referee Steve Mazzagatti crouches close to the fighters. The crowd grows louder. Rogan screams that Rua is in trouble.

Shogun taps on Griffin's leg. Now Goldberg screams that it is over. I run to toward the Octagon

Forrest jumps up and runs across the Octagon, arms flailing in exuberance. I'm the first man in and meet him just inside the gate. He collapses to his knees and I again go to work on the gash. My handiwork between rounds two and three kept his hopes of upsetting Shogun alive, and now I'm cleaning the wound in victory.

Griffin circles the cage and I stand in the middle of it like a proud father. We meet there and I wipe the wound again as he cuts loose with a triumphant yell.

Bruce Buffer makes the call as I wipe off the remaining sweat and blood from Griffin's shoulders. Joe Rogan interviews him and I stand in the background next to Randy Couture. We shake hands. "You did a great job Stitch," he says.

The compliment is particularly meaningful coming from the heavyweight champ. No doubt this moment and this fight is one of my favorites out of the thousands I've been a part of. Through hard work and determination I've risen to an elite level in my exciting profession. UFC 76 demonstrates just how important I, and those like me, can be to the fighters and the sport.

It wasn't always this way. There was a time long ago when people knew me by my given name, Jacob Duran, not Stitch, and I was just another farm worker living in a dirt-poor migrant camp in central California, a farm worker with big dreams.

1

GROWING UP
1950S
HADLEY'S FARM

SOMEBODY WAS STIRRING, taking care to be quiet, but in such close quarters it didn't take much to wake the others. I opened my eyes. They adjusted to the darkness and I saw the silhouette of Tio (Uncle) Miguel as he pulled the blanket back over his bed. Without another sound he left the room and I continued to listen. I heard the deep breathing of my seven brothers and sisters. They were all still asleep, crammed together in the bunk beds in the tiny room.

I heard my mother Maria Inez in the kitchen. The darkness outside of the small window matched the darkness in the room. The sun was still too far away to make even the thinnest of lines on the eastern horizon, but she was already working hard at making tacos to sell to the farm workers who came over on the Bracero program. It granted them special permission to come to the U.S. to work the fields. These workers needed to eat so my mom sold them tacos.

It would be only minutes before my father, Benjamin, came in to rouse us. The fields, the fruit, the vegetables, the cotton, all of them waited patiently, just as they always did. The people in the San Joaquin Valley and more specifically my family and the other eleven families living on Hadley's farm, understood this all too well. Life was centered on those fields. They literally put food on the table.

I knew that soon I would be doing my part by picking my share of cotton, but for now I thought it best to try to get a few more minutes of sleep.

I closed my eyes and Disneyland popped into my head. My friend and neighbor Marcial Ybarra had mentioned the new theme park only a couple hundred miles to the south, and Ralph Gonzalez (we called him Chulo), one of my other best friends, had chimed in that he heard there was a castle there. I thought of this place and wondered what it would be like to go. My thoughts faded and I began to slip back to sleep when I heard my father's soft, but strong voice. "Levanta Te (wake up), we've got work to do."

Despite being exhausted I hopped out of bed and hustled through the already hot kitchen. I said good morning to my mom and pushed through the creaky back door then crossed the yard on the way to the outdoor toilet, careful not to step on chicken shit. With the great number of chickens this task was harder than imagined. All too often I stepped right on the stinky feces and it squished between my toes. To this day the chicken shit smell is fresh in my memory and I don't like chicken because of it.

This time I made it to the restroom without finding a pile of chicken crap. Getting to the toilet in such a hurry was a pain, especially in the winter. But it was even more of a pain when I had to wait for my sister Linda.

Once finished, I returned to the house. Now the sun had managed to cut a line on the horizon, the day would be like so many others, hot, cloudless, and long. My mom had a plate of beans, potatoes, and handmade tortillas ready and poured me a glass of goat milk. "Mom I don't want any goat milk," I said. "It tastes terrible."

The beginnings of a smile appeared on her lips. She knew what I wanted and she added a bit of chocolate then stirred it in. "There that should make it better. Now drink up, it's good for you. Besides, you know your little brother is allergic to cow's milk."

I knew that Ernie was allergic, but didn't see why everyone else had to drink goat's milk. At least the chocolate made the taste somewhat bearable, and I knew I'd have to drink it anyway.

With a belly full of goat milk I was soon in the cotton fields. My big brothers grabbed their six foot long burlap sacks and my dad handed me an empty five pound flour sack. "When do I get a big sack dad?" I said.

"It won't be long son," he replied.

One after another I picked cotton bolls. Sometimes I had to reach in with all five of my small fingers and they got scratched and cut by the plant. There wasn't anybody to cry to, just more cotton to pick. I kept at it as the sun found its place high in the empty sky and scorched the fields. I kept at it and imagined what it would be like to see that castle at Disneyland. I wondered if the rest of the world was similar to Hadley's farm. If not, I wondered what it was like.

The cotton picking was hard, but there was a reward at the end of the day. In order to empty the sacks, my dad, the foreman of Hadley's farm, set up a plank across the trailer. We kids balanced along the plank and then dumped the cotton into the container. By days end it was nearly full and I asked my dad, "Can we jump in?"

He always let me and soon my friends jumped in too. We rolled around and played in the cotton for a few minutes. It wasn't Disneyland, but it is what we had, and it seemed pretty good. After all, what can a kid born on a migrant camp with a birth certificate and address that reads California Packing Corporation #12 expect?

THE CANAL

The fields dominated everyone's lives, but that didn't mean there wasn't some time to play too. Besides the cotton trailer at the end of a tough day, we also had the canal. The water was a lifeline for the San Joaquin agricultural industry. It was also the main source of fun.

In the winter it was drained, leaving nothing more than a trickle. As the valley shook off the cold, it was filled once again. It was on one of these days that Marcial and I played in the canal. We were just six years old and had our long pants rolled up to our knees. We were kicking the puddles of water, throwing rocks, and arguing about who had the best arm, when we heard a low rumble in the distance.

"Weird time for the planes to be spraying poison," Marcial said.

The fields were doused in it, so much so that our family still jokes that mosquitoes won't bite us anymore because we're so loaded with pesticide. But this wasn't a plane. I grabbed Marcial's arm. "It's the water. They're filling the canal."

We scampered up the side and stood on the bank with moments to spare. The wall of water churned closer and I saw the shoes were still below. "Go get the shoes, go get the shoes!" I said.

"No way, you go get them," Marcial said.

Losing a pair of shoes wasn't a good idea when you didn't have a closet full of them. I checked the water and took a step down the bank. I thought I could make it. I took another step. The water thundered now as it splashed up the canal's sides and I realized there was no way. "There's not enough time," I said over the rumble.

"I'll get them." Marcial said and took a hesitant step down the bank.

"It's too dangerous," I said and grabbed his shoulder

A few seconds later the water crashed in front of us. The shoes were swept away and we ran along the bank between the water and the cotton field trying to catch sight of them, but they were long gone. We returned home to tell our parents what happened. They wouldn't be happy, but we figured it was better that it was the shoes and not Marcial or me being washed away. Our parents probably agreed, but we couldn't tell by the punishment we received.

A few months later I was involved in another incident at the canal. A large group of kids splashed and played in our backyard swimming pool as we liked to call it. We roughhoused, tossing each other around the slabs of cement that worked with the pumps to send water to different canals. Jimmy, my oldest brother by seven years, pushed me into the water. My right hip caught the corner of one of the slabs and as I swam to the surface I felt the stinging pain of an open wound.

I hobbled to the bank, trying to fight off tears because I didn't want to cry in front of the bigger kids. "Come on," Jimmy said. "It isn't that bad."

I was mad at myself because my lip quivered and a few tears ran down my cheeks as I lowered my shorts. Everyone gasped at the quarter-sized area oozing a steady stream of blood. "Oh man, I better go tell mom," Jimmy said.

He started off, but Michael, my older brother by a year said, "When mom and dad see this we aren't going to be able to play in the canal anymore."

I could see the thought register with Chulo. "If you're parents don't let you play in the canal, I won't get to either."

Noe Trevino, the fourth friend of the Jacob, Marcial, Chulo, and Noe quartet, shook his head back and forth while keeping his eyes on the bloody abrasion. "Man, you know I won't get to play here either. Plus it wouldn't be fun to swim all alone."

Jimmy looked at my hip and then at the group. "Well look how bad it is. I've got to tell. We'll just say it was an accident."

Everyone's eyes were on me and I realized that even though it wasn't my doing, the fate of the canal rested on my shoulders. "Wait Jimmy," I said. "Let's clean it up. I'll be alright and we won't have to tell."

Everyone liked the idea and pretty soon I was walking through the kitchen door with semi-clean raw skin on my hip. It hurt like hell, but I tried not to wince, even when I sat down for a serving of goat milk.

MOVING TO PLANADA

It didn't happen often, but at this particular moment we were all left speechless. All us kids sat in our small living room and tried to process our father's words. "We're moving off the camp, leaving Hadley's farm."

I was now in second grade and the camp was the only life I'd known. It wasn't much, but it was mine. I looked at my oldest sister Dorothy. She wore the surprise well. Jimmy did too. Benny's mouth hung open and a number of questions were forming. Linda tried to appear as calm as Dorothy. Michael, my brother closest in age, beat Benny to it. "What do you mean moving, to where, when?"

Our father stood in the living room next to his brother, Tio Miguel. He raised his calloused right hand and ran it through his thick black hair. "Moving to Planada and soon. Buying a house is one of the reasons I've worked so hard as the Campero (the foreman of the camp), so we could move one day. It's also why your mother has spent so many mornings making tacos to sell to the workers."

"Will we change schools? Benny said. "I've never gone anywhere but Plainsburg."

"Yes, you'll be going to Planada. It's only six miles away so it won't be a big change. Besides soon your friends will be moving there too."

I knew my dad meant the Gonzales's, the Trevino's, and the Ybarra's. It was great to hear that my best friends, Chulo, Marcial, and Noe would be in Planada with me, but the prospect of moving was still scary.

The meeting broke up and later that night we lay in our bunk beds. We talked of the move and wondered what it would be like. We talked of the school, the town, the new house, and probably would have talked late into the night if it wasn't for Tio Miguel telling us all to shut up and go to sleep.

While my dad, Tio Miguel, and older brothers moved everything out of the two bedroom house on Hadley's farm, I was stuck in my second grade classroom. The day was in no rush to end, but finally it did and I handed my mother's note to my craggily teacher. I knew it said that I was to walk home with Leroy Ramos and his family. They lived across from the school. The teacher glanced at it then raised her wrinkled eyebrows and in a voice thick with distrust said, "You'll ride the bus."

I was too dumbfounded to argue and in a matter of moments I was bouncing along in the beat up school bus toward a home that wasn't mine anymore.

The bus dropped me off and I pushed through the front door. The house was bare except for a few boxes in the corner of the living room. I looked into the two bedrooms, dining room, and kitchen, all empty.

I didn't check to see if the Gonzales's, Trevino's or Ybarra's were home. I knew they'd help me, I mean there were times when my little brother was a baby when Mrs. Trevino would actually breast feed him. Maybe we weren't related, but we were all family.

Instead I just stood in the empty kitchen. This house had been my home for my whole life, but suddenly I felt alone. I remembered the good times swimming in the canal and playing with my friends and I remembered the hard times chopping cotton and picking fruit. I sat down on the wooden floor and a few silent tears slipped down my cheeks.

I thought of and cried about the move until I heard an engine out front. I headed for the front door and saw my dad pull up in his old white International pick up truck. "What are you doing here?" he asked.

"The teacher wouldn't let me walk with Leroy. I had to take the bus and nobody was here when I got here."

Rehashing the time alone brought a couple more tears. My dad wiped them with his sleeve. "It's not that big of deal. I'm here now and you're alright."

I sniffed a couple times. "Help me load up these boxes," my dad said.

It felt good to play at least a small part in the move and once the boxes were in the truck we pulled away from our old house on the migrant camp and turned north onto Plainsburg Rd. I felt caught in between. I was sad to leave behind what I knew, but excited for the new adventure only a few miles away.

PLANADA

The town wasn't much different than the migrant camp in the sense that it lived and breathed with the fields. The population hung around 1,500 in the winter time, but when summer rolled around Planada swelled to close to 6,000. The seasonal farm workers came from all over: Mexico, Texas, Arizona, Colorado, New Mexico – they all came to the San Joaquin Valley because there were always jobs to be found, low-paying, but work just the same. Not much of that work could be found in the town where the bars outweighed the stoplights by three to zero and the men lived by the mantra of work hard and drink harder, but the surrounding fields needed tending during harvest time.

Our family settled into life in Planada. Our new house rested on the outskirts of town and a tomato field dominated the view from the living room. It was nice except when the pesticides drizzled over our property. The house was much bigger than the one on Hadley's farm, plus it even had a real yard.

I made new friends, like Rudy Salcido, Jerry Zarate, the Garcia brothers, the Bonilla brothers, and Alfred Sanchez, a lefty pitcher with a great pick-off move. And I had my old friends, Marcial, Chulo, and Noe since they soon ended up in Planada too.

We kids, just like the adults, still had to work in the fields. Now we were just a little farther away. The canal was a little farther away as well, but that didn't mean it wasn't still a main source of fun. We even found a better spot than the one that ran through Hadley's farm. About a mile outside of town was a wide area named Peter Deep that even featured a couple small water falls.

Every chance we got, after a long day in the fields or a boring day in the classroom, me, my little brother Ernie, and the crew bolted for the soothing waters. We'd swim and splash and I'd do my best to avoid any chunks of cement. The scar from a few years earlier ensured the memory stayed fresh in my mind.

Le Grand road ran along the canal, and on the other side a fig orchard stretched as far as the eye could see. On a hot Saturday in July, some of us took a break from swimming and climbed out of Peter Deep on the fig orchard side. The watering of the trees left the ground in a soggy mess, but Noe thought it looked pretty inviting. He got a running start and dove into the mud belly first. Marcial, Ernie, Chulo, and I watched as our friend slopped around like a pig. Alfred Sanchez rolled up a ball of mud and hurled it. The ball hit just in front of Noe and spattered his face with brown droplets. Everyone laughed and pointed as he wiped the mud from his cheeks. "You got no arm Sanchez," he said. "What are you guys waiting for? It feels great. The dirt's soft and the water's warm!"

I shrugged and Marcial said, "Why not?"

And with that, all five of us dove in. We flopped around, stirring up the mud until it covered our entire bodies. We wrestled and threw mud at each other, and pretty soon the Bonilla's, the Garcia's, Rudy, and Jerry, were neck deep in it too.

Eventually we settled in and relaxed in our impromptu mud bath not realizing that people paid good money to do the same thing at the spas.

While the sun baked the mud onto our skin, I stared at the crisp sky. Just like back when I lived in the camp, I thought of what it would be like to experience more of the world. With the move I at least knew a little more than I once did, but I also knew there was so much more than Planada.

Thoughts of the outside world led me to Pittsburgh Pirates great Roberto Clemente. The star outfielder was fast becoming my hero and I wondered what it would be like to play Major League baseball, to see the United States while smacking home runs off big-time pitchers or running down long fly balls. I liked Clemente because he was a great ballplayer, and loved him because he was a better man. Clemente had made it during difficult times and he inspired others.

I also thought about my other hero, Cesar Chavez. The activist for farm workers was just getting started, but he'd already done a lot for us, especially in the San Joaquin Valley. I wondered what it would be like to have the power to fight for what you believed, to really make a difference.

The mud was dry and crusted before any of us stirred. "Let's jump in the canal with all this mud on us," Chulo said.

We thought that sounded like a great idea and I pulled myself up. I headed toward the canal and left my dreams of the future in the makeshift mud bath. They might be just that, dreams, not a lot of people ever made it out of the poverty-stricken town of Planada once they were there. Besides, I knew I'd be back to the warm mud and back to my thoughts of one day becoming somebody who could inspire others much like Roberto Clemente or Cesar Chavez.

The mud broke apart as soon as I hit the water. A cloud of brown formed around me and I wiped away the rest. My skin was smooth and I felt refreshed. So much so that I didn't even think about all the pesticide that was mixed in with the mud.

SUNDAY AFTERNOON

The park was alive with the sights and sounds of baseball as the farm workers from all over the United States and Mexico geared up for another day of action. Some swung bats and joked with each other. Others played catch in the outfield. And some sat in lawn chairs sipping on cold beer, content to just watch.

Alfred Sanchez and I played catch on the far side of the lawn chairs down the left field line. Alfred's a lefty and he spun a curveball my way that broke nearly a foot. I snagged it. "Nice, sharp break," I said.

"I've been working on it," he replied.

Once my arm was good and loose, I began putting a little more on each throw. I wasn't a pitcher, but had a strong arm and didn't mind showing it off at the Pony League games by firing the pill from my position at third across the diamond to the first baseman.

Alfred scooted back a couple steps and unleashed another curve. This one broke into the dirt and I scooped it up with ease.

Before I returned the ball, a voice caught my attention. "Hey kid!"

I looked to the field where a farm worker who was built lean and strong, much like a shortstop, of course they all were built like shortstops, was pointing my way. It was the oldest of the Ortegon brothers. I'd watched him play numerous times. He wasn't on Roberto Clemente's level, but he could hang with many professional ball players. I said, "Me?" the guy was looking in my direction, but I figured he wanted Alfred. Left-handed pitchers with great pick-off moves were harder to come by than slick-fielding third basemen.

Ortegon replied in Spanish, all the farm workers spoke Spanish, "Si chico, quieres jugar?"

In an instant my hands got sweaty and my throat tight. "Uh, yeah ... sure I can play," I stammered, also in Spanish.

I was one of the best Pony Leaguers, but at 14 years old I wasn't entirely confident that I could play with the adults. I thought it might be best to back out. Then I remembered laying in the fig orchard mud bath and dreaming about what it would be like to be Roberto Clemente. In order to be like my hero, I knew I'd have to challenge myself, even if it made me nervous.

Ortegon raised his arms as if to say, *so you in or what?*

I tossed the ball to Alfred and jogged toward the field.

Minutes later I was smoothing the rough dirt at third base. The pitcher told me to scoot in a bit because the leadoff hitter liked to bunt. I took a couple steps forward and bent my knees and hips. The pitcher began his wind up and I hoped my nervousness wasn't visible to everyone else in the park. The batter acted as if he'd drag bunt and I took a few hard steps toward the plate. The pitch was high and outside for ball one.

After a long, slow breath I moved back to my spot. I figured the guy had decided to test me and expected another bunt attempt. The pitcher cut loose again, but this time the batter turned on it. The screaming line drive was just to my left. I reacted and the ball skipped in the dirt inches in front of my glove. It kicked up and in a smooth motion I nabbed it. The momentum took me off balance so I spun around, squared up to first, and fired a strike. The runner was out by two steps.

The oldest Ortegon looked over from his shortstop position and nodded. "Nice play chico."

I let out a long breath and my heartbeat slowed. "Gracias," I said.

It was a nice play and I was glad I had the balls to give myself a chance to make it. The game went on and I fielded a couple more chances. Alfred came in and pitched a couple innings too. I did okay at the plate, going 1 for 3 with a single up the middle and scoring a run. And then it was over.

Afterward I shook hands with the men and was told I was welcome any time. It all happened so fast. One pitch, one play, one baseball game on a Sunday afternoon with a bunch of men who traveled to Planada to work the fields, and I began to really believe that I was capable of one day getting out of those same fruit fields for a better life.

SUNDAY NIGHT

The Sunday baseball games had become a regular thing and hanging out with friends afterward did too. One night I was at the normal spot in the park in the center of town with Alfred, Rudy, Chulo, Marcial, and a handful of others.

The streets were near empty so the rumble of an old Chevy truck caught our attention. It bounced along the rough road between the park and the public library. We watched for a second, not recognizing the driver. The old man looked over his left shoulder at the group then nodded his head upward and we all returned the gesture. The conversation began where it left off and everyone's attention shifted away from the truck when I heard a slight thud and saw something clang against its undercarriage.

The driver tapped his breaks and they squeaked in protest as the truck slowed. After a quick check into his mirrors, he seemed satisfied nothing was amiss and picked up speed again. I walked across the park to see what the man had hit.

There in the middle of the road was an almost four foot long garter snake. Thanks to the truck's tire, a portion of it was flattened and it was dead. "What the hell is it?" Rudy asked.

"A big ass garter snake," I replied.

Although we were in high school and had seen hundreds of them, we couldn't resist the wonders of a snake. Everyone headed to the street and we all stood around it. A number of snake stories arose and Alfred told of the day his mother, Katie, found one in their bathroom. Said she screamed so loud she woke up the neighbors and almost peed all over herself. We all laughed because as was the case with many mom's in Planada, Katie was something like a second mother to many of us. We could imagine the scene perfectly.

"I've got an idea," I said.

Before anybody responded, I bent down and scooped up the dead snake. Chulo said, "What are you doing Duran?"

I answered by hissing and shoving the snake toward him. "Get that out of my face man!" I obliged and trotted off toward the library.

Everyone gave chase, wondering what I was doing. The library was closed on Sunday night, but the front door offered a nice wide slot for book returns. I carefully fed the snake through the slot and down the shoot.

Someone said, "Oh my God, Mrs. White is going to shit herself when she sees that."

I eased the snake into place until it was resting on a tattered copy of Ernest Hemingway's For Whom the Bell Tolls and said, "That's the idea. She's going to do just like Alfred's mom."

It wasn't that I had anything against Mrs. White. She was really a pretty nice lady. She was just a victim of circumstance. Everyone began to recognize the brilliance of the prank and patted me on the back.

News soon came that her reaction did in fact top Alfred's mom's reaction. Mrs. White let out a blood-curdling scream, damn near had a heart attack, and then called Constable Clyde McMenemy.

The stunt earned me a fair amount of acclaim, but it was nothing compared to what I'd do a couple years later.

HIGH SCHOOL

I continued to play baseball, both with the adults and in school. Roberto Clemente was never far from my thoughts and I followed Cesar Chavez's actions, marches, and protest's with interest. With each day I recognized that I was closer to the time when I'd get a chance to turn all my dreaming into a reality.

My hopes didn't deter me from being a mischievous high school kid and sometimes the jokes were on me. Back when I first started playing ball with the adults I stayed the night at my biggest brother Jimmy's house. Jimmy had just gotten married to Phyllis and was something of a second father to all of us. Often my dad spent his days working and his nights drinking. He was in and out of the house and us younger kids needed somebody who we could look up to. Jimmy was the oldest boy, so he naturally fell into the roll.

Jimmy, his brother-in-law Danny, Michael, and I were all sitting around the living room when Jimmy said, "You're looking kind of shaggy Jacob. How bout I give you a hair cut?"

I ran a hand through my black hair. It was getting a little thick and although it was the 60s, long hair wasn't in just yet, at least in the central valley. "Yeah I could use a cut. Do a good job though. I've got a baseball game tomorrow."

"Don't worry. I'll do you up right."

I sat down in a chair in the middle of the living room and wrapped a towel around my shoulders. "I'm serious Jimmy, don't screw it up."

He didn't screw it up. He did just as he intended, shaved me bald. I didn't know my hair was being lopped off and Danny and Michael laughed as the locks tumbled to the floor. I chuckled with them, unaware I was the butt of the joke. After a few minutes Jimmy declared he was done.

I looked at myself in the mirror and screamed, "Aaahhh!"
My light-skinned scalp had a tinge of blue and tears welled up in my eyes. "What the hell is wrong with you Jimmy?"

"Oh come on, it looks good that way."

"I'm bald! Bald doesn't look good."

Michael stopped laughing long enough to say, "You're right, it doesn't look good."

I drilled him in the chest with a solid right hand and then gave him a left to the shoulder. He gave chase, but as usual I outran him easy. I locked myself in the bathroom, called Michael a few names, and then looked at my bald head once again.

Minutes passed before Jimmy knocked. "It's not that big of deal Jacob. You gotta come out. Danny has to pee."

"Danny can piss in the yard for all I care, and it is too a big deal. I told you I have a game tomorrow. I'm not coming out unless you get mom to bring me my baseball hat. I won't leave the house without it."

"Fine, I'll get your hat."

I wore my hat a lot over the next couple weeks, until new hair began to form on my blue-skinned scalp.

Not long after the shaving incident I was tricked again, but this one ended up giving me something of a claim to fame. The six miles of road between Planada and Le Grand, the town where the high school was located, was a dark, desolate stretch. Jerry Zarate, one of my buddies who found the fig orchard mud baths with me, was also one of the first guys to get his driver's license. One night he called me asking for help pushing another car out of the mud by those very same fig orchards at Peter Deep. Jerry talked me into it by saying, "Hey, if you help push it out we'll give you a beer."

That was an offer I couldn't refuse, so minutes later I was in the back of Jerry's station wagon alongside a couple other suckers in Able Bonilla and Bobby Burolla. We approached Peter Deep and Jerry flicked his lights a couple times. I wondered why but didn't ask. The car sputtered and eased to the side of the road, the canal on the right and the fig orchard on the left, but due to the pitch-black night neither could be seen. "Shit, the car's dying," Jerry said.

Before any of us could respond, a creature appeared from the darkness and banged on the window. We screamed and clutched each other and crammed together as far away from the window as we could get. Jerry fired up the car and took off, but it wasn't long before he pulled over again because he was laughing so hard he was crying.

The whole story came out and it was just another kid wrapped in toilet paper. But in the darkness on Le Grand road a toilet paper-covered high school kid was scary as hell.

This got the wheels turning for Bobby and me. A few months later we enlisted the help of another friend, John Burks, and the three of us swiped some toilet paper from Bobby's house and headed out to Peter Deep.

We found a good spot along the side of the road and Bobby and John wrapped me up real good. It was a frigid December night and we chose it because a basketball game was going on at the high school in Le Grand. We knew a steady stream of cars would come along after the game.

Soon the first unsuspecting carload came by and I stayed along the side of the road. Far enough away so everyone would catch just a glimpse. As the car passed I walked stiff-legged and stiff-armed, much like a mummy, and then faded into the trees. One car after another we played the prank. After each we laughed and came up with new ideas for the next. We also wondered if we were scaring anybody.

The answer to that was a definite yes. We were in fact scaring the crap out of a lot of people. After thirty minutes or so the cold air was getting to us so we called it a night. Bobby and John ripped the toilet paper off of me and we left it on the side of the road.

The next day's headline in the Merced Sun-Star read *Mummy Seen on Le Grand*. The article went on to explain that Constable Clyde McMenemy investigated the seen and found nothing but toilet paper thrown a strewn.

Making headlines led to a whole lot of bragging and in a matter of days everyone knew I was the mummy. I was considering my newfound fame as I sat in math class the following Monday.

Three sharp knocks broke my reverie and my mouth went cotton-dry when Constable Clyde poked his head through the door. His hat in hand he took a couple steps, planted his booted feet, and surveyed the room. His leathery face was streaked with lines of anger. "Sorry to disrupt the class," he gestured to the teacher, "but I need Mr. Jacob Duran to come with me."

Everyone's eyes burned into me as I rose from my desk. My face felt hot and I struggled to smile as I passed Jerry's desk. I knew there was nothing to smile about. Someone must've filed some kind of charges and now I was going to pay the price for my mummy escapade. Jail, community service, hard labor, fines, I didn't know what, but I knew it'd be bad.

It turned out to be nothing like that. After his brief investigation, the Constable knew it was just kids pulling a prank, and since we had done so much bragging, it didn't take long to find the culprits.

Constable Clyde hauled me down the street to see the Judge. The old man didn't quite get the prank and advised that

I organize something like a Halloween party or maybe have something like a dance.

I never did become a dance organizer, but from that day on I was a legend in Planada because I was the Le Grand Mummy.

SMUDGING

It wasn't all baseball and pranks during my teen years. I was expected to work the fields just as hard as the adult men no matter the season or time, summer, winter, day, night. I knew I had to be ready to work whenever I got a call and often the work was dirty and difficult.

Smudging was something of a right of passage into manhood in the farming town of Planada. The fields demanded constant attention, even on cold nights in the dead of winter.

It was 2:30 in the morning when the phone woke me. I snatched the receiver and said, "Yeah."

"It's freezing. The truck will be there in five."

I hung up the phone and like a fireman, threw on my clothes. They were dirty, old, warm, and just what I needed for the job. I trudged into the kitchen, keeping as quiet as I could, grabbed a glass of water and downed it in one gulp.

I then slipped through the front door as the truck's headlights bobbed along the road. It had barely stopped before I hopped into the back and it was on its way again. I scanned the crowd, around a dozen in all, nodded to a couple of my sleepy friends, and then sighed. My breath looked like smoke in the cold air as it trailed away and vanished.

We were heading to the tomato fields because the temperature had hit freezing. The tomatoes couldn't handle the cold and there was only one way to heat them up, smudging.

Upon arriving, we all hopped from the truck. A man stood with torches, just like those from the Frankenstein movies. Everyone nodded greetings. There wasn't time to socialize. Each of us grabbed a torch and one by one, a second man lit the cloth end of each and the flames danced into the air.

I picked a row and headed down it. Every few steps I stooped at an old ten gallon paint bucket filled with diesel. I then touched the flame to the surface and pulled it back as the fuel caught fire with a whooshing sound. Despite leaning away from the blaze, I always felt it on my face. Sometimes it even singed my eye brows and I was careful to not inhale the smoke.

After a few more steps, I repeated the process. On and on, I lit hundreds of cans filled with diesel. Once done I made my way back to the group and we talked and watched as the buckets burned like a thousand camp fires between the rows of tomatoes. It really was beautiful despite the rolling smoke that hung thick in the air.

The night passed and the fire and smoke worked to heat up the entire field, protecting the fragile tomatoes in the process. At about 4:30 in the morning the farmer gave the word. Again we fanned out. I headed into the thick gray and black smoke, down the same row I'd been in a little less than two hours before. Now I didn't need a torch. Instead I used a metal lid. At each of the flaming cans I stooped down and quickly thrust the lid over the flame. Each fire was ended just as fast as it had been started. Again one after another I doused the flames, pitching the fields back into darkness.

The smoke burned my eyes and seeped into my lungs. The soot settled all over me and caked in my ears. Finally the last flame was extinguished and the dirty work was over. I piled into the truck and looked around at the other boys. Their eyes and teeth appeared whiter against their soot-covered faces, and I knew I looked the same.

It was 5:30 in the morning by the time I pushed through the front door. I removed my grimy boots, and despite the bitter stench of smoke that still filled my nostrils I could smell the bacon my mom was frying in the kitchen. "Take off your shoes and don't sit down," she said.

I replied that I'd already taken them off. My mom poked her head out of the kitchen. "You going to school?"

Everyone knew the town lived and died by the fields, so all those who spent the night smudging to keep the tomatoes safe were excused from school. "I've got to," I said. "I have a test in math."

"Well you'd better get in the shower then before your sister does."

I nodded in agreement and loped toward the bathroom, ready to scrub away the grime. I stripped and then coughed up some acrid, black stuff and spit into the toilet. The shower helped energize me and I spent minutes scrubbing away the soot. I knew there'd still be some left. One shower never got it all. I also hoped my math teacher would notice and take it into account when she graded my test.

A few hours later, red-eyed and aching, I completed the last problem and handed in my test. I was sure I did fine. I usually did even if I spent half the night in the smoke-filled tomato fields. I was also sure that it was about time to leave the fruit picking, cotton chopping, and smudging behind.

I'd made the best of my days in the little town in the middle of the San Joaquin Valley, but with my senior year coming to an end it was time to start a new chapter in my life.

2

LEAVING HOME
MERCED COLLEGE

THAT NEW CHAPTER DIDN'T TAKE ME VERY FAR. I decided to attend Merced Junior College just nine miles away. It wasn't something I had a burning desire for, but there weren't a lot of options for farm workers from Planada, plus the fairly new college had a pretty good baseball team.

I didn't know anything about scholarships or financial aid. I simply went out for the team and started playing. The coach knew me from scouting the high school team the previous year and was ecstatic to have me on his squad. We met in the dull locker room and he handed me a couple of t-shirts that read Merced College and a couple pairs of baseball pants. Reluctantly, I took the uniforms and wondered if I had to pay. As if he read my mind, "These are your practice uniforms. They're paid for by the athletic department. Try not to rip 'em up too fast."

"Yes sir," I said and thought *damn this place is pretty nice*!

It wasn't long before I fell into a routine. Each morning I hitched a ride with a friend. It wasn't too hard since so many were attending the college. Then I struggled to stay awake during class and after a quick lunch I was on the baseball field.

I worked out at third base and the coaches pushed us hard. Despite sore hamstrings, I used my slick glove to impress. I was also swinging the bat well. During practice there was nothing else to think about but baseball. The fruit fields, the boring school work, my home nine miles away, nothing else mattered when I was between the white lines of the baseball diamond.

Unfortunately, baseball practice didn't go on forever, but it did go on long enough to cause problems. By the time practice came to an end all my friends had already headed back to Planada. With daylight slipping away I had to beg, borrow, and steal to find a ride back home. If not, it was a long, lonely stretch of highway I'd have to walk.

This went on for a few weeks. The days were long, my finances were dwindling, and I realized that I never was going to find out what it was like to be like Roberto Clemente. It was a tough time and a tough decision. All those dreams as a kid, all those thoughts of playing baseball for a living, and I had to give them up.

I'd been talking with my childhood buddy Marcial, and we were working on an idea. It was a much bigger step than Merced College, but seemed right. So one day I went to school, ate a quick lunch, practiced hard, struggled to find a ride home, and then didn't return to Merced College. I didn't tell anybody. I'd made up my mind and although disappointed I was ready to become a proud member of the U.S. Navy just like my brother Miguel.

JOINING UP

I remembered the play clearly. I'd singled down the left field line and stretched it into a double. I slid into second, just beating the tag, but my foot caught the bag funny and I tweaked my left knee.

Now, over a year later, I sat in the doctor's office in Fresno and winced as he twisted on my leg and the knee popped again. The doc shook his head back and forth and frowned. He asked about the injury and I told him what happened but that it didn't really hurt.

He pushed his black-rimmed glasses up his nose. "I understand son. I can tell you really want to join, but you need surgery on that knee so I have to flunk you."

The words hit me hard. Baseball at Merced didn't work out and now my next plan to join the Navy had unraveled with a twist of my knee. A lump formed in my throat as I thanked the doctor. There wasn't any reason to argue, even when I hopped off the table and put my full weight on the knee with only a little pain. The paper in my hand told the story, REJECTED.

Marcial's jaw hung open as the news sunk in. "Shit Jacob. They won't give you another chance? I mean you've been running around playing ball on that knee."

"No second chance until after surgery, and there is no way in hell I can afford it. Looks like you're on your own Marcial."

"Screw that man. It is crazy enough joining up with a friend. No way I'm going alone."

I empathized with him. With my failing of the physical it had in essence doomed Marcial as well. I looked up from the corner on which we were standing. The town seemed to move in slow motion. The smell of fruit hung in the air. And down the street the edge of a tomato field ran into the horizon. There was nothing wrong with all of it, but I knew I couldn't settle for a life here in Planada.

"Screw it Marcial. I can't go to the Navy, but there's still the Army, Air Force, and Marines. Let's get our asses back to the recruiting station."

The bell dinged when the glass door opened. A Mexican man with a square jaw, intense eyes, and rounded shoulders, jumped from his seat and strode over. He was dressed immaculately in a brown uniform that had never seen a wrinkle in its life. He stuck out his hand and introduced himself, we did the same.

The man was a Marine recruiter and it looked like he stepped out of the movie screen into the office. He told us what it would be like to be a U.S. Marine and despite our desire to leave Planada and serve our country, both of us were uneasy with getting shot at in Vietnam in some six months time.

"What about the Air Force?" I said. "I've always been amazed by those planes."

"I'll tell you what," the Marine replied, "I'm going to come by your house tomorrow. We'll go to Castle Air Force Base."

We left the building and I said, "What do you think?"

"I'm not sure. The Marines, the Air Force. It's all kind of overwhelming," Marcial said. "We've never really been out of the valley and now we're talking about going to a whole different country."

I could see the thought made Marcial uneasy. It made me uneasy as well, but it was also exciting. I stepped off the curb and felt a twinge of pain in my knee, but pushed it aside in a hurry. "It is overwhelming, but this might be our last opportunity."

"It might be," Marcial agreed.

CASTLE AIR FORCE BASE

I stared through the spotless car window as the Marine turned onto the base. A blue sign with a yellow lightning bolt read 93d Bombardment Wing, an American Flag fluttered in the breeze not far behind. I pictured flying in a B-52 and unleashing hell on the bad guys.

The Marine's booming voice brought me out of the fantasy. I glanced at him and even though the man was sitting, his blue uniform with its red stripe down the pants fit perfectly. No wrinkles to be seen and his shoes shined like the sun. "Just look around men. Do you really want to be like that? That Airman's pants haven't been ironed since the start of the war. And look at that one, his pants are shrunk up to his calves." He pointed across the way at two more. "You'd never catch a Marine with boots scuffed like those."

I nodded. I really couldn't see the scuff marks from so far away, but believed the Marine one hundred percent. He asked again, "Is this really what you want?"

"Well Sir, I've got to be honest. I want to serve my country, but I'm not so sure I want to be in Vietnam as a marine getting shot at every day. Besides, I can always iron my pants and shine my shoes."

The man looked at me without really moving his head. The muscles in his jaw clinched and relaxed and for an instant I pictured his thick hand leaving the steering wheel and landing directly onto my nose. Then he nodded, a hint of a smile crossed his lips. "I can respect that. You feel the same way?" he said to Marcial as he glanced in the rear view mirror.

Marcial did and the Marine whipped the car around and out of Castle Air Force base.

Back at the recruiting station he handed me a piece of paper. "You're going to go down to Oakland to do your physical for the Air Force. And don't tell them about that damn gimpy knee."

I thanked the man and the bell dinged as Marcial and I exited the glass door. To this day I don't remember the Marine's name, just as the man probably wanted it. The Marine Corp isn't about being an individual. It's about doing what has to be done whether your name is remembered or not, but I'd like to thank him just the same.

On the same street corner in which we stood not long ago, I said, "Well it's off to Oakland."

Marcial turned to me and cast his eyes downward at the dirty street. "I don't know how to say this man, but I can't go."

I had recognized that Marcial was having second thoughts, but figured that was all they were, thoughts. "What do you mean you can't go? We're in this together. How do you expect me to go if you don't go?"

"I know Jacob. I'm sorry. It's just that Carmen and I are getting along great. We're talking of getting married and starting a family. I can't do that if I'm in the Air Force."

"Shit Marcial, we've been in this together, and now you're leaving me just like that?"

"I'm sorry. It's been a damn hard decision, but I've gotta do what I think is best for me. I hope you'll forgive me."

Before I could answer Marcial turned and walked away, right back into that slow moving town where the smell of fruit drenched the air. And I stood, feeling stuck between Oakland and Planada.

DECISION TIME

The night before I was to board the bus to Oakland, I lay in bed staring at the ceiling and considered whether or not

I should go. I thought of Hadley's farm and the canal in which I swam as a young boy. I remembered the day my family moved to Planada and how I was left in the house alone. I thought of my friends in the small town, the good times we'd had. Chopping cotton, picking fruit, smudging; all the work in the fields flashed in my head. It was hard, but it'd also shaped my work ethic.

It wasn't so bad. And the thought of hopping on a Greyhound and riding into the unknown made my stomach a little queasy. Who was I kidding? I was a small town farm worker, not ready for the world. Then again, I'd been dreaming of making something more of myself for as long as I could remember. The bus tomorrow might be the very beginning. Thanks to the Marine recruiter I was getting a third chance to follow my dreams. I just wasn't sure if I should take it.

Just before I drifted off I thought of the dead body I'd seen recently. The Bracero Program had ended and immigration often raided the fields. We'd yell "La Migra" to warn the illegals and we'd run too, just to mess with them. I was in the driveway picking up rocks and hitting them into the tomato fields with my baseball bat, when a bunch of cops flew by with sirens blaring.

I grabbed Ernie and we took off after them. Since there wasn't much in the way of entertainment in Planada, my dad had been taking us to follow sirens for years. We walked up to the cop cars and learned that immigration had raided the fields and one of the workers attacked an officer. The officer shot him dead with a 357. The sheriff recognized me because I worked with his wife at the Juvenile Hall at college. He let me under the tape and I stood over the body. There a man was pruning less than an hour earlier and now dead in the dirt with a hole in his chest. It wasn't the first death in the fields by any stretch, but it was the first I'd seen and the last image I remembered as I fell asleep.

Out of habit, I was awake with the sun. Before rolling out of bed I thought one last time about what I should do, and in an instant I knew the answer. Making the decision was a weight off my shoulders and I hoped Marcial wouldn't feel too bad about it.

After a quick breakfast, goat milk and all, I did a few chores around the house. I then headed to the fields. There wasn't much work to do, but I wanted to take it all in: the smells, the sounds, the colors. I watched as a plane buzzed over the adjacent field and grinned as the fine mist of pesticides was released. The central valley and the fields were my home, and despite the hard work, I was glad.

The bus wasn't scheduled for departure until the evening. When the time came I shook my brothers' hands, and then my father's. I hugged my sisters and the youngest, Belen, looked at me as if she was asking if I'd hold true to my word.

"Don't worry Belen," I said. "I promised I'd write and I will. I'll write to you all the time."

She fought to smile through the tears. Then my mother was in front of me. She squeezed me tight and her eyes moistened. "Make us proud Jacob," she whispered and squeezed a little tighter.

I nodded, making another promise I was going to be damned sure to keep. When she let go I scooped up my bag and had a funny feeling in my chest as I walked out the front door.

The Greyhound was already idling as I climbed aboard. Jacob Duran was finally leaving Planada. That is if my knee would hold up during my Air Force physical.

OAKLAND

With a hiss the Greyhound pulled into the station. I had been jarred awake moments earlier when the bus slowed to enter the city. I'd watched the buildings pass, close together and dirty. I'd watched the people too. Despite it being one in the morning, many were still out, wandering the sidewalks or sitting against the walls.

With a shudder the bus turned off. I gathered my belongings and headed for the street where I stopped and turned a circle in an effort to get my bearings. I then consulted the street names and the address of the hotel in which I'd take my physical in a matter of hours. I started right, paused for a moment and then reversed course. It was my first time alone in a large city. I walked with my cumbersome belongings clutched tight in my hand, my chin down and shoulders hunched forward. The hotel was only a couple blocks away, but it seemed like miles.

At the first intersection, a black man in a black coat, hands in pockets, approached. He stood uncomfortably close and his eyes darted back and forth as he leaned closer. "Listen bro," he said. "I'm with Huey Newton. You know Huey Newton of the Black Panthers?"

"Yeah, yeah I know," I said. I'd heard of the founder, but didn't know much about the Black Panthers.

"Good, some shit is going down and I've got to get out of town." The man leaned back a little and looked over his shoulder. "So you got any cash I can have?"

Without really considering, I dug in my pocket and fished out a few ones. The man pulled his hand from his pocket and palm up rubbed his fingers together. I handed over the wad of money. He snatched it, looked up and down the street once more, leaned in and nodded his chin up and down a couple times. He then turned and hurried off, jamming the money into his coat as he walked.

I crossed the street and could see the hotel in the distance so I picked up the pace. I thought about the man and how I'd handed over my money so easily, and decided I probably needed to be more careful. The guy could have been thinking about mugging me or scoping it out for someone else. I glanced over my shoulder. Nobody was behind me, but I checked again to be sure. The rest of the way my eyes darted back and forth much like the man's I'd just given the money to.

The following morning my heart thumped as the doctor examined my legs. He tugged on the right leg first. Nothing like the doctor did in Fresno, just a quick pull. He then gripped my left leg and gave it a pull. Since he didn't twist it there was no pain. "I see from your charts you were an active young man working in the fields and playing sports," the doctor said. "No injuries to speak of?"

I wasn't sure if he was asking because he felt something wrong in the knee or if he was just asking. I thought of the Marine recruiter's words; *don't tell them about that damn gimpy knee.* "No Sir, no injuries. I've been pretty lucky I guess. Why do you ask?"

Once I asked the question I was cussing myself for it. No reason to invite further conversation. "Asking questions is my job," he said. "I've got to make sure Uncle Sam doesn't get any damaged goods. You seem to be a pretty solid young man. I think you'll make a fine Airman."

With that he signed and stamped the paper. This time it read, PASSED instead of rejected. There was no turning back now.

BASIC

It was Continental airlines that carried me away from my home. I boarded the plane and looked around the cabin. I'd seen the inside of airplanes on TV, but except for the crop dusters, never in real life. I found my seat and stared out the oval-shaped window. The plane backed up and some of the people in the terminal waved good-bye to their loved ones. I scanned the crowd even though I knew I would not recognize any of the faces.

In an instant we were in the air and I marveled at the barren land as it grew smaller and smaller with each passing minute. The anticipation of the flight and the actual act of leaving zapped me. I dozed for a while and soon the plane touched down.

The heat was oppressive in San Antonio. I stepped off the bus at Lackland Air Force Base with the other recruits and everyone fished out their suitcases from underneath, everyone except me. I had a wooden foot locker filled with a bunch of clothes. I didn't realize I wouldn't need all of my stuff and wanted to be prepared. Now I'd pay the price.

The training instructors screamed at us as we walked through the heat from one place to another in order to in process. I didn't want to stand out, but it was hell hauling around my big ass foot locker and I began to fall toward the back of the pack. I was hanging in there though, that is until one of my handles broke.

Instantly it was that much harder to carry. Sweat dripped off my forehead as I struggled to keep up. The training instructors yelled at me, called me names, and told me to get my ass in gear. I did, but it was a tough haul. All the others had it much easier with their smaller suitcases, handles in tact.

Thankfully, another recruit took mercy on me and helped me carry the foot locker. I made it through the day and it turned out to be my toughest during all of basic training. Being a good athlete, I sailed through the physical tests. I was faster and stronger than almost everyone else and I had spent so much time working so hard when I was younger. If it wasn't for that damn foot locker, basic would have been a breeze.

Basic came to an end and I was given my first assignment. I was heading north.

3

THAILAND
FROM WHITEMAN TO U-TAPAO

I SAT AT MY SMALL DESK in my barracks at Whiteman Air Force Base in Missouri and worked on another letter to Belen. I wrote about my job as a Security Policeman and how I worked with the Minuteman missiles. I told of how I led the convoy as we moved the missile from one place to another, or how I sat out in the cold on the top of a silo guarding the weapons. I wrote about it being a great experience and as always let her know how much I missed her. My mom had told me that Belen kept each of the letters and this made me write them with even a little more frequency.

After a couple pages, I wrapped it up and signed my name. I then folded the paper carefully and placed it in an envelope. I pushed my chair away from the desk and the leg caught the edge of the foot locker. This made me think of the day some ten months ago when I'd hauled it through the heat in San Antonio. I'd come a long ways in a short time and as I glanced at another letter on the desk I realized I was going even farther.

I picked my orders up and read them one more time. I'd received them earlier in the week and was disappointed to learn that I was going to a place called U-Tapao, Thailand. I didn't even know where Thailand was; let alone where or what U-Tapao was. What I did know was that Korea had Tae Kwon Do. I'd told myself that when I joined the military I was going to learn martial arts, so I figured Korea was my best shot and put in for a transfer there.

It seemed the Air Force could care less about my wants, and now I was heading to a front-line base in the Vietnam War.

Soon I was on another plane for the long flight across the Pacific and left the Minuteman missiles behind.

The plane touched down at three in the morning on April 14, 1974 and with stiff muscles I stepped into the stifling Thailand night. The flight-line was wet with rain and humidity and in an instant sweat beads formed on my arms.

GI's in jeeps complete with 60 caliber machine guns mounted on them raced toward the plane, other GI's stood alert on towers holding their weapons across their chests, and I thought *shit, where the hell am I?*

Hours later, I was beginning the normal briefing process. The Airman entered the room and bellowed, "Alright, anybody play baseball?"

I raised my hand and the man said, "What position?"

"I play third base sir."

His eyes lit up like *shit I got me a Latin ball player*, and he clapped his hands a couple of times. "Good, you're on day shift!"

Of course day shift was much better than the swing or graveyard, so despite not knowing exactly where I was; things were getting off on the right foot.

Unfortunately, for the man who thrust the good fortune of the day shift upon me, I never did play baseball in Thailand. I fell in love with something else.

THAI KICKBOXING

Only a few days into my tour in Thailand I was driving along a dusty road toward downtown Sattahip with a few friends that I knew from Basic Training and Whiteman. The others had been in country for a couple months and asked if I wanted to see some fights. Never one to shy away from watching a good scrap, I jumped at the chance.

We drove through a small town with narrow dirt roads before heading into the city. Mopeds raced between the cars and buildings and traffic thickened while the streets remained narrow. Finally, we made it to downtown and the place was alive.

Men and women were selling strange food from battered carts, barefoot and shirtless kids were playing in the dirt, music could be heard from all sides, and everyone was smiling and having a good time.

We weaved our way through the crowd and underneath the lights strung across the street until we found the arena, if one could call it that. It was nothing more than a ring in the center of an open area with chairs up close and bleachers encircling it.

The energy outside was high, but in here it was at a fever pitch. I followed the others lead and ordered a Singha from an old woman. She was missing most of her teeth, but smiled widely after handing me the cold beer and taking the few coins I offered. A drum beat frantically as we pushed to our seats on the floor just twenty steps or so from the ring.

I sat down and took it all in. The same type of lights that were strung across the street stretched from the tops of bleachers all the way across the makeshift arena. They hung on black wires, giving them the appearance of floating. Just below the lights, the bleachers were packed with screaming men. Some held up pieces of paper, some money, and others flashed two, three, or four fingers in the air. All were animated as they hollered back and forth.

"What the hell they doing up there," I asked my buddy.

"Betting, don't ask me how it works, looks like they're all about to fight each other."

He was right. It did look like at any minute they could break into a brawl. I watched as the spectacle continued and then the drum beat stopped. It was replaced by music and the fighters headed toward the ring.

One passed close, wearing colorful blue shorts with stars and strange Thai writing. His hardened muscles were slick with sweat, his bones pointy, and an odd-looking rope thing sat on the top of his head. Later, I learned that this was a Mongkhon, given to the fighters by their teacher after they'd learned a great deal about Muay Thai.

The fighter tapped the bottom rope three times, climbed the steps, and leaped over the top rope. The music continued and I took a step back to consider where I was. It was surreal to think that just a little over a year before I was picking fruit and wondering if I'd ever get out of the fields.

I forgot all about Planada when the fighters began a slow dance. They moved their bodies in a choreographed fashion, stretching their arms, raising their knees, turning circles. I raised my palm in the air as if to ask my friend, *what are they doing*?

"They're paying respect to their teachers, their parents, praying for victory, that kind of stuff. I think it's called Wai Khru Ram Muay."

I turned back to the dance. The men had both been kneeling in the center of the ring, now they stood and the one in the blue shorts acted as if he was swinging something through the air while the other, in red shorts with yellow stripes, stomped hard on the canvas. The whole ring shook with each thunderous footfall. And then the men made their way to the corners. Their teachers removed the rope thing, Mongkhon, while the fighters bowed their heads.

The fight was finally about to start and the crowd built to a continuous buzz. I took another gulp of my Singha and realized I was on the edge of my seat and my hands were slick with nervous sweat, not like the rest of me that was just sweating due to the heat. I also realized that I was loving every minute of this spectacle. The men met in the middle, received instructions, and returned to their corners.

A bell rang and again I was dumbfounded. I'd grown up with boxing, two men using their hands to win, but after a moment of circling, the fighter in the blue shorts, whipped his back leg around and blasted the other in the thigh. The sound of flesh on flesh snapped through the crowd. I leaned closer and said, "What the ..." I didn't finish because the red-shorted fighter responded by throwing a leg kick of his own.

The pace quickened and then the blue-shorted fighter locked his hands around the other's head, he pulled it down and kneed once, twice, three times to the stomach. They broke apart and then it happened.

Amongst the hanging lights, the screaming men, the beating drum, in the heart of Sattahip, the man in the blue shorts whipped a roundhouse to the head of the other. He caught him across the neck and the red-shorted fighter went stiff as he fell to the ground out cold.

I spilled a little of my beer as I jumped to my feet. The arena erupted in chants and cheers and the losing bettors, and maybe even some of the winners, threw things into the ring.

To no one in particular I said, "What is this?" I didn't get an answer and didn't know what I'd just seen, but a couple things were for damn sure, I loved it and I was going to find out!

BECOMING A MARTIAL ARTIST

As soon as I got a break the following Monday I headed to the Rec Center to sign up. The man behind the counter, complete with bushy gray hair and a tattoo of a shapely woman on his forearm said, "We got Tae Kwon Do, that what you looking for?"

"Yes Sir, that works for me," I said. Prior to my weekend trip to the Muay Thai fights I would've been happy to take Tae Kwon Do. Now I didn't think it was exactly what I was looking for, but then again they both sounded the same at the start, Tae Kwon Do and Thai Kickboxing, so they probably were the same.

The man directed me to a shop off base to get fitted for my uniform, called a Dobok in Korean. Once finished with my day shift patrolling the U-Tapao perimeter, I headed to the shop. The bone-thin Thai man kept rubbing his lips together as he measured, and I thought he was measuring too big. The man adjusted a bit and told me it would be ready soon.

During lunch on Wednesday I returned to the shop. The uniform was waiting for me, but I didn't have time to try it on. I thanked the old man and grabbed a quick lunch on the way back to duty. That afternoon, as I patrolled the base, I had a gnawing nervousness in my stomach. Finally I recognized that it was because in a matter of hours I'd be in my first Martial Arts class.

Soon I was headed to the gym. I snatched my crisp white Dobok off the hanger and ripped off my military uniform. First I put on the top. It squeezed against my shoulders and was tight on my lat muscles. I stretched my arms and brought them in front of my chest. The uniform stretched a bit, but it was like putting on a dress shirt that was too small, it seemed that it could tear at any minute.

Next, I slipped on the pants. I couldn't believe it but they were just as tight as the top, plus they were short, so short that I had flashbacks to the day Marcial and I had our pants rolled up and lost our shoes when the canal was filled. To say the uniform pants went to just above the ankle would be kind. It was more like they stopped at mid-calf.

I looked in the mirror and shook my head. I then squatted down a few times to see if I could move in the painted-on uniform. I moved okay, but it wasn't very comfortable. Earlier, another student had showed me how to tie my belt, so after a few tries I had a halfway presentable knot. I glanced in the mirror one more time and thought, *what the hell, you wanna learn don't you?* And with that I shoved my bag in a locker and headed for the gym.

I felt ridiculous as I crossed the concrete floor to the corner where class was about to start. A guy shooting baskets glanced my way and then did a double take. I knew my face was a little red, but I could handle some embarrassment if it gave him the ability to kick like those guys I'd seen at the fights.

Almost thirty GI's lingered about getting ready for class and I approached Mr. Kit, the Thai man I'd talked to earlier. During our previous conversation, Mr. Kit, a small and somewhat serious man especially for a Thai, had told me that Tae Kwon Do was the assigned martial art at all bases in Thailand, but their instructor, Seop Joo Ahn, had left months ago, and his replacement, Master Toddy, had recently left as well. They followed the traditional Tae Kwon Do belt structure and teachings because Muay Thai was reserved only for the Thai's. However, Mr. Kit also confided with me that they would incorporate Thai kicks, leg checks, elbows, and knees on the sly.

Mr. Kit guided me over to another Thai man. This one was about the same age or maybe a little older, probably almost ten years my elder in his early 30's. He was taller with broad shoulders and his angular jaw and cheek bones made him look as if he should be in the movies instead of kicking ass in a Military gym. Mr. Kit introduced me to Mr. Wanna, who offered a broad smile and a deep bow. I returned the gesture and then we shook hands. "Welcome to our class Jacob. Have you trained before?"

"No sir, not really, but I'm ready to learn."

"Good, let's get started."

Class got underway and despite the small uniform and the fact that it was more Tae Kwon Do than Thai Kickboxing, I ate it up. My muscles hurt much like they did when I was playing baseball at Merced College, except the pain was a little deeper from all the torturous stretching and repetitive kicking. My feet blistered and tore. My uniform went from bright white to dull white, and I wouldn't have had it any other way.

I was a dedicated and fast learner and it was only a month before I was flipping front kicks, roundhouses, and side kicks with speed and accuracy. Mr. Wanna, Mr. Kit, and Mr. Pe, a student instructor who'd just earned his black belt before I'd arrived, were impressed with my enthusiasm and skill.

In a matter of months I climbed from white, to yellow, to orange, to green belt and every time Mr. Kit's younger brother, Mr. Ken, came from Bangkok where he was working on his Physical Education degree, he commented on how fast I was coming along. Then with an enthusiasm that maybe even outpaced mine, he'd throw kick after kick with lightning-fast accuracy. The four of them recognized that with each day and each training session, they were forging me into a warrior. And maybe even more importantly, we were becoming friends.

FRIENDSHIPS AND TRAGEDY

For months I trained religiously, two, even three classes a day and usually seven days a week. When I was on duty I practiced my technique at the gate or on the guard tower. With my shirt soaked through I'd keep practicing and stretching. The day I did the splits to where my nuts touched the ground was truly momentous.

I couldn't get enough of it and that was fine with Mr. Kit and Mr. Wanna. Often I'd work with them outside at the tennis courts or on the grass, and sometimes they'd just watch me do countless round houses and spin kicks without saying a word to me. They'd whisper amongst themselves, but wouldn't talk to me. I regret that I never asked them what they were saying. I was becoming so close with them. It was as if they were my brothers.

It was at a demonstration at the NCO Club not too far from those tennis courts where I had just witnessed Mr. Wanna do the unthinkable by breaking a football-sized rock with his hand, when I decided to ask Mr. Pe about my other friend and instructor, Mr. Kit. "You know I love him like he is one of my brother's Mr. Pe, but I notice he does not smile or talk so much. Can you tell me why?"

Even though we were such good friends, I felt uneasy asking the question, but Mr. Pe waved me off. "You are like our brother, so I think you can know."

He then told the story about Mr. Kit and his younger brother Mr. Ken, the one who attended the University of Bangkok. Their father, Narong Kaewpadung, was the head of law enforcement in their village. He was so honorable that no matter their rank or social status, he did not let the bad guys get away. This earned him a great deal of respect amongst the law-abiding villagers, but not so much with the criminals. In 1963 he arrested a local gangster. This made Officer Kaewpadung a target to the most dangerous criminals and not long after making the arrest, he was assassinated.

Mr. Ken was eight years old at the time and Mr. Kit was a teenager. The news was obviously devastating to their mother. She had a nervous breakdown and couldn't care for her sons. The brothers had lost their father and mother and were separated. Mr. Kit went to live with a family in the north and Mr. Ken moved to Pahkai village.

The years had passed and the two had taken different routes to U-Tapao. Mr. Pe was unsure if the tragedy affected Mr. Kit more because he was older, or if it was just in his personality to be more subdued than his younger brother.

I raised my shoulders up then let them fall back down as I blew out a long breath. "I had no idea they went through that."

"And don't treat them differently because you know," Mr. Pe said. "they are warriors and want no pity."

I understood and agreed to continue to treat them both with respect and dignity. It was even easier after hearing the story and one of the best ways I knew to honor them was to keep learning and training my hardest.

Through my friendships with my instructors, I was easily accepted by all the Thai's, and I was building quite a reputation. The Thai taxi drivers loved giving me a hard time. Every time I walked by the line on the way to my barracks at least one of them would hop out and say, "Sah-wah-thee (hello) Bruce Lee!" he'd then get in a fighting stance and throw kicks my way. We kicked and punched at each other with no malicious intent and all the other drivers would howl with delight. Then another would step up and I'd repeat the process. On more than one occasion I had to pass the gauntlet of taxi drivers before getting to my barracks.

There were other, much tougher opponents and I had to face them too. The Thai guards who lived on base and trained in Muay Thai liked to come to practice to spar with the GI's. Because of my dedication, height, and great kicks, Mr. Wanna and Mr. Kit almost always gave me the assignment of taking on the Thai guards. I relished the opportunity and always fared well, so much so that I was rewarded in another way.

INTO THE JUNGLE

Mr. Wanna offered me a spot on the demonstration team. The group often headed out into the jungle to do demonstrations at small villages. One day toward the end of my tour in Thailand, we all boarded the baht bus, which looks like a pick up with seats running along the back. We sat on benches on either side of the bus facing each other. Only a cover protected us from the night. We drove a good ways along a pockmarked road and as we were jostled about, the jungle got thicker on each side. Sometimes the road became so skinny that we had to lean forward to avoid getting smacked by the tree branches as they passed.

Eventually we made it to our destination. It was similar to my first experience when I went to the fights in Sattahip, except on a much smaller scale. The villagers stared at me, but I was kind of used to it. I was the only American on the team and we were so deep in the jungle that many of them had never seen a Farang, the Thai word for foreigner.

We went through the paces on a rickety, makeshift stage held together with bamboo. Mr. Kit used his agility and speed to wow the crowd as he flew through the air. Mr. Pe used his strength to blast through boards as if they were sticks of butter. And Mr. Wanna broke blocks that were no match for the rock he broke at the NCO Club.

Soon it was my turn to display my skill. I removed his glasses, and although the brick was just a blurry gray image, took aim. Then with a tidal wave of power I did a spin kick and blasted through the brick. Pieces flew in all directions and the crowd applauded.

Moments later everyone was in the Monastery changing back into our clothes. Mr. Pe came up to me with a worried look on his face. "Hey there's a bunch of people outside pissed off at you," he said.

"What are you talking about?" I said. "Why?"

"When you broke that brick a piece flew off and hit a baby on the head and scratched it. They are mad because you didn't acknowledge it and say sorry."

"Man, I didn't have my glasses on. I couldn't even see. I guess I should go apologize to them now."

"No, it's too late," Mr. Pe said, "they won't understand. We just need to get out of here!"

I considered it. I didn't know how these villagers would respond and after all I was in the middle of the jungle. I agreed to just hit the road and we piled into the baht bus. With the trees closing in around us and as we rumbled along the bumpy road, we saw lights behind us. "Shit man, they're coming after me," I said.

I beat on the back window and in Thai asked Mr. Wanna to step on the gas. Mr. Wanna didn't quite understand and Mr. Kit hastily relayed the message. Mr. Wanna glanced in the rear view mirror and pushed on the pedal. The bus lurched as it gained speed. Everyone held on as we were thrown around in the back.

The mood was tense. Nobody knew exactly what to expect if we were caught, and although we could take care of ourselves, we didn't want to fight our way out of the jungle against a bunch of angry machete-wielding villagers. Fortunately, we didn't have to. After five minutes or so the trees opened up and the bus whipped onto the main road where it accelerated and we left our followers behind.

The close encounter with the villagers made me think of the other time I felt like I was in danger in Thailand. I was often paired up with a Thai guard named Jote, and we became friends. Jote took me to his village over by the Cambodian border. It was a great experience as I got to spend time visiting with and eating rice with a Buddhist Monk.

Later, as I drank rice wine with the villagers, a woman wearing nothing but a sarong that covered her lower half, breast sagging to her belly and teeth black from chewing betel nut to get high, approached me. "You a nice Farang," she said. "You can have my daughter for the night."

I politely declined and soon it was time to leave Jote's village. We loaded up into a baht bus and just as we sat down we were rocked by what seemed like an explosion. We were thrown around the back of the bus and I feared the Vietcong had attacked us. It was actually a car that slammed into us from behind. The crash threw us around the back of the bus. I found myself on the floor looking at the smashed up front of the car lodged in the back of the baht bus. My head was a little woozy, but after a quick inventory I realized I was fine.

Jote wasn't so lucky. He was sprawled across the side of the bus and the bench. His eyes were closed and blood was running from the other side of his head.

"Jote, you okay? I yelled

Slowly his eyes opened, but they were out of focus. He lifted his head and more blood leaked from it. I said again, "You okay?"

"My head, my ear," Jote said.

I worked my way around to the other side and saw that a piece of glass had literally cut Jote's ear almost all the way off.

He'd also banged his head on the side of the bus and a welt had formed above his right eye.

Despite the gruesomeness of the injuries, I felt I was calm and in control. I kept telling Jote that he'd be alright as we raced to a hospital. He seemed like he would truly be okay, but the wound looked nasty. He spent hours getting sewn up and he did turn out to be fine other than a headache and a horrible gash. And for me, I wasn't really physically injured, but it was a scary experience. I thought about where I was, a small village along the Thailand Cambodia border, and thought about how I was pretty much all alone. The aloneness is what bothered me. I never gave all the blood a second thought.

Despite the crash and the fear of being chased by the villagers, I was happy I'd ended up in Thailand. I had a new love in the form of martial arts and I was good at it. Now though, after a year and some four hundred hours worth of training in Tae Kwon Do and Muay Thai, my time at U-Tapao was running short. I'd have to figure out how I could keep practicing Thai Kickboxing while in the United States.

LEAVING THAILAND

I tried everything I could to make it where Mr. Pe could come to the States with me. Not only had we become such close friends, but Mr. Pe had even started writing to my youngest sister Belen and they'd become friends as well.

When I broke the news to him that he was not going to be able to come, tears formed in the corners of our eyes. In order to fight them off I said, "Remember that time you carried me across that puddle?"

Mr. Pe smiled and I could tell he was thinking about that day months ago. One of my training partners, Ramiro Rossel, and I were with Mr. Ken and Mr. Pe in a zone that was restricted to GI's. Despite the location, I didn't feel unsafe since I was with a couple of the toughest people in Thailand. It had just rained hard and as we walked down the street we came to a muddy water puddle. There was no way around it so Mr. Ken grabbed Ramiro and Mr. Pe grabbed me and the men put us on their backs and carried us across the water in order to keep our shoes dry.

As I rehashed the story with Mr. Pe I realized that it was something that could only happen in Thailand. The Thai people were like that, once you were their friend, they'd do anything for you.

It had been an amazing year. I'd become a brown belt in Tae Kwon Do and had a ton of experience in Muay Thai, but as it is with the Military, you often don't get to stay in one place too long even if you really want to.

Mr. Ken didn't stay in Thailand much longer either. In 1977, he followed Master Toddy to England where he trained thousands of Westerners in the art of Muay Thai, and is now known as the quite famous Grandmaster Sken. Despite all those students and hours of training, he remembers the day in 1975 when I got my brown belt, because he was the one I had to fight to earn it.

4

RETURNING TO OAKLAND
"SHOW ME DURAN" AND SOUTH DAKOTA

I WAS ON LEAVE AND HANGING OUT and drinking with my friends in the park, the same one where we found the dead snake, when my little brother Ernie started telling everyone how much of a bad ass I was now. I didn't tell the family I was training over in Thailand. Upon returning, I had Ernie hold a baseball glove about head high and I kicked the shit out of it. He was impressed with my newfound skill so he was talking about it. "You guys should see Jacob. He kick's like Bruce –"

Juni Montano cut Ernie off by stepping in front of him and squaring up to me. Juni was a Marine and had just returned home as well. With his best steely-eyed Clint Eastwood stare and in a voice to match he said, "Show me Duran," and crossed his arms in front of him, fists down, then slid his left arm over his right and brought his right hand back to his hip in a karate stance.

Now we were all a little tipsy and I almost laughed thinking Juni was messing around. "Show me Duran," he repeated.

"Naw, naw, naw, Juni I'm –"

"Show me Duran."

I started to protest again, but the Marine wanted to show the Airman what was up. "Show me Duran!" He deepened his Karate stance.

Juni was a hell of an athlete, and he was a Marine so you know he was tough, but that night in the park while in his karate stance he never saw it coming. Just like the night in Thailand when I was introduced to Muay Thai by the head kick KO, I threw a roundhouse into Juni's neck. I didn't want to knock him out so I popped him on the side of the head and pulled it back.

Juni just stood there and didn't say a word and that was the end of it. Then a couple beers later Juni came up to me. "Duran, I don't know what hit me."

It was funny, but there's even more to this story later on.

A week or so later I was a few states away at my next duty station in South Dakota. PKA Kickboxing was just getting started and an American trained in Muay Thai was damn near unheard of, so Ellsworth Air Force Base with its flat surroundings that ran into the Black Hills, didn't offer much in the form of training for me. I headed to the Rapid City YMCA without a Thai friend in sight just hoping for a place to train.

The Y had a room with a couple heavy bags so in the Thai shorts Mr. Pe had given me and an U-Tapao t-shirt, I blasted away on the bag. I remembered the words of Mr. Wanna and Mr. Kit and practiced my technique as if they were standing in the room watching me.

Soon I fell into a routine. Once my duty day ended at Ellsworth, I made my way to the Y where I'd stretch until it hurt. It was a lot of work getting my nuts to the floor and I wanted to keep them there, and I practiced Tae Kwon Do and Thai Kickboxing techniques while blasting away at the heavy bag.

One day I didn't realize I'd stayed longer than usual. After hundreds of spin kicks I was working on a jab/cross combo followed by a jab/fake cross/high kick. The combo wasn't difficult, but I'd learned in Thailand to drill the techniques until it was fast and perfect. Sweat spilled from my face and drenched my U-Tapao shirt as I repeated the combo over and over.

Finally, I felt it was on the money and called it a day. I turned to grab a towel to wipe up the puddle of sweat and noticed I had an audience. A man with about the same build as me and wearing a black Gi that matched his black hair, seemed to approve what he'd just saw. As if being noticed was an invitation, he crossed the gym. "You've got some very nice kicks," he said.

I responded with a thanks and the man introduced himself as Robert Salazar. He taught Kenpo Karate at the Y and invited me to stay for the class. I did and soon I was training with Robert. It was good, not quite the same as in Thailand, but it kept me busy and I learned some techniques that I was able to add to my arsenal.

I got to put that arsenal on display at a Karate tournament on Ellsworth. I was still a brown belt but entered in the black belt division. I knew that because of my training in Thailand I was more capable than most. I just wasn't sure how much, and entering the black belt division seemed the best way to test myself.

The tournament got underway and I dispatched of my first opponent in brutal fashion.

I was staying loose, ready for my second bout when the guy I was scheduled to fight came up to me. "You're hitting too hard man," he said.

I wrinkled my nose and looked up into the guys small intense eyes. "Okay, isn't that the idea?"

"No you're just supposed to score points," the man said. "So you'd better not try that shit on me."

I didn't appreciate his tone, but he was gone before I could respond. I didn't know if the guy was full of crap and just trying to get me to go easy or what, but the idea of holding back didn't compute. I mean I wasn't out to hurt anybody, but this was a competition, and besides I was used to plowing into my opponents in Thailand and knew they came back at me just as hard.

Moments later we were facing each other again, this time on the mat. The guy shot me a menacing look as some kind of warning. I met the glare and thought *alright then asshole, you're asking for it.*

The fight started and I set up a step-in sidekick and landed it perfectly to his ribs. He doubled over and fell onto his butt. The referee jumped in and told me to take a knee.

I waited while he recovered. It was obvious a fire was beginning to burn in his belly. After a few minutes he stood and rolled his neck a few times to indicate he was okay, and then with his jaw and fists clenched, huffed to the center of the mat ready to destroy me.

The referee edged between us, placed his hand on our chests and forced us to step back a little. Then he yelled, "Fight!"

It seemed a fight was exactly what the man had on his mind. He charged recklessly throwing a few wild kicks and punches. I dodged them easy and planted a roundhouse into the exact same spot where I'd just landed the sidekick.

A high-pitched groan shot from his lungs and he fell once again. This time the fight had been knocked right out of him. All it took was two kicks and I was in the finals.

I had no problem winning my third fight either. None of my opponents came close to matching the skills of my Thai friends.

Since I was representing Robert Salazar's class from the Y, the man bear-hugged me and lifted me off my feet. His brown belt had just mopped the floor with the black belts and I'd only used my legs in doing so.

Unfortunately for Robert, I wasn't long for South Dakota, or the Air Force for that matter. It was time to become a civilian once again. My big brothers, Jimmy and Michael, were working for R.J. Reynolds Tobacco Company, and two weeks before I was to leave, my sister Linda got a job with them as well. I had already sent my household goods to Oakland thinking I'd get a job there too, but with three Duran's already on the payroll, and as I started to learn about the corporate hiring process, I wasn't so sure if I'd be working for R.J. Reynolds or not.

BACK HOME

In Oakland, I sat down across the desk from Bob Wheeler. The assistant manager asked me a few questions in an Oklahoma accent and then held up a piece of paper. "Looks like your brothers are hard workers." It was a recommendation letter from Jimmy's manager. "I figure we'll give you a shot. You're hired."

We walked outside and Bob pointed to a 1975 Ford LTD. "That'll be the car you're driving. Welcome to R.J. Reynolds."

As a salesman for R.J. Reynolds, I was planted in the middle of Oakland, not far from where I climbed off a bus as a young man unsure of himself. Now a few years and a whole lot of punches and kicks later I was back.

Just days after moving into my new place, I walked to a convenience store down the street from my house. A man approached, much like the one did years before when I'd just gotten off the bus for my physical. "Hey give me a five spot man. I got to eat," he said.

This time I didn't reach into my pocket, instead I squared up to him. "Naw you're gonna have to find another sucker," I said.

The man considered his response and I continued to look him dead in the eye. Finally he just turned and walked away. I watched him go and then walked to the store and bought some bread and milk with my five bucks.

The job was fine, good in fact. I liked the work and was making a decent salary, but the itch to train was strong and I couldn't find a place. Finally I hooked up with a friend, Alfredo Sanchez, who was actually my barber. Some barbers like to kick ass too and Alfredo was one of them.

We hatched a plan to enroll in school at Alameda College because they offered martial arts classes for free. Before long we were "college students" who only showed up for the free Tae Kwon Do.

Since it was a new place and I just wanted to get in a little work, I went in as a white belt. The black belt instructor was good and he liked to let everyone know it. Only a couple classes into it he lined up the students then called us out one by one to spar. He wasn't into educating during the sparring session. Instead he pretty much beat the shit out of one student after another.

I watched and shifted my weight back and forth as I waited my turn. The instructor blasted a lower belt with a roundhouse and followed it up with another. The man was done, but the instructor popped him again for good measure.

This type of behavior would never fly in Thailand and I caught myself clenching and unclenching my fists while I rolled my neck in lazy circles. The instructor, sweat beading on his head and breathing a little heavy, pointed at me and then tightened the knot in his black belt.

The pointing finger was all I needed. I stepped out of the line, bowed to him, and then got in a fighting stance. He snapped a roundhouse. I rolled with it and fired one back at him. It caught him in the hip and he winced and stepped back with his eye brows raised.

He let out a loud Ki-yap, switched feet and tried a roundhouse followed by a back kick. I circled out of the way again and got him in the back and stomach with a double kick.

The instructor's face grew red, those beads of sweat became rivers, and he continued to push the pace. I countered each move and scored point after point.

After a few minutes of frustration, he called it quits. He swallowed hard as he called class to an end and everyone bowed to the flags and to him. I noticed he kept glancing my way as he rounded up his bag and packed his stuff, as if wondering how a white belt just handed him his ass.

Outside, Alfredo said, "You kicked the crap out of him."

"He kind of deserved it didn't he?"

"Yep," we nodded to each other and Alfred turned to leave. "Hey you better come in for a hair cut tomorrow, you're looking scraggily."

"Okay boss," I replied.

I turned to go and the girl I was sitting next to in class was standing in my path. "I just want to thank you. I was about to quit because I really didn't see any benefit until I saw what you did tonight. Now I'm staying for sure."

This was really cool to hear. I know that it isn't just about beating people up, but sometimes you had to lay a beat down on somebody to prove a point, and maybe I did that.

Not long after, I got to see if my instructor had gotten the message *don't pick on people just because you can, it'll come back on you.* I was pumping gas at a nearby station and he pulled into the next pump. He hadn't really talked to me since being embarrassed, but now he said, "So where have you trained before?"

"Thailand for a year and in South Dakota."

The man's face visibly relaxed and his shoulders lifted. "Oh I see, no wonder you are so good."

He left the gas station happy to know he hadn't been beaten up by a newcomer, and maybe he learned not to pick on others as well.

The class at Alameda College was good, but you can only pretend to be a student for so long. Besides, I wanted to take my game to a new level. I was great with my feet, knees, and elbow, but I needed to add my hands to the mix.

KING'S GYM

It was a seedy area. Bars and strip clubs lined the streets and a fair amount of prostitutes could be found walking along the cracked sidewalks. I drove through the debauchery on my way to and from work. Usually, I just cruised through with the tunes on the radio and selling tobacco products on my mind, but one day I kept my eyes peeled. I wasn't searching for a hooker, rather I'd heard from my barber Al Sanchez that a new boxing gym was opening soon.

I found it at the corner of east 14th and 23rd. Nestled amongst the bars was a plain building with a few windows on either side of the door. A small sign announced that it was Charles King's gym, but not open yet.

I cupped my hands against one of the windows and saw movement, so I walked to the door. It was cracked a few inches and I heard music coming from inside. I pushed the door open a little further and slipped in.

A thin man who was unloading a box noticed me first. He smiled and asked if he could help me. I introduced myself and said, "I want to learn how to box."

The man's smile grew a little wider and he introduced himself as Charles King. "We'd love to teach you, but as you can see, we still have a ways to go before opening."

He was right. They did still have a lot of work. A couple of heavy bags hung from the ceiling, the beginnings of a ring had started to form, and one mirror was attached to the wall, but that was it. We talked a little longer and the other man who'd been painting the back wall wandered over. He was a little bit sturdier than Charles and his brow was thick with scar tissue. "This here is my man Maurice Harper," Charles said. "Former pro boxer, retired with almost 30 wins."

I introduced myself once again and the three of us talked some more. Finally, I had to cut out for work, but the gym remained with me during the day. After seeing the beginnings of it I realized I desperately wanted to get in there and start throwing my hands.

A week later, on my way home from work I stopped by the gym again. I noticed it was coming along, but still had a ways to go.

A few days later, I was back at King's Gym. Now a row of heavy bags waited to be punched and a few speed bags had been installed. I watched as Charles and Maurice prepared to hang another nine foot tall mirror on the wall. The brackets were in place and the men stood on either side. I asked if I could help, but they said they had it.

They lifted and the mirror slipped and tilted a bit. The top hit the wall hard as they set it down for another go, and I watched as a crack formed at the top and snaked down the middle. Maurice grumbled under his breath and Charles eyed the crack for a few seconds before saying, "Looks like we got to get another mirror."

Finally, the day came. The gym was scheduled for a ten o'clock opening so I arrived a few minutes early. The place looked nice, a row of nine foot mirrors with no cracks, rows of heavy bags and speed bags, a nice ring, jump ropes hanging on the wall, and a few weights in the corner. I turned in a circle and told Charles and Maurice that the place looked great. I then took in a deep breath. The smells of new leather and paint came to my nose, not sweat and blood.

A lined sign up sheet sat on the counter and I signed my name. It was the first on the list. I then paid the $15 monthly dues and was ready to start boxing.

On that morning in the late-70s, I became the first to sign up at the now famous King's gym. And I've been followed by a host of boxing legends and MMA stars. Olympic Gold Medalist Andre Ward calls the gym home, and greats like George Foreman, Pernell Whitaker, Julio Chavez, James Page, Bone Crusher Smith, James Toney, and Joe and his son Marvis Frazier have all trained at King's. Nick and Nate Diaz and Jake Shields have also let their hands fly at King's. Even Bob Dylan has gotten a workout or two in there.

But the first ever member was Jacob Duran, and I planned on spending a whole lot of hours there learning the sweet science from Charles and Maurice.

BECOMING A DAD AND BOXING AND COACHING AT KING'S

Years before returning home, I had married at the age of twenty. I'd spent most of the years in the Air Force away from my wife. So much so that it wasn't really like we were married at all. But in Oakland we were together. Our relationship was full of ups and downs. One of the ups came on March 31, 1978. My daughter, Carla, was born. Years later, in August of 1984, we'd have another up when Jacob Jr. was born. The relationship didn't last much longer after Jacob's birth though. We were both just too young, but later on I would meet somebody who was perfect.

With a baby at home, I was often sleepy during the day, but the sounds of King's gym always woke me up. I was in the middle of those sounds, arms crossed and hands still a little sweaty from holding pads, as I watched the 16-year-old kid shadowbox in the ring. I looked at my friend Pete Alvarado. "You think Chapo will do alright?" I said.

"He'll do better than alright," Pete said. "He's gonna win the damn thing."

I uncrossed my arms and shook my hands a couple times. "Hope you're right."

"I was right when you cornered Lopez for the first time wasn't I?"

I couldn't argue with that. After a few months of training at King's with Charles and Maurice, my hands were catching up with my legs. My combinations became crisper, my footwork smoother, and my head movement natural. Then

Pete Alvarado showed up. We became friends right away and Pete, thanks to his dad who trained fighters, had been in boxing gyms all his life in Puerto Rico and New York.

The months passed and we watched as more and more young kids began training at King's. Soon Pete and I started helping out those kids in between our own training sessions, and after a while we found ourselves coaching a team of six amateur boxers.

The time of which Pete was talking about came when Gabriel Lopez, a tough kid the same age as Chapo, was fighting in an event in Hayward. It was my first time in the corner with Pete and I was amped. The first round ended, Lopez sat down and I started working on him at about a hundred miles per hour. Pete laughed and said, "Hey relax man. One minute is a hell of a long time."

I did relax, and he didn't know it at the time, but that advice would help me a great deal in the future.

Chapo finished up shadowboxing. "Looking good Vargas," I said. "You're ready to go this weekend right?"

He nodded and threw a couple of sharp jabs in response. "Good, hurry up and get cleaned up. I got something for you guys," I told all the fighters.

While Chapo was changing, I headed to my R.J. Reynolds van and pulled out a box that sat atop all the cigarette cartons, the same van in the same parking place in which it had been broken into only a month before. The idiot thieves smashed the window and stole the stereo, leaving behind thousands of dollars worth of cigarettes. With the box under my arm, I double checked to make sure the van was locked before heading back into the gym.

The kids went crazy as I cut the tape and lifted a pair of black and white shorts with King's Gym embroidered on the back and front out of the box. They'd never had a uniform before and these took a little doing on my part. I'd gotten donations from my accounts with R.J. Reynolds so we were going to the Golden Gloves Tournament in style.

"You guys are gonna look damn good while representing King's Gym this weekend," Pete said. "So make sure you fight good too."

They all did fight well. Gabriel took third and Chapo made it to the finals in his division. He was out-pointed early, but delivered a few body shots that made his opponent grimace. He kept at it, landing more body shots and firing off snapping jabs that kept his opponent off rhythm.

With one round to go, Chapo sat on the stool and steadied his breathing. "He's worn down," I said. "Keep at the body then mix in a couple of overhand rights."

Pete agreed. "This is it Chapo. All that hard work pays off this round."

The boys touched gloves and Chapo went to work on the body. His hands were as fresh as they were in the first round and he did just as I said by firing off a big right hand. It connected flush and his opponent stumbled, but held on until the round was over.

Chapo claimed the decision and with it he became the first Golden Gloves winner from Charles King's gym. And he was coached by the first ever member of King's gym. I continued to coach and train, but I also wondered what it would be like to promote an event. Only one way to find out!

HENRY J. KAISER AUDITORIUM

It was early in the afternoon and the newly renovated Kaiser Auditorium was empty. Pete supervised as the guys finished installing the padding on the turnbuckles. I helped two men pull a banner tight that read *Amateur Boxing Presented by King's Gym and Budweiser.*

Once the banner was in place, I turned to Monte Poole. "So what do you think?

The writer for the Oakland Tribune replied, "Looks fine, but why isn't your name on it? You're the one putting this on."

"Yeah, but Budweiser is sponsoring it and Charles is the one that got me going in boxing," I said.

"Those Budweiser posters are all over the area," Monte said. "How'd you get them anyway?"

"Their sales force has been hanging those things everywhere haven't they? I got them because I hustled, made some calls, contacted a guy who knew another guy, until they were on board with the sponsorship," I replied. "You know what it takes Monte, you always gotta be hustling."

"You got that right. You still have 16 fights on the card?" He asked.

We started walking toward the ring. "Yep, still 16, gonna be a full night of fights."

Pete needed help with some paperwork so I had to cut my talk with Monte short. I thanked him for the articles he'd already done, and Monte said he looked forward to the fights.

Since I got off work at five o'clock the day before, I'd been going from one thing to the next to ensure my first promotion was a success. I had everything in place, the sponsorship, the advertising and media, the fighters, the officials, and I'd managed to continue to train, coach, and keep up with my sales for R.J. Reynolds. I was ready for the event, but as I finished up with Pete and unfolded a few chairs at a table next to the ring, I wondered if it was all worth it.

A few hours later I read off the schedule to a room full of people and still wondered if it was worth it. I'd only had time to grab a bologna sandwich for lunch and ate it while on the move. I'd just changed from my old jeans and t-shirt into pants and a button down shirt and asked Pete to make sure the doors would be open in five minutes.

After assurance from Pete, I made the rounds checking with each boxer and their corners to see if they had what they needed. Some of my guys were on the card, and despite being dressed up, I grabbed the pads and held them for Chapo for a couple minutes. Each pop of the pads reminded me why I was doing this and also made me recognize that there was nothing better than it.

Pete found me in the hallway. "Shit, this place is filling up fast," he said.

We headed out of the tunnel and into the arena. Pete was right. I estimated close to a thousand people had already filed in.

After another check with everyone around the ring, it was time to get underway. The fights actually provided some relief for me. I mean I had to make sure each aspect of the promotion was going as planned, but the fights went off without a hitch.

Once the event ended, Monte tracked me down. "What'd you think?"

"I thought it went well," I said. "A lot of people here tonight."

"For sure. Bet you had 2,500 people here and it ran real smooth."

Monte wasn't the only one to call the night a success. Pete was fired up and Charles told me it was a great event. It seemed this kid from the fruit fields of Planada had found a niche in which I might have a great deal of success. But I was a fighter at heart, I loved the action and those couple minutes of padding out Chapo were the best couple minutes of the night. I needed to be in the middle of it. Besides, it was time for another move and a new challenge.

5

KICKBOXING
DENNIS AND STITCH

THE ROUNDED, METAL QUONSET HUT looked like it had been over in Vietnam around the same time I was in Thailand. It was dull and dented, but served its purpose well and was only miles away from my new home in Fairfield. The wide open space was fully equipped with everything a combat sports athlete could need.

I had just finished work on the speed bag and a little shadowboxing, and was getting warmed up on the heavy bag. King's gym had taught me the art of using my hands, and while there I'd kept working on my legs, but I'd let them slip a little bit.

I started blasting and sank into another one of my routines where the world around me gets lost. With each crushing blow my legs seemed to return to their old form, and in between kicks I fired off jabs, crosses, and hooks.

After a flurry of kicks and punches, I drilled the bag with an overhand right and turned away from it. A young man, maybe in his mid-20s with a dark complexion, short curly hair, a thick mustache and pearl white teeth, was stretching some ten feet away.

He nodded as I unraveled my wraps. "Damn, where'd you come from?"

"Been at King's in Oakland the last few years, but before that ... that's a long story brother."

"I got some time," the guy replied. "And I could use somebody to train with. Name's Dennis Alexio."

I recognized the name right away. Dennis was already the light heavyweight kickboxing champ and on his way to winning titles in other divisions. We talked and I told him about my time learning Muay Thai in U-Tapao and my more recent days at King's gym. Before long we were kicking and punching at each other on an almost daily basis.

The first time we sparred, I saw Dennis' amazing athletic ability. The man was so fast and strong it was obvious why he was a three-sport star who had his number retired at Vacaville High. I had to focus on technique and rely on my own snapping kicks and precise footwork just to keep up with Dennis. He moved like my Thai friends, but had power coming out his ears.

The days passed and we became closer while kicking the snot out of each other. Pretty soon we'd stop while sparring and I'd point out how Dennis could change his foot position slightly in order to be faster, or move in order to create better angles. After a while the sparring was less and less and instead I started holding pads and working with him more as a trainer.

While I worked with his legs, boxing trainer Al LaGardo worked with his hands. The two of us lifted his already incredible game to a new level.

Dennis was scheduled to show off his ever-improving kickboxing skills at the Vallejo County Fair. The ring was set up in an auditorium that doubled as a livestock building and the place was packed with fans. But before Dennis fought, one of his sparring partners, David Rooney, was set to enter the ring.

With Al and me in his corner, David looked sharp. His opponent was a big man, but much slower than Dennis. David picked him apart in round one, but in round two the man caught him with a right hand. A cut opened up just below his left eye and a thin line of blood slid down his cheek. The round ended and Al and I jumped into the ring. I'd never worked a cut before. I'd been in the corner many times, but never stopped blood.

Instinctively I wiped away the blood and checked the gash. It wasn't big, but it was a cut nonetheless. I applied direct pressure while Al talked to David about keeping his hands up and keeping better distance. Just before the minute between rounds came to an end, I removed the cloth and the cut was not bleeding. I applied a dab of Vaseline, unsure of how much to use, and David was back out for round three.

David returned to picking apart his opponent and I watched and shouted instructions, but I kept thinking about the cut. I wondered if I did what was needed. By the end of the round a trickle of blood had begun to leak once again, nothing like before though.

After the fight, I wiped the wound clean and Al said, "Might need a few stitches Dave."

But I'd remembered seeing someone butterfly before so I tore off a piece of tape and cut it into a thin strip. Then with my left hand I pinched the cut together and placed the tape over it with my right so it would keep the skin in place.

"I think that's gonna work," Al said.

"How does that feel?" I asked.

With a big smile David said, "Feels good. Looks like you saved me some stitches ... Stitch."

"Stitch," I said, "Guess that's got a nice ring to it."

Al agreed and at the Vallejo County fair three fights before I was to corner Dennis Alexio, Jacob Duran fixed his very first cut and became known as Stitch.

LEARNING TO BE A CUTMAN

Word got out that Al and I were helping Dennis Alexio, and other fighters wanted to train with us as well. Much like Pete and I did with the amateur boxers at King's gym, Al and I built a solid stable of kickboxers. Our guys were cleaning up in the International Kickboxing Federation and aspiring champs from all over California were soon heading to the old Quonset hut.

I found myself working days at R.J. Reynolds, spending my evenings training kickboxers, and many of my weekends at kickboxing events. I liked being up close to the action, and after working that first cut a new door was open.

Of course learning how to fix cuts was pretty much on the job training and it wasn't easy figuring out what to do and not to do when stopping the flow of blood. I went to the Fairfield Public library and chuckled when I saw a slot much like the one I'd stuck the dead snake in to scare Mrs. White. I approached a lady at the desk. "You have any books on blood, how to fix cuts?" I said.

The silver-haired woman peeled off her angular glasses and frowned. "Books on blood?"

"Yeah on learning how the blood flows in the face and head so I can figure out how to stop cuts from bleeding better," I said.

The woman shook her head back and forth while still holding the frown. "Let me see what I have."

A few minutes later, I left the library with two books under my arm and hopes that they'd shed some light on how I could become a better cutman.

After getting past the technical jargon, I did find some useful information in the books. I learned how the blood flowed and used that information to begin to formulate ideas on how to better treat cuts. But books could only take me so far, so one Saturday night when I wasn't at a kickboxing event, I headed to the Richmond Auditorium.

It was playing host to a pretty high-profile boxing card with Marvis Frazier taking on James Bone Crusher Smith in the main event, and I, hungry to learn about the cutman business, was looking for some spilled blood.

I got my wish. It didn't come from Frazier or Smith, but on the under card Manny Gonzalez suffered a gash above his right eye. In between rounds I moved around in my seat and stared intently as the cutman went to work on Gonzalez. In moments the blood had stopped and the boxer was out for the next round.

With a minute or so left in the round, the cut opened again, and again in between rounds the cutman stopped the bleeding. After the fight I headed back into the guts of the arena and found him. I introduced myself and the old man, cheeks sagging over his jaw and suspicious eyes, looked me up and down.

"Nice job on that cut. You mind if I asked what you did?" I said. "What'd you use to keep it dry?"

"Fuck you," the man said, "I learned from my master and you're gonna have to do the same. I'm not telling you shit."

He then turned and lumbered down the hall and around the corner.

I played out the conversation in my head to see if I was out of line. I knew that cutmen liked to keep their trade a secret, but this guy was a complete ass. I headed back toward the ring and right there in the Richmond Auditorium decided two things. I was going to become the best damn cutman in the world and I was not going to be an ass. If people wanted to learn from me I'd be happy to teach them. That is unless you're the guy who worked the Gonzalez cut in Richmond, California on February 23, 1986, you can piss off.

KIEV

I didn't have much luck learning about the trade from other cutmen, but I did learn a lot from the ringside doctors. They were much more willing to give information and I soaked it up. With their help I learned about the bone structure of the face and more on how the blood flowed. I still watched cutmen and tried to mimic what they did, however I wasn't always sure who was good or not.

One thing was for sure, Will Edgington knew what he was doing. He trained the likes of Bobby Chacon, Tony Lopez, and Loreto Garza and I watched him wrap their hands. Part of being a great cutman meant being able to wrap good hands, so I watched Will and then started practicing on my own. Over and over I practiced on myself, wrapping my hand in different ways searching for the perfect formula, and many of today's fighters would tell you I found it. One day I wrapped my own hands and tested the wraps on the heavy bag. Then while cutting off the tape I took a dime-sized chunk of skin off my forearm. It hurt like hell and it was bleeding pretty badly. I thought *shit what should I do*. Then I thought *shit, I'm a cutman, I'll just fix it myself.* So that's what I did and I've still got a little scar on my arm from it.

Just because I was heading down the path of becoming a cutman, it didn't mean I was slacking off with my other duties. I continued to spend most evenings in the battered Quonset hut forging kickboxers into champions.

I also took those same kickboxers and boxers to fights and tournaments throughout California and the United States, but our longest trip was to Kiev, Ukraine. It was December in 1991 and the Soviet Union had literally just collapsed. As a matter of fact, our event was the first professional fights in Ukraine after the break up.

It was December 15 when the plane descended through the thick clouds into a deep grayness and the sunshine disappeared for a few days. Kiev is a beautiful city. Its buildings have so much history and the magnificent churches with their rounded spires are definitely something to see, but it was hard to enjoy them. Everything was draped in a massive shadow and the temperature was biting cold. Even during the middle of the day it seemed like it was early morning or late evening and most cars drove with their headlights on. I guess I should have expected it, but being from California it was quite a shock.

The way I understood it was that many of the former KGB members had made sure they had nice "retirement plans" and stashed away a good chunk of money. They also loved the fight game so they decided to get into promoting. I don't know how much of this story, if any, was true.

The American kickboxers and boxers were brought over to take on the Ukrainian kickboxers and boxers and we trained at an old military base. The soldiers were more like salesman and they hawked everything from their uniforms to their equipment. I left Kiev with a pretty nice collection of belt buckles and hats with the old Soviet symbols on them.

We fought on December 18 and it was a pretty lively event. The Ukrainians basically kicked our asses. One exception was Mark Longo. Mark was a sparring partner for Dennis Alexio and the big man knew how to fight. He met up with Victor Doryshenko for the FIKB title and lost a controversial decision. Even with the loss he impressed the promoters so much that they had him sit at their table at the after party and he downed high-dollar Vodka and Caviar all night.

A trainer from New York named Freddy Corteone and I decided to head down the street to a local bar. The place was a dive but it was a good experience. We sipped drinks that burned, and talked about the event. We finally decided to go and I noticed Freddy was looking for something. "What'd you lose?" I said.

"I can't find my freaking glove," he said in his thick New York accent.

Now normally I wouldn't have considered losing a glove to be such a big deal, but we were in Ukraine a week before Christmas and it was damn cold. We looked all over the place for it, with no luck.

After a few choice words Freddy decided that he was just going to have to shove his hand in his pocket and we started to leave. Then the old lady running the bar came out with the glove. We thought she found it and was returning it, instead she was hustling us. In barely understandable English she said, "Five dollars," and held up five fingers.

Freddy and I looked at each other. "Can you believe this shit?" he said.

I chuckled. "Good thing she didn't get both of them. You'd be out ten dollars."

Freddy didn't think the joke was too funny. He said to the woman, "We are here for kickboxing," and threw a couple slow punches. "You know Columbus? He's the promoter."

I don't know if the woman understood what he was saying, but when she heard the name Columbus she understood alright. Her already pale face turned a ghostly shade of white and she handed Freddy the glove.

Maybe those stories of the promoters being former KGB were dead on the money. In any event, both of Freddy's hands were at least semi-warm as we walked back to the hotel. Despite getting our asses kicked it was a fun trip. I also remember meeting a couple of young Ukrainians that did not fight on the card. The oldest was barely 20 and his brother was just a teenager, but they towered over everybody and it seemed many thought they had a bright future in combat sports. They introduced themselves to me as Vitali and Wladimir Klitschko and I didn't realize it at the time, but years later I'd get to know them a lot better.

ASK

After a handful of years and a whole lot of success, I felt it was time to move on. I finished padding out a promising kid and sat down on a bench next to Al. "We've outgrown this place," I said.

"What do you mean?"

"Look Al, we've got guys begging to train with us. We've got IKF champs and we've been working with the best kickboxer on the planet. Maybe it's time we look into getting our own gym."

Al scratched his arm and grimaced a bit as he thought. "I don't know. We've got a good thing here. We're successful. We don't know if we could do the same in our own place. Besides, neither one of us has any money."

"You're right, we don't know how it'd go, but it might be worth it to give it a shot," I said.

"Maybe," Al said, "but think how much it'd cost to start a gym."

It would be expensive, and after talking about it a little more I realized that my friend and fellow trainer wasn't ready to go. And for sure we didn't have the money to open a new gym, but I wouldn't let something as trivial as not having enough money stop me.

I talked to my girlfriend Charlotte about it. We'd known each other for almost a year before I finally asked her out, now we knew we were on our way to being married. Charlotte had the same concerns as Al, but once the idea set in, it stayed with me.

It continued to eat at me and in January of 1992 I was calling on one of my clients. I parked my company car outside of the mini-mart not far away from the awning that housed a single gas pump and noticed that not all the lights were on. I found the owner outside his office door. The man waved me in and we sat down to do business. We talked for a while and I said, "What's going on with the other half of the building?"

"Had to shut it down. Business is too slow."

The reply sank in and I ran the building's layout through my head. "So are you going to rent it out?"

"Haven't really thought about it. Why, you know somebody who wants the space?"

"I might," I said, even though I knew I couldn't afford it.

We talked a little more and it turned out rent would be reasonable. Still, I didn't know if I'd be able to swing the deal.

I walked outside and looked at the building then peeked through one of the dozen or so small windows. It would be perfect. I then turned and looked at Armijo High School on the other side of Texas Street. The location was perfect as well.

I talked to Charlotte and drove her, Carla, Angela, and Jacob by the location. They agreed it would work. We considered the possibility of getting a loan, but I had a faster, albeit slightly crazier idea. I'd just gotten a credit card with a low interest rate, so the next day I headed back to my R.J. Reynolds client and plunked down $1,500 to get in the building, and then it was time to use that credit card to do a little shopping.

I bought mirrors to cover one wall, new carpet for much of the building, and all the necessary bags and equipment. I continued to sell tobacco for R.J. Reynolds, continued to train my kickboxers, and worked on getting my school ready. The days were long, but after a month I was putting the finishing touches on it.

I knew I needed a name for the place, but nothing was jumping out at me. Then one night as I lay in bed it came, ASK, the American School of Kickboxing.

Soon it was time for the grand opening and I hoped the place would be packed. I needed it to be because my damn low interest credit card was maxed out!

GRAND OPENING, TYING THE KNOT, AND FRANCE

On the morning of February 29, 1992, a leap year, the parking lot to the east of the building that now housed a mini-mart and the American School of Kickboxing, filled up with cars. Some even had to park across the street in the Armijo High School parking lot.

I had been at the gym since the sun came up making sure everything was ready. Now it was late morning and the place was packed. My kickboxers were there, including Dennis Alexio who had gone on to win the light heavyweight, cruiserweight, and heavyweight belts all at the same time and was just a few weeks away from a huge fight with the undefeated Branko Cikatic at the Thomas & Mack in Las Vegas. I was in Dennis' corner for it and it was a wild ending as Dennis lost his foot pad and then the ref didn't really break them apart. Cikatic wasn't acting like he wanted to fight and Dennis dropped him with a couple lefts but the fight was ruled a technical draw.

Fortunately there wasn't anything crazy about my grand opening and even though it was different than the opening of King's Gym in Oakland some 15 years before, I couldn't help but think of that day. I was so eager to learn and now so many people were eager to learn from me. It made sense. I'd become known as a man who could turn kickboxers into champs and fix them up in a hurry if they happened to get cut. The Daily Republic of Fairfield had even begun referring to me as the guru of kickboxing.

After the opening, I immediately had full classes. Each day Monday through Friday I taught classes from five to nine each night. I continued to train my professional fighters, but now I had an opportunity to train others as well. I loved this aspect of the gym and poured my energy into each class.

Another exciting event took place in 1992. I had popped the question to Charlotte and we were married on June 13th. Charlotte was stunning in her wedding dress and despite sweating a bit underneath my suit; I didn't look half bad either. I stood at the altar and glanced at Carla as Charlotte walked toward me and the music played. Carla looked beautiful, and next to her was Charlotte's daughter Angela. At 11 years old, Angela was three years younger than Carla, and she looked beautiful in her dress too.

After the ceremony, my son Jacob, who was almost eight and looking handsome in his suit, walked up to me and shook my hand, trying to act big for the occasion. I returned the handshake with appropriate solemnity and realized that my family had come together with Charlotte's and I knew it was right.

With my new family, new gym and old job at R.J. Reynolds, my days were full and exhausting, but I'd grown used to working from dawn until dusk. Besides, it was worth it. And I actually decided to promote again. My entrepreneurial spirit probably got jump started back when I was five years old and I'd watch my mom make her tacos for the farm workers and it stuck with me ever since.

For my first kickboxing event I teamed up with the Solano College baseball team and held the fights in the field house. The players worked the gate and concession and I took care of everything else. This event piqued the interest of some Airmen at Travis Air Force Base and I ended up doing three shows there called Battle at the Base. Each was a success, but promoting still wasn't my thing. I liked being up close to the action, not behind the scenes making sure everything ran smoothly.

I was close to the action in March of 1994. Mark Longo, the kickboxer that drank the Vodka and ate the Caviar in Kiev, called me up to work his fight in Marseille, France. The promoter wanted photos in his shorts and Mark, who'd been training himself because he lived in Denver, was totally out of shape. The promoter called me and he was pretty concerned. He wanted to know if he was in shape at all. I couldn't lie so I told him that he was not but he was working on it.

The promoter was so worried that when we arrived in Marseille he met us at the airport with a scale! Thankfully Mark had been working on his conditioning and he was fine. Then we saw the posters and realized that the photos Mark sent had been airbrushed to make him look thinner.

It was crazy how worried the promoter was about looks, especially when considering what went on between the rounds of Mark's fight. He tangled with Serge Melchionne for the Light Heavyweight title. It was an exciting fight and in between rounds I was in the ring coaching and working on Mark's face. I kept hearing the crowd going absolutely crazy and wondered what the hell was going on.

Finally, as the third round came to an end, Mark's brother Mike hit me on the shoulder. "Check out the ring girl between rounds."

I was in the middle of work and looked at him like he was a dumb ass, but he said, "Trust me."

In between rounds I worked on Mark and glanced over my shoulder when I sensed the ring girl was just behind me. She was dressed in a sexy leopard print bikini and prancing around with the ring card above her head. She was nice looking, but I didn't see what all the fuss was about. Then I happened to look down and it all came crashing on top of me. Spilling out of her bikini bottoms was a forest's worth of bush. I mean if she was side by side with Don King, Don would look like a skinhead!

I stifled my shock and whipped my head back around and gathered my composure. As the fourth round started I looked at Mike in disbelief. "Told you," he said.

The crowd only got to see the show one more time. In the fifth Mark ended the fight with a beautiful KO. Unfortunately for Mark I think the ring girl upstaged him.

It was a fun time and I'd make many more trips to France, but I'd soon get to work on a much bigger stage, albeit one without bush. That was okay though because I was happily married.

6

BOXING AND LAS VEGAS
MONTERREY, MEXICO

I HAD JUST GOTTEN OFF THE PHONE with my boss at R.J. Reynolds. My gym was doing great, but I couldn't quit my day job, and months earlier I'd put in for a transfer to Las Vegas. The desire to become a cutman full time had grown, and I knew the best place to reach this dream was in Sin City.

There was nothing available at the time and my boss again told me I'd take a pay cut if I moved, but I reiterated that I wanted to transfer if it was possible. The phone rang again. This time it was my old friend James Gogue. "Stitch, you wanna have a shot at working with Tony Lopez?"

"Nice to talk to you too James," I said. "And yeah I want to work with Lopez."

"I figured you would. They're expecting you next weekend. Want you to wrap his hands to see what you can do and maybe work with him for his next fight."

The following weekend I was face to face with Lopez in his gym in Sacramento. I wrapped his hands then smoothed the tape and packed it tight. Then all I could do was watch.

Lopez hit one fist into the other and wiggled his fingers. He then threw some punches for a couple minutes and made his way over to the speed bag. I thought he liked the wrap, but he wasn't giving any real indications.

In a matter of seconds the bag was bouncing back and forth making the familiar sound as it rattled between his fists and the platform. He sped up his hands and the rhythmic sound sped up as well. And then a loud pop threw everything off. He stopped and reached up to touch the bag. He'd busted the rubber inside and the bag was partially deflated.

I stood just a few feet away, and he turned to me and said, "I'll see you in Mexico."

Just like that I would be working my first world title fight as Lopez would be tangling with Julio Cesar Chavez for the WBC light welterweight belt. As I pulled away from the gym, I realized this was a huge step toward reaching my goal of being a sought-after cutman.

On December 10, 1994, I turned a circle inside the Estadio de Beisbol in Monterrey, Nuevo Leon, Mexico. It seemed fitting that my first world title boxing match would be in a baseball stadium. With empty chairs and bleachers on the field, it didn't look too much like a baseball stadium, but it still brought back memories of my first dream and first hero, Roberto Clemente. It had been over 20 years since Clemente had died in a plane crash, but being here made images of his awkward yet wildly successful baseball swing flash into my head.

I walked down an aisle and entered the dugout. I turned and planted one foot on the top step then leaned onto my knee. It could have been a lot different if I would have stayed at Merced and pursued baseball, or stayed in the fields of Planada. As it was, a few hours later I'd return in the middle of thousands of screaming fans.

Underneath the stadium as I was preparing to wrap Lopez's hands, his promoter Cedric Kushner came into the locker room. "Kid you might be able to wrap a good hand, but I got my own cutman," he said. "He'll be taking care of Tony at the ring."

I paused and looked up at Cedric's long face with its thick mustache and recognized that I might be a well-known name in kickboxing, especially in California, but in the boxing world I wasn't well known. If it was what Cedric wanted there was no point in arguing. Besides I would still wrap Lopez's hands.

The locker room filled. A few people sat in chairs in front of the baseball lockers. Others stood and talked to each other while watching the fights on the closed-circuit TV. I was ready, determined to do a damn good wrap. Then Emanuel Steward entered the room. The legendary trainer was working with Chavez at the time and during title fights the other side sent a representative to watch their opponents get their hands wrapped.

The pressure was on. I remembered all the hands I'd wrapped and the hours I'd spent perfecting my style while working on my own hands. I massaged Lopez's fingers and hands and looked at the hardened bones. They weren't any different than so many others, and just because Emanuel Steward was looking on wouldn't change how I did my job.

I went to work and in 15 minutes Tony "The Tiger" Lopez's hands were ready for battle. "This fighter will never have problems," Emanuel said. "His hands will never break because that's a great wrap."

"Thank you," I said. Then I added, "Can I use that as a quote?"

Emanuel smiled. "Any time."

Underneath the Monterrey night sky, Lopez and Chavez went back and forth, digging punches to each other's body and ripping shots at each other's head. The crowd chanted and played drums and I enjoyed every minute of it. About halfway through Lopez got cut. I didn't think it was too bad, and Cedric's cutman kept it dry for a round or two, but by the tenth it was bleeding a lot. The doctor came in and called the fight even though Tony and his corner thought it should continue.

On the flight back to California I was sitting with Tony and the rest of the team. "If you want my opinion you could've continued to fight," I said. "The cut wasn't that bad."

Maybe he would have continued to fight if it was me who was working on the cut. I'll never know, but soon I got to find out if I could stop the blood from flowing even if my man was suffering from multiple cuts.

VEGAS

Carla, Angela, and Jacob had just left the room and Charlotte and I sat at the kitchen table. I'd just told the kids that we were moving and I thought of the day my dad and Tio Miguel told the family we were moving off the migrant camp. The move to Planada was a tad smaller than this one, but it didn't seem like it at the time. Daniel, the baby Charlotte and I had the summer before last, was asleep in Charlotte's arms and she looked down at him. He'd be coming to Vegas with us, Angela would too, but Carla and Jacob would stay with their mom in California.

It had been almost ten months since the title fight in Monterrey. I had continued to work and while at an event in Laughlin, Nevada one of the inspectors, Tony Lato, watched me wrap Ramona Gatto's hands. Lato said, "You wrap as good of hands as Julio Cesar Chavez's trainer, you should move to Vegas."

I wanted to. I'd been trying to get there but couldn't afford to do it without R.J. Reynolds. Lato's words stoked the fire even more and just a couple weeks later I boarded a plane to fly to England to work a fight and realized I was sitting next to the famed Ugandan boxer Cornelius Boza Edwards. I knew who he was, but had never met him. We realized we were working the same event and talked at length.

"I'm hoping to get to Vegas," I said.

"Yeah, you know a lot of people want to get there Stitch, but it isn't easy," Edwards said.

"What do you mean?" I knew Edwards spent a lot of time in Vegas and now lived there.

"I mean you have to have a job, a place to stay, and you need money too. You have to make connections and just because you are there it doesn't mean you'll make it. You can't depend on this game for money."

Now as I took a sip of my iced tea and looked at Charlotte holding Daniel, I remembered what Edwards had told me and for just a second wondered if I was making the right decision. It had been a crazy day. My manager called with the news of a transfer to downtown Las Vegas, but it would come with a ridiculous $25,000 pay cut and I had to be there in a week. I hung up with my manager and called the manager in Vegas, "I've got my kids, my house, my gym," I said. "I can't be there in a week."

The manager understood, at least sort of. "I can give you two weeks," he said.

Charlotte, being supportive as always told me that we could do it, so we delivered the news to the kids. "How do you think it went with them?" I asked her.

"As well as it could have," Charlotte said. "The kids are good."

"Yeah I know," I said, "but this is hard on them and it's happening so fast."

"It is, but that's how life goes sometimes right?" Charlotte replied.

I got up and put my glass in the sink. "Right. And it's going to lead to big things. I'm sure of it."

In a matter of two weeks I closed ASK, sold my house, packed up the goods in the back of a U-haul, and feeling like the Beverly Hillbillies, made the drive from Fairfield to Las Vegas. I swung by the gym in the loaded down U-haul to turn in the keys. I opened it just three years earlier, but it had become a part of me. I stood in the doorway one last time and looked around at the empty room. The carpet still looked fresh and I thought about how crazy it was to use my credit card to get the place up and running. It paid off and I'd come to believe that in order to make it in life you had to take chances, but still, a credit card? I turned off the light and pulled the door shut. I had made many moves in my life, and wondered if this would be the last.

On the way to Las Vegas we stopped in Bakersfield to stay the night. Just outside of the hotel a man who'd robbed a store was shot by the police. I looked out the window and could see the body, lifeless in the street. I hoped it wasn't a bad omen for the move, but brushed if off. I wasn't going to Vegas to rob anybody, but to wrap hands and fix cuts.

FINDING WORK AND DON KING

The coffee was lukewarm and turning bitter, but I took another sip as I waited for Don King in the Mirage's 24 hour restaurant. I was meeting King to receive $5,000 training expenses and he was already an hour late. While I waited I considered my time living in Las Vegas.

Once the family had settled into the new house and I'd settled into my new position with R.J. Reynolds, I started heading to the gyms. I was anxious to get to work and I needed it. With the big pay cut and the loss of income from the kickboxing school, money was a little tighter.

I ended up at Golden Gloves. It was a classic boxing gym with two rings and a whole bunch of hungry fighters. It took a little work getting through all the egos, but it wasn't long before I was wrapping hands, and former champ Jamaican Mike McCallum took notice. I worked with him a little, but realized that he was hooked up with Eddie Futch and that I was probably stepping on toes by working with him.

I had watched the other trainers closely and noticed that they weren't doing anything special. I'd come to Vegas to be a cutman, figuring all the best trainers were already here. They weren't. I'd started holding pads and working with a few guys. The first was Terry Davis. He happened to be from Vallejo, California and he turned out to be my first payday in Las Vegas.

The plan was to focus strictly on being a cutman, but my talents as a trainer kept me busy too. My meeting with Don King came about when my old friend James Gogue, who I now say could have been my agent with all the work he threw my way, gave me a call. "Stitch, I got a big one for you," he said. "My man Ray Lovato is scheduled to fight Felix Trinidad for the IBF welterweight belt. He needs a cutman."

"Looks like he's got one now James," I said.

I met with Lovato and pretty soon I was holding pads. That led to an even bigger opportunity. One day after a training session Ray said, "Stitch, I need a head trainer. Can you come to Big Bear?"

The offer was tremendous and I mulled it over before saying, "Let me see if I can use my vacation time at R.J. Reynolds, if so I'm in."

I was able to use my vacation time, so now I was waiting to get the expense money from Don King. I took another sip of coffee. The waitress had topped it off so it was a little warmer. I set the cup down and saw King crossing the restaurant. The people sitting at the tables did double takes and whispered as he walked by. His shoulders were pushed back and his hands gripped the lapel of his jacket. His hair appeared to be running from his forehead and he was showing off his perpetual promoter's smile.

He sat down across from me with a flourish and we talked about the fight. King tossed out a number of impressive words when he described his champ Felix Trinidad. I was much lower key when talking about Lovato. Finally, King said, "I got your money. I hear you are training at Big Bear."

He pulled out a roll of hundreds from his jacket pocket. "Yeah, training at Larry Goossen's," I said.

"Lovato's not going to need the lungs," he said with a laugh. "You know Trinidad is going to knock him out early."

He finished counting off a stack of hundreds and put them in a pile. "Count that for me Stitch. Should be $2,500."

While I counted the first stack King started another one. He glanced a couple times and noticed I was paying attention to the second stack as well. The kid from Planada had learned a lot since the day I gave money to the guy claiming to be a Black Panther in Oakland. "There's only two thousand here Don."

"What? Count again, I'm sure it's $2,500."

I kept my composure and counted again while King kept laying down Franklin's in the second stack. "Nope, only two thousand," I said.

King didn't flinch as he finished the second stack and I made sure to count it too. There was $3,000 in it so I got what I came for. We parted ways and as I left I thought *damn, Don King tried to hustle me*. It seemed the famed promoter always wanted the upper hand, even if it was for small peanuts.

BIG BEAR AND THE BIG FIGHT

I pulled through the security gate and headed toward the building that sat not far from the small airport's runway. With an elevation of almost 7,000 feet, many famous boxers had used Goossen's gym for their training camps. The few cotton-white clouds seemed closer at the higher elevation and as I parked and walked toward the non-descript gym, I marveled at both the quiet and the beauty of Big Bear.

Once inside I surveyed my surroundings. The gym housed two boxing rings, a variety of bags, and a bunch of strength training equipment. Off to one side there was a locker room and what looked like an office. The gym was empty, and as I made my way toward the office I looked at the photos on the wall. I saw the Rueles brothers, Rafael and Gabriel, Oscar De La Hoya, and I even found a shot of Mike McCallum, the Jamaican I'd worked with briefly a few months earlier.

Finally, I met up with the rest of the team. Lovato had already been at Big Bear for a couple weeks to work on conditioning and Larry Goossen and James Gogue were both there too.

We settled into the routine. Lovato took the opportunity for a crack at the undefeated Trinidad very seriously. He ran along the lakeshore each morning at five and then after breakfast we worked conditioning while the sun was still low in the sky. After a few lazy hours at the house, where there wasn't a damn thing to do, we trained in the afternoon. I had watched tape of Trinidad and Lovato and I worked on how we could exploit any faults in the Puerto Rican's impressive skills.

After a few weeks the fight was growing near and the camp was going great. Then Gogue got a telephone call. He walked into the gym looking like his dog had been shot. "Mike got cut."

It took a second for the news to sink in. The fight was on the same card as Mike Tyson vs. Bruce Seldon. The fullness of his statement hit me and I said, "They're pushing the whole card back because Tyson got cut?"

"Yeah, at least six weeks."

It was as if Big Bear's thin air became thinner. The camp had to break apart for a while and I had used up too much of my vacation time with R.J. Reynolds to continue as head trainer. I went back to Las Vegas and worked from Monday to Thursday and then made the almost three-hour drive to Big Bear each weekend once camp restarted.

The fight took place at the MGM Grand on September 7, 1996, the same arena where Mike Tyson had decimated Frank Bruno in three rounds some six months earlier. The hype was insane. Lovato's team, Goossen as head trainer, me as the cutman, and Gogue as the other corner, felt that despite the interruption in training, the camp had gone well. All of us were confident that Lovato had a good chance of handing Trinidad his first loss.

Don King and Trinidad's team must've thought Lovato would give Trinidad fits as well. King couldn't have one of his main attractions lose. The dressing room was even more crowded than when I had wrapped Tony Lopez's hands in Mexico. Camera's snapped photos and filmed, and Marc Ratner, the Nevada Executive Commissioner, looked on. And then there was the member from Trinidad's camp watching as well.

The wrapping was going well until I began using the Power Flex tape that I'd made sure was approved by the Nevada State Athletic Commission. Trinidad's trainer had a fit, saying, "What is that? You can't use that kind of tape."

"It's been approved," Ratner said.

The man wasn't happy and before I completed the wrap he stormed out of the room. A few minutes later we got word that Trinidad's father (and manager and trainer) Felix Trinidad Sr. wouldn't come out if the tape was used.

Everyone went back and forth on the issue and it seemed Trinidad Sr. was going to stick to his guns even though the tape was legal. Finally Ratner came in the dressing room. "I know it's approved," he said. "But can you take it off so we can have the fight?"

I asked Lovato and he was fine with it, so instead of adding to the ridiculous situation I removed the Power Flex tape.

Minutes later we were in the ring and referee Mitch Halpern got the fight underway. The welterweights got after it with Trinidad holding the slight upper hand for the first five rounds. It seemed the training at Big Bear was paying off. Lovato was rocked by a big right hand in the fifth and ate a number of punches, but between rounds he wasn't winded at all.

In the sixth Lovato again took a barrage of punches, but this time Mitch Halpern jumped in to stop the action. Lovato thought the fight was stopped too soon and much of the crowd agreed, but it didn't matter. We had been building to this fight for months and in minutes it was over. The electricity of the night sank into my bones. I was disappointed that the fight didn't go as we'd hoped and I was more than ready to jump back into the fire. Later I learned that Lovato had spent his $80,000, the biggest payday of his career. Like many fighters, he bought a car, gave his parents money, and spent it on who knows what else, and in just three months the money was gone.

I worked a few fights over the next couple months and then Gogue called me up again. This time it would lead to a monumental effort, one that would show the world just how valuable I could be.

MIKE MCCALLUM AND RAUL MARQUEZ

In November I headed to Tampa with Mike McCallum. He was set to fight Roy Jones and on the last day of preparation I padded him out and it was the best pad work I'd ever done. We worked like a fine tuned timepiece and I knew he was ready to fight. Unfortunately he was meeting up with a prime and undefeated Roy Jones. Mike hung tough but lost the unanimous decision. The last time Roy had even been to decision was two years prior when he beat James Toney. And it just so happened that Mike's next fight was against Toney.

We were at the Mohegan Sun in Uncasville, Connecticut and on a small stage for the weigh in. Toney often had trouble making weight and this time was no exception. I watched as he climbed on the scale and noticed that he was standing in kind of an awkward position. I then looked behind him and saw his trainer, Freddie Roach, kind of supporting Toney to take a couple pounds off the scale. I called him out on it and got a wild reaction. Freddie went nuts on me. "Fuck you, who the fuck are you," he yelled. "I'm not cheating!" He's kind of got a high voice and he was fired up.

Well I knew that it was an act and stuck to my assertions, but nothing else came of it and Mike lost a decision to James and then retired.

A few years later I had Freddie on my radio show (I did a show for years called The 13th Round with Nick Ward). I brought up the McCallum/Toney weigh in incident and he admitted that I did in fact catch him. He decided his only defense was a good offense so he cussed me out. What a moment and no hard feelings to Freddie, he's a good guy.

Not long after the Freddie Roach lambasting, James Gogue came through once again and I was glad we'd become such good friends. Back when I had my gym, Gogue was working with Diego Corrales and he'd bring the 16 year old by to train. The kid usually wore out my pros, but the beatings spawned a friendship between Gogue and me and he recognized that I had a talent for taking care of fighters that few others possessed.

This time he hooked me up with Raul Marquez because the light middleweight was having trouble with his hands. He was scheduled to fight Anthony Stephens for the vacant IBF title and needed to make sure he kept his weapons safe.

I auditioned by wrapping Marquez's hands while his father looked on. I passed with flying colors and on April 12, 1997, a national TV audience saw Marquez claim the title over Stephens with a little help from me. Marquez was cut on the forehead early and I kept him in the fight until he scored a TKO in the ninth.

In July, the lefty Marquez defended the title easily by TKO'ing Romallis Ellis in the fourth and it set up a match up with Keith Mullings on September 13, 1997. The fight took place in Las Vegas at the Thomas & Mack Center on the same card as Oscar De La Hoya vs. Hector Camacho for the WBC welterweight strap.

The crowd was abuzz as the Marquez vs. Mullings bout got underway. The two men went at it and I quickly recognized that my wraps were especially important. Mullings kept dropping his head each time Marquez fired off a right lead jab or threw a straight left. The blows often caught the top of

Mullings' head and for a fighter with bad hands it wasn't the place Marquez wanted his punches to land.

It also became obvious that it wasn't just the wraps that would play a factor. Marquez got a nice gash over his left eye and I went to work on it between rounds. I stopped the bleeding and Marquez went back out. A couple rounds later Marquez was cut over the right eye. The gash was about the same and now I had two cuts to contend with. I shut down the blood flow and Marquez remained in the fight.

Mullings, sensing that he'd hurt Marquez, tried to pour it on. The crowd was on their feet and the fight was only halfway over. Marquez fought off the onslaught and returned the favor, another round in the books and another cut for Marquez, this one on the nose between the eyes.

The gashes above his eyes were leaking and the one on his nose was bleeding freely. Using both hands to stop all three cuts, I worked at a frantic pace, but with an air of confidence. The doctor checked Marquez and saw that the cuts were under control.

To the delight of the fans the fight pressed on. Each man landed on the other, one minute Mullings seemed to be getting the best of Marquez and the next it would be the other way around. I cringed as Marquez landed a left flush onto Mullings bald dome, but it didn't seem to hurt his hand at all.

A couple more rounds and Marquez had suffered more cuts. I was now working on a swollen face that looked like it had been placed in a blender. The cuts above the eye were the ones that had the best chance of resulting in a fight stoppage, so I made sure they stayed dry. I then worked on the bridge of the nose between the eyes and the two cuts on the cheeks all at the same time.

Finally, the fight made it to the twelfth and those at ringside marveled at this fact. Marquez looked battered and beaten, but Mullings wouldn't be taking family photos any time soon either. Everyone knew it was close on the cards and I was glad I did my part to put it in the fighters' hands.

They finished out the final round and waited for the decision. Bernie Cormier and Tom McDonough gave the nod to Marquez, while Bill Graham saw it Mullings way. Some thought the win was controversial, Marquez thought he did enough to retain his title and he never would have gotten the chance if I wouldn't have been able to keep him in the fight.

In the locker room Marquez pulled off his gloves and I cut off the tape. His hands were severely swollen from all the punches to the top of Mullings' head, but they weren't broke. And later when Marquez was sewed back together, the doctor had to use 75 stitches! No wonder after the bout the inspector in Marquez's corner said, "Stitch, you absolutely saved the fight. Great, great work."

He wasn't the only one who thought I had done a tremendous job. It was on that night, September 13, 1997, in the Thomas & Mack Center when many people realized just how important a great cutman is to the fight game.

YORI BOY CAMPUS

Less than three months later I was back in Marquez's corner in Caesar's in Atlantic City. Marquez's IBF title was on the line against Yori Boy Campas. At the weigh in, legendary cutman Chuck Bodak came up to me. I didn't know him all that well at the time, but he told me I did a great job on Raul's cuts against Mullings. It meant a great deal coming from him and it was then that we became friends and he took me under his wing. Chuck was a teacher and I learned a lot from him. To give some perspective of how much of an impact he had on the fight game, he worked with Rocky Marciano, Ali, and Oscar De La Hoya and many more in between.

Seeing Yori Boy brought back memories of the first time I met him back in 1992. I cornered a fighter by the name of Will Hernandez who got a shot at Campas in Tijuana, Mexico.

I made the trip mainly because I wanted to meet Campas. The tremendous body puncher was as good as they come and he was once a catcher in baseball, so of course I liked him.

I watched from Hernandez's corner as Campas entered the arena. The Mexican-Indian came out with a large plume headdress and walking next to him was an Indian carrying what looked like a large deer's head. Another man danced around them and shook rattles like the Yaqui Indians.

It was quite the spectacle and more entertaining than the fight. Campas stopped Hernandez in the first round. Afterward, Hernandez's manager paid me my cut for working the corner and it was fifty dollars short. I told him so and the squirrely man who many referred to as "Is a cock" because well, he was, and it sounded like his name said, "That's to pay for your license."

"Look," I said, "I came down here to help you out. I'm not paying for the license."

"Doesn't matter, you got to pay so I'm taking it out," he said.

It was just fifty bucks, but it was the principle of it that pissed me off. "No you're not. I'm not coming back to Mexico. If it was California or Nevada it'd be a different story."

"Mexico, Nevada, all the same, you owe the money," he said.

"You know what," I said, "if you don't give me that fifty bucks, I'm gonna give you fifty bucks worth of ass kicking."

I left Mexico with my money and as I watched Campas make his grand entrance once again, this time at Caesar's in Atlantic City, I laughed about that conversation.

I was all business when the fight got underway though. It was pretty much even going into the eighth and I had once again needed to work some magic on Marquez. Then Campas ended the fight with a TKO. Later Marquez realized he took the fight way too soon. His face had not healed from the Mullings fight just three months earlier and he said as much after the loss. I think this fact again goes to show just how bad Marquez's face was after the Mullings fight. Years down the road I met up with Yori Boy Campas again, I was in his corner for his 100th fight.

JOHNNY TAPIA, MSG, AND NEW OPPORTUNITIES

Not long after Marquez lost to Campas I ended up working with Johnny Tapia. He beat up Rodolfo Blanco in his hometown of Albuquerque, New Mexico and then it was set for him to fight in New York City at Madison Square Garden on the Evander Holyfield/Henry Akinwande card. I was really fired up because I always saw the Garden as something of a symbol. Once I'd worked there, I'd know that I truly made it.

Charlotte doesn't go on many of the trips with me. Truth is she'd be bored out of her mind half the time, but I made sure she was with me for this one. We got to New York City early and enjoyed all it had to offer. Then on Wednesday we got the news. The whole fight card was postponed because Akinwande had tested positive for hepatitis B. I had the same feeling I had when Lovato's fight was postponed. It sucked, but there wasn't any reason to bitch and moan about it.

Later that day Charlotte and I continued to do the tourist thing and we came across the famous Copacabana. We wandered inside and the management group was there. The club was near empty preparing for the night and they asked us what we were doing. I told them about the fights and working with Johnny Tapia. They thought that was cool and invited us back later that night.

I had also met a guy who had a limousine business and he took us out to dinner that evening. Afterward he drove us to The Copa in a beautiful black stretch limo. A line of a couple hundred waited to get in and he stopped right by the main entrance. We got out and could feel the eyes on us. I'm sure people thought we were famous and were trying to figure out who we were.

The manager saw us almost immediately and met us on the sidewalk. He shook our hands and ushered us inside. Talk about feeling important! So yeah I didn't get to actually work at the Garden on that first trip, but I did get dropped off by a limo and treated as a VIP at the famous Copacabana nightclub, so it turned out alright.

What didn't turn out all right was the next fight I worked with Johnny. It was at the Hilton in Vegas against Carlos Francis Hernandez. Johnny got cut in the second and I went in to fix him up. Oddly enough, his trainer Jesse Reid was pissed about me going into the ring. He said he'd work the cuts. I was kind of wondering why they'd hired me if they didn't let me do my job.

During the fight I told Teresa, Johnny's wife and manager, about what Reid did. She told me just to work with Jesse and she'd deal with it after the fight. I knew they were having trouble with him, but I didn't know what would come of it. Turned out that Reid wanted half my pay for working cuts and Teresa gave it to him!

I met with Johnny and Teresa at a later date and I think Johnny knew that Jesse and Teresa were in the wrong, but he felt he had to stick by his wife. I figured it wasn't worth the headache so I told them I understood, but at the end of the day they were wrong. I also never worked with them again and it was too bad because I like Johnny and he was a damn good fighter.

Next I worked with Frans Botha. His trainer was Panama Lewis and Lewis was banned for life from working the corner because of an incident back in the 80s with Luis Resto and Billy Collins. He had taken some of the horse hair out of Luis' glove so the punches would cause more damage. Billy kept telling his dad, who was working his corner, that it felt like he was getting hit by rocks. Afterward Billy Sr. called for an investigation and everything came to light. Panama denied it, but Luis and he were found guilty of assault and both spent time in prison for it.

The incident also left Billy with double vision and he couldn't fight. He died less than a year later in a car wreck when he drove off a cliff. His family thought that he committed suicide because he couldn't fight. It's a terribly sad story all the way around.

When Panama called it had been about ten years since he had been released, but like I said, he couldn't work the corner. He asked me to be the pad man. I'd been working with so many guys though that my shoulder was busted up (I couldn't even lift my arm above my head), but I decided I needed the money and Botha was fighting Mike Tyson, so why not?

Frans' timing was so horrible at first that he was routinely punching me in the face, but a crazy thing happened. After the second day of holding pads I went home and showered and my shoulder felt great and I could lift my arm above my head. I guess my nerves and muscles were so twisted in my shoulder from years of holding pads that when I started working with Botha his punching power must have kind of shook them back into place. To this day I haven't had any problems.

After six weeks Frans was sharp, so sharp that he was beating Tyson through four rounds. Tyson was coming off his ear-biting of Holyfield and Frans was making the ring rust show. Then with only ten seconds left in the fifth Mike got him with a short right and it was over. Frans will tell you to this day that it was the biggest mistake of his life.

My list of fighters was long and I was so busy that I was concerned about being able to continue to work for R.J. Reynolds. Then one day they came to me. "We're downsizing," my manager Augie Ponce said. "You've been with us a long time Stitch (even my boss called me Stitch) so you'll stay on board, but they want to offer you a buyout."

The offer couldn't have come at a better time. I took the buyout so I'd have almost a full year to concentrate on training and cornering boxers. Then I got another interesting offer. This one was to play a role in the movie *Play it to the Bone* with Woody Harrelson and Antonio Banderas. I checked my schedule. The audition was for three o'clock on my last day with R.J. Reynolds and I was supposed to be at work until five.

I thought the chance at the movie was gone. "I had a shot at a movie," I told Augie, "but the audition is on the last day of work."

"What time's the audition?" Augie said.

"Three, so I can't make it in time."

"You kidding me Stitch, a chance to be in a movie!" Augie said. "I'm working with you on the last day so we can fill out all the proper paperwork. I'll have you out of here by noon."

Augie was true to his word and on the day I left R.J. Reynolds, I became an actor.

Play it to the Bone

Chuck Bodak and I were slotted to play the role of cutmen for *Play it to the Bone*. I really wanted to be Antonio Banderas' cutman because he was Latin. Chuck and I arrived on set together and he went straight to Antonio. I was stuck with Woody Harrelson. Now don't get me wrong, I loved watching him in *Cheers* and I even enjoyed *White Men Can't Jump*, but I'd hoped to work with Antonio. As it was, I played the role of Vince's (Harrelson's) cutman and Chuck was Cesar's (Banderas') cutman.

It worked out for me because Woody was great to work with and his character, Vincent Boudreau, gets cut and his promoter and trainer tell him that he's got the best cutman in the business. Plus I got all the airtime. Later Chuck said, "Hell, your getting all the cuts Stitch!"

At one point during the filming Woody got pissed because his moves weren't quite right. He stormed off and since I'd been wrapping his hands every morning I figured we had a pretty good relationship. I yelled after him, "Woody, do you need some help?"

He kept walking and I'm thinking, *shit what did I just do?* Then he turned. "Sure," he said.

I followed him outside the Mandalay Bay Arena and showed him how to stand properly and how to throw his punches from a boxer's position and how to use rotation to add snap to his punches. We worked for a while then went back in. He finished the scene perfectly.

During breaks the make up artists took pictures of the actors so when we started again they could ensure the cuts looked the same. Woody was made up to look like boxer Angel Manfredy and he just happened to be ringside. We took a picture with me in the middle and Angel on one side and Woody on the other. I asked the make up artist if I could have a copy. He said, "No problem," but the next day he came to me and said, "I'm really sorry, but the picture didn't come out."

I remember thinking it was a photo I would've liked to have. I got something else that was meaningful though a few days later. It was Chuck's birthday and the director, Ron

Shelton, framed one of the cornerman jackets. Everyone signed it and he presented it to Chuck in the middle of the ring. He thanked everyone and said, "When I cash in my chips," then looked down at me, "Stitch will be the next, best cutman in the business."

When I heard that, chills literally ran through my body. It was an unforgettable moment.

Hollywood calls it a "wrap party" and it's thrown after shooting is finished. I took Charlotte, my sister Belen, and my friend and former world champion Livingstone Bramble. Most of the cast was there and we were having a blast. Then I was surprised when Woody said he had something to present to me. Everyone stood in a semi-circle and he handed me the 8 x 10 framed photo that the make up artist said he didn't have. It was signed, "Stitch, you are so cool. Thank you for all your help, Woody Harrelson."

If that was all, it would have been a great experience, but then I got invited to the Hollywood premiere. Here I was a kid from Planada walking down the red carpet with my beautiful wife on my arm.

We all saw the first screening and then attended a party. Charlotte hadn't met Antonio Banderas and he was standing across the room. We made our way over to him and I introduced them. Being a romantic Latino, he grabbed her hand and kissed it. She melted right then and there.

On the way out Charlotte and I took one more picture with Woody and his wife and Antonio and his wife, Melanie Griffith. We left and I thought *shit like this only happens in the movies.*

It was a great experience and then another offer came rolling in. This time a guy named John Barnthouse called wanting to know if I'd train him. I told him that I didn't work with amateurs and then he had another offer. "I read an article about you and it said you wanted to put a video together," he said. "I just graduated from the American Film Institute and I'd love to help you do this."

I considered, "How much do you charge?" I asked.

"No charge. It'd be an honor for me," he said.

I couldn't say no to that and suddenly I was on the other side of the camera. It was a good thing I'd watched director Ron Shelton as much as I did while on the set of *Play it to the Bone*. The results of the partnership between Barnthouse and me were pretty crazy. So much so that many in the boxing world, including Don King, Gary Shaw, and a host of others, weren't too interested in the documentary ever seeing the light of day.

MAKING BOXER'S NIGHTMARE

We sat at lunch and talked about the documentary. John leaned forward with his elbows on the table and plans for how everything would go down. The tentative title was *Chuck Bodak: the Shaman of Boxing*. The legend had mentored me during a time when one cutman mentoring another was almost unheard of.

I listened to John's ideas and it was hard not to get excited, but as the younger man talked I couldn't help but think of a scene from the movie *Colors*. Sean Penn plays a young police officer and Robert Duvall is the veteran. He says to his new partner, "There's two bulls standing on top of a mountain. The younger one says to the older one, 'Hey pop, let's say we run down there and fuck one of them cows.' The older one says: 'No son. Let's *walk* down and fuck 'em all.'"

John was that young bull. He was ready to run and his energy was contagious. He'd put together a proposal to do the project for $60,000, but he was fresh out of the AFI and I was now known in boxing and kickboxing circles, but not so much in the circles that would want to invest. We didn't have a lot of funding, but that had never stopped me before and it wasn't about to stop John either.

We planned on doing interviews during a couple big upcoming fights at the Mandalay. Lennox Lewis was set to face David Tua on November 11, 2000, and almost a month later Fernando Vargas and Felix Trinidad were scheduled to touch them up in the same arena. We hired a boom mic operator and set out to make a documentary. We did the same a month later and in a matter of days we compiled an unbelievable amount of interviews from an unbelievable cast of boxing insiders.

I caught up with Dr. Margaret Goodman at the Lewis/Tua press conference and she talked at length about cutting weight and dehydration. Referee Mills Lane talked of the same issue while we sat in the empty arena prior to the fight. Over lunch Chuck Bodak talked about how boxing gives those who don't have many other opportunities a chance to be successful, but it's a hard road. Fernando Vargas' conditioning coach John Philbin talked about diet and training. Dr. Flip Homansky talked about the importance of education and how trainers were instead trying to control the fighters based on where the next purse was.

We also spent time talking with Hall of Fame trainer Emanuel Steward, Nevada State Athletic Commission Executive Director Marc Ratner, Hall of Fame trainer Doc Broadus, famous boxer and trainer Eddie Mustafa Muhammad, promoter Tony Holden, referee Richard Steele, referee Joe Cortez, cutman Miguel Diaz, former world champ Rocky Gannon, the list continues. John and I added it up and we'd interviewed over 600 years worth of boxing experience!

Originally I interviewed Fernando Vargas in the gym where he was training, but when I listened to it there was a lot of background noise. I mentioned this to him and he said, "I'm about to head back to the hotel, jump in the car with me and we'll do the interview there."

We did just that and in the back of Fernando's Lexus SUV limousine he talked about how boxing helped him and how hard it was to make it. He was so open and helpful. Fernando had walked down that road, he made it to the top, but he still wanted to help other boxers by sharing his experiences.

Thanks to a friend of mine called "Crocodile" I was able to hook up with Mike Tyson prior to one of his training sessions. Croc was a friend of Mike's as well and he told him that we were putting together a documentary to help young fighters. Mike was more than happy to talk so we found a corner of the gym. He'd been through so much during his years and like Fernando, he too was all for helping out other boxers.

He talked about the discipline that it takes to make it and said, "You have to take the pain ... discipline is a form of doing what you hate to do but doing it like you love it ... without discipline you're nothing."

He also talked about the body and the brain. When you want to get the best out of an individual you have to get them in a hundred percent physical condition because when their body's at a hundred percent physical condition, their mind tells them that ... the only purpose for our body really is to carry our brain ... you have to love it more than anything in the world. More than you love yourself and that's when your ego comes in. You have to have that to be a fighter, but you have to be humble too. You have to be brutal, you have to be cruel, and you have to be humble. It's interchangeable and it's really complex, but it's really simple. And that's what you have to understand about the discipline for boxing, wrestling, martial arts, or whatever it is. It's really complicated, but still it's really simple."

Mike went on to make so many other great points and when John and I left the gym we were amazed at his candor. He had given me his heart. His words were sincere and he wasn't talking just to hear himself, but to really educate other boxers.

With the editing and interviews all wrapped up, I was confident we had a product that the world would want to see. It didn't turn out to be just about Chuck Bodak (although that would've made a great documentary). Instead it was about all the pains and sorrows boxers had to go through to make it in their chosen sport. It highlighted both the good and bad and showed that changes were desperately needed for the sake of the boxers.

Then I screwed up. I had all these people in the boxing industry willing to provide input in an effort to educate and make the sport better. I assumed that the big promoters and TV people, those in a position to get the documentary to the public, would want the same. I went to them, Don King, Gary Shaw, Larry Merchant, guys at HBO, Showtime, and in varying degrees of hostility I got the same answer. None of them wanted it to get to the public.

I didn't really see it as portraying boxing in a negative light. Instead, it showed the current state of the sport and offered ideas on how to make it better. The boxing powers didn't agree. From where they were sitting everything seemed perfectly fine.

I couldn't believe the reaction and it was very disheartening. I'm sure we could have found other avenues to get *Boxer's Nightmare* to the public, but I think we would have continued to get resistance and it would have made things tough for me. Besides, I ended up getting a really interesting offer to work in a different sport.

7

UFC *(THE EARLY DAYS)*
A WHOLE NEW BALL GAME

THE SLOT MACHINES MADE CONSTANT background noise and a craps table exploded with applause, but I didn't break stride or even glance over. I was heading toward one of Bellagio's ballrooms to work a K-1 Kickboxing event and wanted to be on time.

The room was small but luxurious and about a thousand fans focused on the ring in its center where two men were about to start a match. After the first fight I made my way around the ring and heard somebody call my name. I turned toward the voice and saw a familiar face. The man had thinning dark hair, wore slacks and a blazer over a button down shirt, and looked up with a slightly askew smile. Although I hadn't seen him in just over a year, I recognized my old friend Dana White immediately. We knew each other from working in the same Las Vegas boxing gyms from time to time and I used to sell Dana a brand of boxing equipment called M and M out of Mexico.

We exchanged hugs and pleasantries then Dana said, "You know me and the Fertitta's, Lorenzo and Frank, bought the UFC earlier this year."

I nodded. "Yeah I heard something about that. How's it going?"

"Really good," Dana said. "I bring it up because right now we've got one cutman, Leon Tabbs, and we'd like to bring another one on board. You interested?"

I was definitely interested but said, "Shit Dana, I stopped watching that stuff because it was too brutal. They don't take care of their fighters and for someone in my position I can't stomach that."

"It's not like that now," Dana said. "We've got a bunch of new rules in place and we're working to make it a lot better. You'd be helping make it safer for the fighters."

The crowd cheered as a kickboxer for the next bout made his way to the ring. We waited until the noise died down. "I'll let you get back to work," Dana said. "Let's exchange business cards. I'll call you tomorrow and you can let me know. We have a big event, the first one back on pay per view, at the Mandalay in a couple weeks."

The next day I had just finished with a faxed order for my new employer, Trepco West. After making Boxer's Nightmare I'd decided to go back to work. My new boss Al Paulis was good about working around my schedule and thanks to my experience at R.J. Reynolds I did a little bit of everything for the company. The other reps went to stores and filled out orders in person. I instead taught my accounts how to fill out their own orders so they could fax them to me at their convenience. Because of this I worked from home or even more often worked from the gym. My wife Charlotte said when she saw how I'd set things up, "Jacob you're barely even working. You've got it made."

I laughed. "All those years busting my ass on the farm. God is just looking out for me now. He figured I needed a break."

Charlotte just rolled her eyes in response.

I was about to head to the gym when my phone rang. It was Dana. "You have a chance to think about joining us Stitch?"

I had thought about it and recognized that it was a great opportunity. "I'm in Dana. When do I start?"

"UFC 33 in a couple weeks."

UFC 33

My instructions were to find Burt Watson in the guts of the Mandalay Bay Arena. I didn't know who Burt Watson was or what he looked like, but I had been told he was African American and a former Marine and he'd most likely be wearing jeans with a pair of nice kicks and to, 'just look for the man in charge.'

I turned down a hallway and a young guy hustled by. "Hey, you know where I can find Burt Watson?" I said.

The man pointed behind him. "A few doors down on the left if he's still there."

A moment later I entered a small room and saw Leon Tabbs talking with a man that had to be Watson. "I'm here to work with Leon as the second cutman," I said.

The man strode over and introduced himself as Burt. "Nice to have you. I've heard a lot of good things. You ever wrapped hands for MMA?"

"No, boxing only," I said.

"Leon will catch you up to speed. Fighters arrive in an hour, you'll only wrap a couple guys since this is your first time out. I'll have the list up soon. I've got to run. Good luck."

I started to reply, but Burt was already at an almost run and out the door.

I looked at Leon Tabbs. The man was a couple inches short of six foot and curly gray hair and a gray beard covered his dark face. He beckoned for me to come over and then turned his slender frame around to a table in the corner and went back to cutting towels in half.

I crossed the room and recognized an odd animosity. It was as if Leon wasn't too fired up about sharing how he did things. Maybe if he wasn't being directed to show me, he'd be brushing me off like the guy back in Oakland. As it was, Leon stopped cutting towels and pulled out his tape. He gave me a quick wrap and explained while he did it. "The big difference is the gloves, only four ounces so you can't put too much padding or they won't fit. Also, some guys like less around the hands so they can grab better, usually the grapplers."

I nodded and asked a few questions as Leon went. The man answered, sometimes reluctantly, and soon he was done. I cut the tape off and about that time Burt Watson burst into the room with a piece of paper. "Here's the list. Stitch you got Dave Menne first in room three and Jens Pulver in room four."

I nodded and Leon took his list then went back to cutting towels. The ones the Mandalay made available were too big, so Leon was stuck with the tedious process of cutting them in half.

After making sure my bag was packed and ready to go, I headed down the hall. I found room three and wasn't sure what to expect. I hadn't watched the sport since the early days and didn't know any of the fighters. I pushed through the door and found a docile room with three groups of men stationed in different corners. All eyes turned my way. "I'm here to wrap Dave Menne," I said.

A man in the back right corner said, "Over here."

Dave offered a thin smile that curved toward his low set ears that stuck out a bit and were cauliflowered like any good wrestler's. I pulled up a chair and slipped into my normal routine. I didn't even know that Menne was about to fight for the UFC's first ever middleweight belt and Menne sure didn't know that this was the first time I had ever wrapped an MMA fighter's hands.

I worked as if I'd done it many times before and was careful not to make it too thick. I asked Dave how it felt. "Good," he said.

He didn't talk much and the whole locker room seemed subdued with anticipation. Finally the job was done and Dave said, "Thanks."

"No problem," I said, and wondered if he would be so appreciative if he knew he was my guinea pig.

Down the hallway in room number four I found a much different atmosphere. It was filled with the same anticipation, but the room popped with energy. A man bounced around along the back wall and another sat on a bench with his arms folded and hard eyes. I found out that the first was Jens Pulver and the second Pat Miletich. I didn't have a clue who either one of them was and didn't know the caliber of their athleticism and training. I did know as I looked at Pulver with his spiked hair and the odd combination of a brown left eye and blue right eye, that the man was the source of the energy. It seemed to ooze from his pores and as he sat down for his hand wrap his right leg shook as if the energy was about to bust out of it.

I went to work, now an expert as this was my second go at wrapping an MMA fighter, and this one, although I didn't know it at the time, was scheduled to defend his lightweight belt.

Pulver was much more talkative than Menne. He joked a bit and talked back and forth with Pat Miletich. The man responded in a gruff voice, but his hard eyes were relaxed when he verbally sparred with Jens

Soon the wraps were complete and Jens stood up then flexed both hands and looked down at them as if he was in disbelief. He shook his hands up and down then threw a couple of short punches. "You gotta feel these Pat," he said.

Two fighters into my MMA career and I had a happy customer. The fights went off and both Menne and Pulver won unanimous decisions. It was actually a boring event as every fight on the main card went to a decision. Afterward I was heading out of the arena and saw Dana White. "How'd it go Stitch?" he said.

"Good, no problems."

"So you're with us now right?"

"Of course."

Dana smiled, but I could tell that it was dulled by disappointment. Years later he mentioned that he felt the event pushed the promotion back several years. Not just because of all the mediocre decisions, but because of the long title fights that featured Pulver and Menne the main event between Tito Ortiz and Vladimir Matyushenko went over the pay per view time and was cut off.

The event was titled *Victory in Vegas* and it was the promotions first in the fight-rich city. Maybe it didn't seem like a victory to Dana White and the Fertitta's, but for me it did. I'd made another turn in my career and was off to a sizzling 2-0 start in two title fights no less.

UFC 34

After UFC 33, I went back to my usual routine of working in the boxing gyms and filling orders for Trepco whenever they came across the fax. I didn't think too much about the next UFC event which was scheduled for November 2.

The day rolled around and I was soon in the middle of a wired crowd inside the MGM. I'd worked wrapping hands and was back and forth between the locker rooms and the Octagon before finally settling in cageside.

A guy by the name of B.J. Penn was about to square off with a Japanese kid who'd lost earlier in the year to Jens Pulver. I looked around one corner of the Octagon and saw Pulver at the announcers' table as he was sitting in during the fight. He didn't have to work too long. Uno came out with a crazy flying kick that Penn side-stepped pretty easily. He then landed a vicious combo that dropped Uno against the fence and finished him with a rapid succession of right hands.

The energy in the building was instantly electric and as I jumped up and headed for the Octagon I had goose bumps on my arms. Penn, only seconds after the KO, left the Octagon in a hurry and brushed by me on his way up the ramp toward the back.

The crowd had barely caught its breath and the next fight, for the welterweight title was underway. Earlier in the day I had heard a little about this one. Pat Miletich, the guy who was with Pulver when I wrapped his hands at UFC 33, had recently lost the belt to Carlos Newton. Now one of Pat's protégés, a young wrestler named Matt Hughes was looking to avenge his coach.

I watched from my seat as Newton and Hughes put on an exciting first round. Early in round two Newton got Hughes' head locked up between his legs. I wasn't sure what the move was called, but the guy next to me said, "That's a freaking tight triangle."

I nodded about the time Hughes lifted Newton off the canvas and walked him to the fence. The whole time Newton kept his legs locked around Hughes' neck. The two stayed in that position for a moment, and then Hughes slammed Newton to the canvas. The fight was over in a heartbeat. Newton was out and it looked to me like Hughes didn't know where the hell he was. But it didn't matter because he was the new welterweight champ and the crowd was bordering on hysteria.

The next two fights did nothing to curb the enthusiasm as Ricco Rodriguez TKO'd Pete Williams and Randy Couture TKO'd Pedro Rizzo to keep his heavyweight belt.

The talk backstage centered on the Hughes slam. I heard one group talking about Hughes being out cold. Then down the hall another group thought he wasn't. Years later, in his book *Made In America* Hughes said, "Maybe the blood ran into my head or maybe it was just the choke, but when I hit, his choke had done enough to me where I was loopy."

UFC 33 had failed to really pull me in, but after UFC 34 I was extremely glad I'd taken Dana up on his offer. I recognized that the UFC had a potentially very bright future and as I looked across the locker room and saw Dana congratulating Hughes, I noticed that the man's smile wasn't dulled by disappointment in the least.

I wasn't disappointed either. I was established in the boxing world as a top notch cutman and I was now grabbing a foothold in MMA too. I pulled out of the MGM Grand parking garage and into the mild Las Vegas night and had the distinct feeling that things were only going to get busier and better.

LYON, FRANCE

Back in the early days of the modern era of the UFC, I'm calling the modern era about the time the Unified Rules of Mixed Martial Arts came into existence and the UFC started following them, there were some big gaps between events. There was enough time between UFC 34 and 35 for me to go to France for six weeks.

I wasn't there for vacation. I'd started working with Fabrice Tiozzo as the previous year he'd lost a unanimous decision to Virgil Hill. It was my first time in France and I know that we Americans have the idea that the French people aren't exactly cordial. Well that wasn't the case for me. Let me preface by first saying that Lyon is known as the culinary capital of France. I'd go out and about in between training sessions and the French people would ask if I was a tourist.

When I answered that I was the trainer of Fabrice Tiozzo, the red carpet rolled out, or really I guess it was the dinner plates that rolled out. Everywhere I went I was getting to eat the best food. Everything from perfectly cooked meats to light and sweet pastries, and that was just for breakfast.

It was a good thing I was working my ass off training Fabrice, because if not I would have put on at least twenty pounds. As it was I stayed pretty fit and we had a solid training camp.

Fabrice then went out and TKO'd Tiwon Taylor in the third round. I guess they were happy with me because some 15 months later I returned to train him for his bout against George Arias. I say they were happy, but maybe not so much. Fabrice's manager put me up in a hostel. That's basically a cheap hotel where nothing is your own. You share bedrooms, bathrooms, everything. I had my own room, but I did have to share the bathroom. I usually waited until late at night to take my showers just so I didn't have to deal with others.

I was pissed at first, but then I decided to roll with it, I chalked it up to being a unique experience. Fabrice beat George Arias by decision and looked pretty good. After two long trips to France though, I told them that it'd be best if I just worked as his cutman in the future. Besides, the UFC was starting to have more events at the time. A couple weeks after Fabrice TKO'd Taylor I was back at the Octagon in Connecticut and the fights were exciting but the food didn't taste near as good!

CONSEQUENCES AND A CONFUSED DOCTOR

Months had passed since the night of UFC 34. I returned from France just in time for Christmas and a couple weeks later I made my first trip with the UFC. I went to Connecticut to work UFC 35 at the Mohegan Sun where Jens Pulver, a guy I was becoming more and more familiar with, scored a decision over B.J. Penn. Still though, I didn't really know the guys in the MMA game.

Back in Vegas at UFC 36, I made my way through the hallway toward my room at the MGM. It had been a long night that was punctuated by a heavyweight title tilt between Josh Barnett and Randy Couture. The elder heavyweight champ Couture had won the first round, but he'd been cut in the process. I watched my counterpart Leon Tabbs as he worked to seal up the small opening above Couture's right eye. Even from a distance I could tell Tabbs had no problem with it.

In round two, Couture went back to taking it to Barnett until about two minutes remained. Then Barnett turned it around and pummeled Couture for about a minute straight. Finally referee Big John McCarthy stopped it and Barnett was the new champ.

Backstage, I planned on grabbing my bag and heading home after the long night, but a gurney came wheeling down the narrow hall. I stopped to make room and the squeak of the wheels grew louder as it approached. One medic pushed and the other guided. They moved slowly and I saw that their passenger was Randy Couture.

The group wheeled by and with my back to the wall I was almost directly over him. It was as if he was on display as he drifted by. I'd seen my fair share of jacked up faces over the previous 15 years, but I was amazed at how destroyed Randy Couture's was. He was swollen and distorted and both eyes were closed and his mouth was leaking blood. The gurney turned a corner on its way to the ambulance and I thought, *man it looks like he got the shit beat out of him by five or six guys.*

Josh Barnett is a big dude. Maybe his elbows and fists did damage that equaled that of numerous men and it wasn't long before it came out that Barnett had tested positive for steroids. But later I found out that Barnett was a really good guy and we spent a whole lot of time together in Japan where he made me a lot of extra cash on the side.

Only a couple months after UFC 36, I also found out that sometimes doctors aren't so sure exactly what to do when they are working cageside. The UFC had taken its show to Bossier City, Louisiana and I sat next to the cageside doctor during the fights. He'd just returned from working on a cut and the doctor in a thick Cajun accent said, "Stitch, you think that guy needs stitches?"

"Naw, I think he's okay," I replied.

A couple fights later another cut happened and I went in the Octagon and did my job. I sat back down and the doc tapped me on the arm with the back of his knuckles. "What about that guy. He need stitches?"

I gave the man a sideways glance. "Yeah he's probably gonna need a few doc."

The man just nodded and turned back to the action.

I did the same, but thought *why is this doctor asking me such crazy questions*? So with my arms folded across my chest and two men kicking and punching at each other in the Octagon I leaned over and said, "Don't take this wrong, but what the hell kind of doctor are you?"

The man's eyes got wide and he turned his palms upward. "I'm a cardiologist. I know nothing about this. If somebody has a heart attack tonight I'll be okay, but I don't know anything about cuts!"

I shook my head and couldn't help but laugh. I also thought *damn, what a crazy place to be.* And it was pretty crazy, but not near as much so as a couple months later when the UFC made its first journey across the Atlantic.

BEST DAMN AND CROSSING THE POND

I, like everybody who worked to make the UFC a smooth running machine, was getting geared up to go to London, England for UFC 38, the organization's first trip to the UK. Then I got a call from the front office. The promotion was holding an impromptu show at the Bellagio because one of the fights would be aired on Fox Sports Net's *Best Damn Sports Show Period.* I checked my schedule and it was clear for June 22.

Soon I was in the same building in which I saw my old friend Dana White almost a year earlier. There were only six fights on the makeshift card and I sat face to face with a kid barely 20 years old. "How's the hands? Any problems?"

"They're good," Robbie Lawler said.

I knew about Lawler's striking prowess and I'd sat alongside the confused cardiologist in Bossier City and watched Lawler win his UFC debut by decision. Now here he was barely a month later fighting again.

With all pre-fight preparations complete and the fights underway, each man wanted to put on a good show because of the possibility of landing on *The Best Damn Sports Show Period.*

In the third fight I worked Lawler's corner as he squared off against Steve Berger, who'd also fought in Bossier City against Benji Radach in a bout that ended in a no contest. The two went at it with Lawler using his heavy hands in the first round. At the start of the second Lawler went nuts and in a flurry TKO'd Berger.

Backstage I cut off his wraps. "How do your hands feel?"

"They feel absolutely great," Lawler said as he pumped them up and down.

He had good reason to be fired up because it was his fight that would end up airing on *The Best Damn Sports Show Period* and it wouldn't be long before I made an appearance on the show as well.

A few weeks after the thrown together UFC 37.5 card I was standing in the hotel lobby in London, England. It had been an odd couple of days. The London media was either bashing the sport's brutality or saying that it wasn't a sport at all. I had stood along the wall at the press conference even though there were plenty of seats available since almost nobody showed up. And the weigh in was pretty much empty too. It was a strange feeling because in just a handful of events I'd gotten used to the growing energy and anticipation as each show neared.

The hotel lobby mirrored the press conference and weigh in, almost empty, when I noticed Josh Barnett coming out of the elevator. He had a much shorter, bald-headed man with him. Josh saw me as well and made his way over. I had worked with Josh a couple times before and we were becoming friends.

"Stitch, what's up?" Josh said. "Hey this is my friend Ian Freeman. He's fighting Frank Mir."

Ian and I shook hands and the man spoke in a thick British accent. Then Josh said, "Can you make sure you wrap Ian's hands?"

"Of course," I said and turned to Ian. "Even if you aren't on my list I'll take of you."

"I really appreciate it," Ian said.

A lot of fighters said they appreciated it when I agreed to wrap their hands, but there was an unusual depth to Ian's words that I couldn't put my finger on.

Later that night I wrapped Ian and he didn't have much to say. He sat with his head down and eyes fixed in concentration. I was getting good at reading each fighter's mental state right before the fight and I had started working to give each man a little extra confidence when I could. After all, they were about to nakedly stand in front of the world and compete in the most unforgiving sport. I figured that most feared being exposed as someone incapable more so than they feared getting hurt.

With Ian though, there wasn't really any words. My contribution in the confidence department would come solely from the tape job.

Inside the red brick of London's historic Royal Albert Hall and underneath the massive dome, I sat ready to work on Ian if needed. Almost four thousand of his countrymen, well below the building's capacity, watched as Ian Freeman TKO'd Frank Mir. The crowd was almost right on top of the Octagon and insane. As soon as the fight was over I headed backstage to grab some supplies for the next bout, a rematch between Matt Hughes and Carlos Newton.

As I returned to the Octagon, I saw Ian on the way out. "Thanks," he said over the still excited crowd and I didn't get a chance to reply. While waiting to apply the Vaseline to Matt Hughes I thought once again that there was more depth in Ian's appreciation, but soon the next fight was underway and I never got a chance to really consider it further.

Hughes was again accompanied by his coach Pat Miletich and he again beat Carlos Newton, but this time he didn't knock himself out in the process.

After the event everyone took a bus to the after party at a huge night club. I was tired and hungry, but loaded up with everyone else. Drinks were paid for by the UFC and the crowd was pretty much shoulder to shoulder. It was a good time, but I'm not much of a drinker so I had a couple beers and was about to call it a night. A whole lot of others were just getting started though.

Just before I headed out, a ripple of excitement shot through those still at the club. Word was that there was a back alley brawl involving Tito Ortiz, the now infamous Lee Murray, Pat Miletich, Chuck Liddell, and others. I considered checking it out, but was sure it was just a rumor, probably a scuffle at best. So I went ahead and left to grab a few hours of sleep.

A handful of hours after the supposed brawl, we all road the bus to the airport. I learned that it was in fact true and the story was still shaky, but supposedly Murray actually knocked Ortiz out.

Pat Miletich sat across the aisle from me and it looked as if he was still drunk. "Red bull and Vodka kicked my ass," he said.

I laughed and then watched as he took a huge bite out of a loaf of bread. He looked like a Viking as he tore off the mouthful. He then pulled a piece off with his hand and launched it at Tony Fryklund who sat a couple seats away. The bread drilled him in the back of the head. Pat laughed and with a mouthful of bread said, "Got you Fryklund," and then repeated the process.

On that trip I learned a couple things. Pat was funny as hell and it was a nice gesture, but probably not the best idea for the UFC to buy booze for everyone.

However I didn't figure out why I noted such sincerity in Ian Freeman's appreciation until years after UFC 38. While being interviewed I was told that when Ian entered the fight against Frank Mir, a man on the fast track to the UFC heavyweight title, his father was very sick with cancer. Ian did not know how his father was, but just before the fight word circulated through the press that his dad had passed away.

After the fight while I was backstage, Ian was given the microphone and he dedicated the fight to his father. All those who knew his dad had passed had to wipe tears from their eyes.

BACK TO VEGAS

It had been such a high energy week. Tito Ortiz's grudge with the Lion's Den fighters that began on his first night in the Octagon back at UFC 13 and escalated at UFC's 19 and 20, was about to begin its drawn out climax as the light heavyweight champ was fighting Ken Shamrock at UFC 40 at the MGM.

Ortiz and Shamrock had appeared on *The Best Damn Sports Show Period* and stood nose to nose while talking trash and the card also featured KO specialist Chuck Liddell against Renato Sobral. Liddell had stepped aside so Shamrock could get a crack at Ortiz. And if that wasn't enough, Matt Hughes was fighting Gil Castillo for the welterweight belt as well.

Las Vegas was buzzing and I was standing cageside when one of Ortiz's cornermen came up to me. He handed me a folded up shirt. "Tito wanted to make sure you get this," he said.

It was a Team Punishment button down shirt with my name on it. I thought it was a really nice gesture because Tito went out of his way to make a shirt for me and I didn't even wrap his hands. He is one of just a couple guys I haven't wrapped because he does his own. I've also never wrapped Liddell's because Chuck's trainer, John Hackleman, wraps his hands.

The excitement continued to grow as the night wore on and there was one big finish after another. The building absolutely erupted when Liddell ended Sobral's night with a stunning head kick. Then it was time for Ortiz and Shamrock.

I stood outside the Octagon as Ortiz made his way down the ramp. Shamrock was already in the cage and Limp Bizkit blasted through the arena. The energy was so thick, it pulsed and felt tangible, like I could reach out and touch it. Chills ran up and down my spine as Tito approached.

Bruce Buffer screamed Ken's name first and then Tito's. Tito jumped high in the air and the fight was underway. It started off at a frenetic pace. Tito was all over Ken and then about thirty seconds in Ken landed a big right, but Tito kept the pressure on.

He battered and bloodied Ken in round one, but with just a few seconds left in the round I looked over and saw my partner Leon Tabbs kicked back in a chair with his arms crossed. The round ended and I didn't have any need to go into the Octagon. I looked at Tabbs and he remained seated as well. Ken had opted to go with his own cutman. The UFC gives the fighters a choice, they can go with us, at the time it was Leon, Don House, and me, or they can have their own man.

Round two was more of the same with Ken hanging on and Tito looking like the champ. It came to an end and again I remained seated and Leon did too. Round three was much like the first two. Ken had moments where he electrified the crowd, but for the most part Tito just beat the shit out of him.

This time when the round came to an end I did head to the Octagon. Tito wasn't in bad shape or anything, but the effects of the fight were starting to show and I needed to make sure he was good. While getting him ready for the fourth round and working on a small cut on his chin, a roar came from the crowd and then I heard Big John McCarthy say, "That's it."

Tito raised his hands in the air fingers pointed to the sky, and then climbed the fence and screamed to the crowd that he loved them.

I congratulated him once he was off the fence and he pulled on a shirt that read *I just killed Kenny, You Bastard.* His shirts after earlier events had helped to fuel the rivalry and this one would as well. I was glad that my shirt from him just had my name, no message!

I had noticed Leon in the Octagon working on Ken and after everyone cleared out and once Leon and I had a moment to talk, I said, "What the hell happened? I thought Ken was going with his own cutman."

Leon laughed. "Shit, after his face was all busted up in round two, his cutman came up to me and said, 'Uh you can take over from here if you want.'"

I couldn't help but laugh about the situation. It made sense though. I'm sure Ken didn't think he'd get cut up and swollen like he did, and when it happened the corner realized they needed a professional in the Octagon, someone who could fix him up the right way. Unfortunately for him, after round three it was too late. His face had been beaten too badly for Leon to keep him in the fight.

Leon laughed again and shook his head back and forth. "Can you believe that? Pulled me in when it got too bad."

Actually I could believe it. I'd already seen so many crazy things in my year and a half with the UFC, and I was about to see a few more in the next few months.

THE FAR EAST

The Pacific Ocean is pretty damn big. I learned that firsthand on April 29, 2003 because I sat on a plane for hours and hours as it arced toward Tokyo, Japan. I was heading there to work with Josh Barnett. He was fighting the huge, and undefeated, Jimmy Ambriz in New Japan Pro Wrestling and asked me how much I'd charge to come along and be in his corner. I gave him my fee, which I thought was fairly substantial, and Josh didn't bat an eye. Just like that I was a part of his team.

With nothing but cold Pacific Ocean below me and sleep impossible in the uncomfortable plane seat, I thought about the last couple of events. I'd met Ricco Rodriguez's family prior to his fight at UFC 41 in Atlantic City. They were nice people from right there in New Jersey where they worked as Morticians. I thought that was a pretty peculiar family business, but hey I guess it pays the bills. Then I watched in surprise as Tim Sylvia KO'd Ricco. Don House, a world class boxing trainer, had been working with Ricco and House had also been brought in to work as a third cutman in the UFC.

It was just one of those things. Sylvia looked great and dropped Ricco to win the heavyweight belt. After UFC 41 I was in Miami for UFC 42. Matt Hughes claimed a decision over Sean Sherk to defend his belt, but the fight that I really remembered was Pete Spratt and Robbie Lawler. I knew Pete from kickboxing and he blasted Robbie's right leg in round one. In round two he got cut above the right eye though. Big John stopped the action and I followed the doctor into the Octagon. The cut was bad, but not too terrible. Phil Baroni was commentating with Joe Rogan for the event and he said something along the lines of me being one of the best and if anybody could stop the bleeding it was me.

I appreciated Phil's kind words, but I ended up not needing to keep Pete in the fight. The doctor asked me what I thought and I told him it was no problem so the fight restarted.

Just seconds later Pete got Robbie with another kick and Robbie quit. The brutal leg kicks had taken their toll and completely jacked up Robbie's hip. If I remember right he even dislocated it.

It was Robbie's first loss and the punishing kicks kind of changed the course of his career.

As the plane got closer to Japan I knew that the course of my career wasn't changing, but it was broadening once again. This would be my first time working in Tokyo and I wasn't sure what to expect. Fortunately, Matt Hume was there too. He knew the culture and took me under his wing. He's a great guy and many people know him for his coaching ability, but he was the one that actually inspired Sheik Tahnoon to begin the now famous Abu Dhabi submission wrestling championships. The Sheik saw Matt submit Olympic Gold Medalist Kenny Monday in under a minute and then asked if he'd train him and his team and one thing led to another.

It had been a couple days since touching down in Tokyo and Matt had struggled to teach me how to use chopsticks and taught me to never stick them into the bowl where they were standing straight up and down, it's very offensive. Now I wrapped Josh's hands in a dressing room in the Tokyo Dome and I met another guy on the card. He was half Brazilian half Japanese and making his MMA debut. There was a lot of hype around him in Japan because he had trained with Japanese wrestling legend Antonio Inoki.

I held pads for Josh in the dressing room and we watched the young kid Lyoto Machida win a decision over Kengo Watanabe and then it was our turn. Soon we were standing on a platform in the middle of thousands upon thousands of Japanese fans and lights were flashing all around us. I looked around and thought, *Damn, I'm standing here in the Tokyo Dome with Josh Barnett.*

We walked toward the ring, Josh with a towel on his head and me just to his right with my medicine bag and my bucket. It really was surreal and a turn in my career that I never thought would happen. But that's something I've learned through the years, you have to put yourself into positions that create opportunities and when they arise you have to grab hold of them.

Minutes later it was Josh Barnett grabbing hold of and kneeing and punching the crap out of Jimmy Ambriz on his way to a quick TKO finish. My first time at the ring in Japan came and went in just over three minutes, but I'd be back many times in the near future and am proud to say that I'd leave my mark on the Japanese combat sports landscape.

MARVIN EASTMAN AND A GOAT'S WHAT?

After the excitement of the trip to Tokyo, I was back in Las Vegas at the Thomas & Mack for UFC 43. I wrapped Ian Freeman's hands again and the card had a crazy disqualification when Wes Sims stomped on Frank Mir's face. The main event was great too as Randy Couture TKO'd Chuck Liddell to claim the interim light heavyweight belt making him the first fighter to win belts in two weight classes. But the fight that sticks with me more than all the others was between Vitor Belfort and Marvin Eastman.

I was working in Eastman's corner and the fight got underway with each man feeling the other out. Marvin threw a few low kicks, but none connected with Vitor, who was sporting a little different look than I remembered with a scruffy chin and longer curly hair. Vitor launched a high kick that just missed and Marvin caught him in the leg with a solid kick. I was settled in and watching closely and then Marvin tried to shoot a double and Vitor got him in a Muay Thai clinch.

As soon as he had Marvin's head between his forearms, Vitor delivered a left knee followed by a right knee both to Marvin's bald dome. The blows dropped Eastman and Vitor pounced landing a dozen or so punches in a matter of seconds.

About the time Big John was stopping the fight, I was climbing up the steps and heading into the Octagon. I couldn't tell exactly what happened, but knew Marvin was hurt. I got to him and knelt down just to his right and saw the extent of the damage. A huge gash was opened up above his right eye and my first thought was, *son of a bitch, I can see his skull.*

I applied pressure to the trench and could tell that he was in semi-shock. The cameras caught a glimpse of the cut and the crowd responded with a collective groan. It wasn't bleeding that bad considering its size and I figured I needed to find a way to see if Marvin was truly alright, not just physically, but mentally as well. After all, at the time Joe Rogan thought the cut looked like Marvin had been hit with an axe. And that's not an easy thing for anyone to stomach, not even a fighter.

I was close to Marvin's ear and I said in as light-hearted of voice as I could muster, "Marvin, this is the biggest fucking cut I've ever seen in my life!"

Marvin responded by cracking a smile and I was glad for that reaction. I then knew that he was okay, at least mentally if not physically. People always ask me what the biggest cut I ever worked on was and I always answer that it was Marvin's at UFC 43. I don't know who it was, but they made a pretty good analogy when they said, "His forehead just opened up, like when you fillet shrimp tail."

Years later at UFC 86, Joe Rogan and Mike Goldberg bantered back and forth after Josh Koscheck cut Chris Lytle open in about the same spot as Vitor cut Marvin. The Lytle cut reminded them of Marvin's and this time Rogan mentioned that Marvin's cut looked like a goat's vagina.

There are a lot of ways to describe Marvin's cut, an axe wound, filleted shrimp tail, or even a goat's vagina, and they're all probably fitting (although I haven't really spent time looking at goat's vagina's so I don't know how huge they are). I do know that it was one damn big cut, the biggest I'd ever seen.

It wouldn't be long before I'd see something else quite shocking, but this happened outside of the cage and involved my friend Mike Tyson.

BOB SAPP VS. MIKE TYSON

It was practically chaos inside the K-1 ring at the Bellagio. Bob Sapp was fighting Kimo Leopoldo who'd fought a couple months before at UFC 43. I'd just visited with Mike

Tyson ringside and now watched the wild display. Each man went down in the first and Sapp wobbled back to his corner. Dr. Davidson, who works with the UFC and would soon be featured in my new DVD, was in the corner checking on Sapp and the Nevada State Athletic Commission Executive Director Marc Ratner, who'd been in Boxer's Nightmare, was in the corner trying to sort out if the fight should be stopped.

It was almost comical. Dr. Davidson was exasperated at Sapp's actions. At one point Sapp raised his hands like the doctor was the referee and Dr. Davidson pulled his hands down and kind of rolled his eyes. Then Sapp screamed over and over, hai, hai, hai.

Finally, round two started and Sapp clubbed Kimo until he was out. Then just when it seemed the insanity would end, Sapp walked over to the ropes and called Mike Tyson into the ring. Mike, dressed in a suit, made his way to the ring with a handful of cameramen in tow, and Sapp charged like he wanted to fight.

Everybody swarmed around them and then the two went back and forth. "If we fight Marcus of Queensbury [boxing rules], I'd love to fight him ... tonight!" Mike said.

This prompted Sapp to say, "They may call you Kid Dynamite. If you mess with me I'll put your fuse out."

"Sign the contract big boy, sign the contract," Mike replied with a smile.

Now I, like the rest of the world, knew that Mike had been going through a tough time financially. He'd recently filed for bankruptcy. But I also knew that if Mike was going to head to Japan to fight Bob Sapp and whoever else in K-1 kickboxing, he needed to learn at least how to defend against kicks and with my background I could teach him what he needed to know.

After the chaos in the ring settled down I caught up with him and told him as much. Mike considered the idea and agreed that it'd be good for us to work together. We left it with tentative plans to get together over the next few days.

It had been a week and I hadn't heard from him, so I decided to head to his house to see what was up. He lived next to Wayne Newton so I drove by the "Casa de Shenandoah" and marveled at its size. Then I pulled up to Mike's place and there were three police cars in the driveway. I thought *shit, what did Mike do now.*

I parked at an angle behind one of the squad cars and walked to the front door. It was halfway open so I poked my head inside. I didn't see anybody so I crossed the threshold. The mansion was almost empty and I stood still, listening. I heard voices and walked toward them, through the foyer and a living room, then down a hallway until I found the source, two uniformed police officers.

They saw me enter the room and turned my way. I didn't know what the hell was going on so the thought occurred that they might pull their weapons on me, but they seemed too relaxed for that. They did give me a hard look and one of them said, "Can I help you?"

"Yeah, I'm looking for Mike. Is everything okay?" I said.

The other officer gestured to the extravagant and near empty room. "Sorry, Mike doesn't live here anymore."

"Doesn't live here anymore, what do you mean?"

"House is no longer owned by him. The state has taken control of it."

The words were hard to process. Mike was having financial troubles, but here I was standing in what was his house maybe twelve, or six, or two hours ago. I didn't know how long ago, but knew that this place had been the epitome of extravagance, I mean it used to have a freaking Bengal Tiger in it, and now it was Mike's no more. I was sure he was once again at a low point in his rollercoaster of a life.

Moments later I sat in my car and stared at the house's magnificent facade. My thoughts drifted to the days when I'd watch in disbelief as Mike would enter the gym with his entourage of hanger ons. One guy to sit in the car with the air condition running to keep it keep it cold, another to hold the door, another to set out his three or four choices of training attire for the workout, and six or seven others to talk on their phones that no doubt Mike was paying for.

I thought of the times I'd padded Mike out and felt the power of his hands, and I thought about the power of the words and thoughts he expressed during the taping of a *Boxer's*

Nightmare. He gave me his heart and spoke so eloquently about the plight of the struggling boxer. It was horribly ironic that much of what he said, had and was happening to him.

As I sat behind my steering wheel I shook my head back and forth. I wasn't under the illusion that my documentary could have helped Mike and saved him from heartache, but I believed that it could have helped many others.

Unfortunately, too many of those in power in the boxing world didn't want to help the fighters, didn't want to educate them, didn't want to make the sport better like I did.

I pulled through and out of the driveway leaving the black and whites and Mike's empty house behind. I had a sick feeling in my stomach and I wondered where Mike was. As I drove past Wayne's house I was glad a UFC event was less than a month away. The new fighting sport had yet to experience the corruption and division of power, and if I could do my small part to keep it that way I vowed that I would.

Mike Tyson and Bob Sapp never did happen. Due to his past felonies Mike couldn't get into Japan and I don't know if he ever made a dime off the deal.

THE CROW AND THE SPANKING

A month after I pulled away from Mike Tyson's lost house I was working my ass off to fix Jorge Rivera's cut up head. I've said many times that David Loiseau keeps me employed because he's got razors for elbows. On this night at UFC 44 in the Mandalay, Rivera was the recipient. I kept the gash as dry as possible and Rivera went on to win the decision.

It wasn't anything like Raul Marquez's five cuts that resulted in 75 stitches, but it seemed that the job I did on Rivera made a lot of people in MMA recognize that I could do more than wrap hands. I could keep guys in fights and that was good for all involved: the UFC, the fighters, and the fans.

A couple fights later I watched in amazement as Randy Couture dominated Tito Ortiz for the light heavyweight belt. Tito had proved himself time and time again, and of course

Randy was no slouch, but the way he fought on that night against Tito was miraculous.

I guess going into it he knew something that none of the rest of us did. I wrapped his hands as I'd done a few times before and he was so relaxed. Here it was a huge and much hyped fight and he wasn't fazed. Randy held the interim belt after KO'ing Chuck Liddell and the champ Tito was nine months removed from giving me the nice shirt and then beating the crap out of Ken Shamrock.

It was the type of bout that would frazzle the most seasoned fighter's nerves, but not Randy's. I sat down across from him and he smiled big. "Stitch, good to see you again."

I told him the same and went through the usual questions to ensure that I was aware of any issues with his hands. Then I wrapped and we made small talk back and forth. The conversation would have fit better if there was a dinner table between us instead of the back of a chair and a handful of tape.

I walked out of the room wondering if he was delusional. Maybe he didn't recognize that he was about to fight Tito in front of over ten thousand rabid fans in the Mandalay and who knew how many millions across the world. Or maybe he was confident because he knew what would happen.

One thing Randy couldn't have predicted came near the end of the fight. He had thoroughly beaten Tito, but Tito being the fighter that he is continued to hang tough. Knowing he was well behind on the cards he was desperate for a finish. He tried for a kneebar, but I could tell that Randy positioned himself in a way that Tito couldn't finish the move.

I'm sure a lot of others could tell the same thing, including Big John McCarthy, and it's a good thing. Randy sat on Tito and then slapped him on the butt three times. He then did it three more times before giving him a closed-fist punch to the ass. Some people thought that Randy tapped, but it was pretty obvious by his relaxed demeanor that this wasn't the case.

Bruce Buffer announced Randy Couture as the light heavyweight champ. I stood two steps behind him and thought of how beat up he looked after his fight with Josh Barnett at UFC 36. One thing was for sure, Randy wouldn't be riding to the hospital on a gurney tonight.

FRANK TRIGG

Nobody was real fired up about wrapping Frank Trigg's hands at UFC 45 at the Mohegan Sun because well, Trigg is kind of an asshole. I didn't really know the man at the time, but I'd spent a lot of time and was friends with Dennis Alexio who many people thought was an asshole, so I figured Trigg and I would be fine.

That's why I didn't hesitate when he requested that I wrap his hands before his welterweight title fight with Matt Hughes. I sat with him while his trainer Rico Chiapparelli looked on. I talked to him briefly and asked if he had any problems with his hands. He shrugged and said they were good.

He did have a gruff personality but as we talked I got a feel for him and I think he felt comfortable with me. Of course a good wrap will make a fighter feel comfortable, especially when he is about to take part in the biggest fight of his life.

I finished with Trigg and the camera crews were in the dressing room. He shoved his taped fists into the UFC gloves and Rico held pads while Trigg popped them with rights and lefts to give the cameras a little footage.

Trigg had a rough time with Matt Hughes and was submitted by a standing rear naked choke in the first round, but I had begun a new relationship with another fighter.

It wasn't until years later that the back story of that night came out. I was on Trigg's Tagg Radio and he told the rest. He didn't tell anybody, but he shattered his hand two weeks before the fight at UFC 45. It was broken in 14 places.

During the pre-fight medicals the doctors tested his hands by squeezing them and tested his punching power and Trigg said, "I'm screaming as this guy's checking my hand ... I'm like okay no problem we're good we're good, I'm losing weight as we're standing there because my hand is hurting so bad. Well Stitch wraps it and there's no way I can use my left hand, I can't use my left hand at all. It's impossible. There's no way I'm going to be able to punch with it. After he wrapped it I started hitting mitts because the camera crews were in there so I gotta hit mitts. Wow I can hit! Holy shit I can hit! He wrapped it so tight. He literally gave me one more round because that's all I had. I couldn't fight. There was no way I could've punched the man with my left hand."

It is incredible to me that Trigg was so tough that he sucked it up while I wrapped his broken hand to the point that he was able to keep the breaks from me. And apparently the wrapping of his shattered hand helped save the night. On the same Tagg Radio show Trigg talked about what MMA journalist Loretta Hunt said, "After the fight, even though I lost ... Loretta Hunt came up and said, 'Thank God you guys fought because you saved the night. Because that [the Tank Abbott fight] was a complete debacle. Your fight actually made the night.' I was like good, but put it on Stitch because I couldn't have gotten out there. There was no way in hell I was going to fight ... well effectively."

When I heard Trigg tell this story I kind of deflected his praises because I really appreciated his words, but I also recognize just how amazing these fighters are. They are a special breed and although I understand just how valuable I am, if it wasn't for these athletes I wouldn't be able to do what I do.

INOKI BOM-BA-YE, LYOTO, AND THE LAST EMPEROR

After my first trip to Japan with Josh Barnett I'd been back a couple more times. It seemed the trip across the Pacific was becoming a pretty regular thing. Now it was New Year's Eve and I was in Kobe, Japan to work with Josh as he was to fight the almost seven foot tall Semmy Schilt.

A funny thing had happened over the course of my visits to Japan. Very few people, if anybody, knew how to really wrap a hand correctly over there. The Japanese fighters learned that I was there to work with Josh and they wanted to know if I could wrap their hands too. Josh transformed into my agent and said, "Sure, he'll wrap your hands, but he charges five hundred dollars."

Back in 2003 there was a lot of money being made in MMA in Japan, so nobody thought anything of it to fork over the money. All a sudden I was getting a pretty nice chunk of extra cash. I don't remember who the first guy I wrapped for money was, but it might have been Kazuyuki Fujita. I do remember a guy in a suit handing me an envelope. I played it cool and shoved it in my pocket and did the wrap.

The whole time I was wondering if there was really five hundred dollars in the envelope. I knew that's what Josh had told them all, but I couldn't really believe that somebody would pay that much for my wrap. I got finished and on the pretense that I needed to take a leak I headed to the restroom. I closed myself in a stall and pulled out the envelope. I blew in it to open it up and sure enough I found five of the crispest one hundred dollar bills I'd ever seen.

I shoved it back into my pocket and thought *I could get used to this!*

Now on New Year's Eve there was such an exciting feel at Inoki Bom-Ba-Ye. MMA on December 31 was absolutely huge in Japan and this event wasn't the only one on the night. There was also a K-1 Dynamite in Nagoya and PRIDE was holding its own show in Saitama.

Fedor Emelianenko was PRIDE's heavyweight champ, but he wasn't in Saitama. Instead he was in Kobe with Josh and me. From what I heard Inoki offered him a higher purse so here he was and it cost him the PRIDE belt for a little while. Earlier in the year Fedor started to earn an air of invincibility that he would maintain for years to come. He shocked many people by beating Antonio Rodrigo Nogueira and then he was rocked by Fujita, the same one that I think I first wrapped for the five hundred bones, but he recovered and won the fight.

Now here he was in the dead quiet locker room sitting across from me. There was just a certain aura around Fedor. His eyes looked as if they'd been burned into his head and then set in a perfect fighter's stare once they cooled. I wouldn't say I was nervous, but I definitely wanted to do a great wrap. As I've said, I try to get a feel for the fighter and if I can give them even a sliver of confidence, I like to do so.

I knew Fedor had broken his hand in his last bout against Gary Goodridge, so I asked if it was okay. He didn't speak, just nodded that it was. I started wrapping and asked him another question or two, he again just nodded. I wasn't sure if he was in fight mode or if this was just the way he always was, a stoic Russian. Either way, I took a hint and didn't say anything during the rest of the wrap except for open and close whenever I wanted him to open or close his hand during the process.

Once finished I said, "How does it feel?"

The Last Emperor Fedor Emelianenko turned his fist upward and looked at it like he was seeing it for the first time. He then opened and closed it a couple times. He was in no hurry to respond as this process took a good ten seconds. Then with his fist still balled up he really looked at me for the first time and said in English with a thick accent, "Super ... super."

He was a man of few words, but that was all I needed to hear!

Something I didn't think was so super happened after Lyoto Machida's fight with Rich Franklin. As I'd mentioned, I'd met Lyoto before his first ever MMA bout earlier in the year at New Japan Pro Wrestling and he had trained a lot with Japanese legend Antonio Inoki. Well just after wrapping Fedor I ended up working Lyoto's corner. He looked good and dropped Rich in the second round then stopped the fight with a barrage of punches.

Immediately afterward I followed him down the steps where Inoki stood waiting. I held my bucket and bag and stood to Lyoto's right as he bowed. Inoki then did something that shocked the hell out of me. He slapped the shit out of Lyoto, first with his right hand and then with his left. I thought, *let me get out of here* and started inching away from them. Then Lyoto responded in a way that was also unexpected. He bowed again and Inoki did the same.

I hustled backstage to get ready for Josh's fight still wondering what the hell happened. I figured Josh probably knew, but didn't want to ask him right before he fought. Later on I did get a chance to ask and apparently the Inoki slap is for the fighting spirit, it's called Tokon, and a lot of people, not just fighters, like to get slapped by Inoki for courage or even good luck. At some events they'd line up and enter the ring, men, women, children, young and old, and he'd smack all of them.

I also found out that although he hit Lyoto pretty hard, he hit him even harder, and once with a closed fist, on that first night I met him back at New Japan Pro Wrestling. And Lyoto wasn't expecting that one! There's a video on the Internet that shows this one and I can't believe I was backstage and missed it altogether.

A couple fights after the second Inoki slap, I was back at the ring. It was actually the second time Josh and Semmy had met. Josh submitted him with an armbar back at UFC 32. I listened to Bruce Buffer make the introductions and then the fight was on. There were so many cameras around the ring that it was hard to see the action when they were on the ground next to the ropes, and I was right against the apron. Josh looked good in the first round, but got roughed up a bit in the second. I jumped in between rounds to take care of a couple of small cuts.

Round three was filled with more back and forth action and then with a bloody nose and time running out Josh caught Semmy in a beautiful armbar. The big screen showed the submission from directly above and it was perfect. I cleaned him up and Josh gave his speech to the crowd.

Fedor was fighting Yuji Nagata next. Josh knew Yuji from New Japan Pro Wrestling so with a nice shiner on his left eye and after putting his warm ups back on; Josh and I worked in his corner. About 30 seconds in Fedor caught him with a straight right and then finished the fight in just over a minute.

Backstage, I had my bag and bucket with me and was walking down a brightly lit hallway. There was an energy in the air that pinged with relief. It is hard to explain but it's there after each event. Win or lose, as long as the fighters believe they fought their best on that particular night, there is usually a sense of satisfaction. All the anticipation and stress that comes with weeks or months of training for a fight is dumped out into the ring or cage and the fighters have learned something new about themselves on their continuous journey to completeness.

I passed a room with the door half open. I thought I caught a glimpse of Fedor on the way by, but kept going. Then after a couple steps I heard what sounded like my name. It came in a thick accent and I paused and turned. Fedor stuck his head out the door. "Stitch, come in."

I figured since I was being invited by Fedor himself, it would only be polite for me to accept. I entered the room and he clasped my shoulder with a smile. "Come drink vodka with us," he said.

I glanced around the room and his brother Aleksander and Amar Suloev, both also fought on the card, were there, as well as a few others from Fedor's team and his family. He handed me a shot glass and filled it to the rim.

"Thank you," he said, "for wrapping my hands."

We then saluted and downed the liquid. It burned like hell, but I played it off acting as if it was as refreshing as an iced tea.

After another shot, I realized I was at risk of getting falling down drunk, so I thanked him for his hospitality and left. I walked down the hall and all I could do was shake my head as I thought, *New Year's Eve in Japan, what a crazy night.*

VITOR AND RANDY

It was good to be back in Las Vegas. I'd been traveling a great deal and with UFC 46 set for January 31, 2004 I was able to spend some time at home with Charlotte and got to take the kids, Carla, Angela, and Daniel, out to dinner a couple times. It was nice to hear all the great things they'd been doing while I was bouncing from one event to another. All three of them made and still make me proud. Carla was actually getting into the MMA business as well and it was great to see how she jumped in and started making a career for herself.

While I was having dinner and spending time with my family, Vitor Belfort, who was scheduled to fight Randy Couture at UFC 46, was going through a family crisis. His sister, Priscila, had vanished on January 9.

I don't remember how I heard the terrible news, but there was a lot of talk about whether Vitor would fight or not. He chose to go through with the bout. So it was with a heavy and worried heart that he showed up in Vegas to challenge Randy Couture for the light heavyweight belt.

I'd worked many cards on which Vitor fought, remember he opened up the "goat's vagina" on Marvin Eastman, but I'd never been able to wrap his hands even though he wanted me to. This time it worked out.

After the weigh in I went to his suite inside the Mandalay. Since this was the first time I'd be wrapping his hands I wanted to give him a pre-wrap so he could get a feel for it.

I could tell the last few weeks had been really tough on him. There had not been any word on his sister Priscila, so he was in Las Vegas gearing up to fight Randy Couture while not knowing where she was or if she was even alive.

I tried to keep the mood lighthearted, I figured he needed that, and I wrapped his hands as well as I could. He liked the wrap and gave me a t-shirt as a token of appreciation. The wrap gave him a little bit of confidence and he definitely needed it. Vitor came into the sport at only 19 years old and was nicknamed "The Phenom" because of his awesome ability, but almost seven years before UFC 46 he'd been TKO'd by Randy Couture and really never quite lived up to everyone's ridiculously high expectations. Now here he was with all this weight on his shoulders and he had to fight Couture again.

I left his suite and hoped that I had given him something that was positive and would help him through his fight the following day. A lot of people might not get this aspect, but what might seem like such a simple thing, wrapping hands, is so important to the fighters. The tape that I apply is literally their only equipment. It is the only thing that enters the cage with them, so what might seem like a small thing to some actually carries a huge amount of importance. I understand this. I see it in the fighters' eyes and hear it in their words, so I was glad to give Vitor that.

On the flipside, I was giving the same confidence to Randy too. I ended up wrapping both Vitor's and Randy's hands for the fight and then it just so happened that I was working in the red corner with Randy. I stood cageside and watched Vitor approach and he wore a shirt with a picture of Priscila on it. My heart went out to him once again.

On the first exchange Vitor threw a left hand that glanced off of Randy's left eye. The men locked up and while against the fence Randy kept blinking over and over. I could tell something was wrong, I just wasn't sure what. I looked at Dr. Goodman and she was thinking the same thing. Finally, Big John stopped the action and I followed her into the Octagon.

She wiped the eye and had him close it and we saw the cut at the same time. It looked as if a knife had sliced Randy's eyelid (it turned out it was the seam of Vitor's glove). I was ready to tell her I couldn't work on the cut. It was something I'd never seen before and in a really terrible place. I didn't get a chance to give her my two cents because to the dismay of the crowd she made the right call and stopped the contest.

Vitor and his corner rightfully celebrated. He needed something positive and it probably wasn't exactly how he wanted to win, but it was a win nonetheless. Randy congratulated Vitor and then he turned toward me. I placed a cloth on the sliced eye and moved it away for a moment. It was already blotted with blood.

In 49 seconds Vitor had become the light heavyweight champ, but he still didn't know where his sister was and he wouldn't find out the whole story for quite some time.

A TITLE FIGHT AND A TORN HAMSTRING

After UFC 46, I was in France to work with Fabrice Tiozzo again. He'd only had one fight since I stopped training him and became his cutman. He won it by TKO. Now here we were back in Lyon where he was fighting Silvio Branco for the WBA light heavyweight title. Things had changed in a big way. Before I'd stayed in a hostel and waited until the middle of the damn night so I could have the shower to myself. Now I was set up in a five star hotel. The day of the fight we loaded up and the mood was pretty tense.

As the car pulled away from the hotel I saw lights behind us. A couple of motorcycle cops pulled in behind us and I thought *man, what a shitty time to get pulled over*. But to my surprise they didn't stop us. Then I noticed two more motorcycle cops in front of us and it hit me that we had a freaking police escort to the arena. One guy would pull ahead and stop traffic at an intersection and then another would do the same at the next. It was a cool feeling, probably on par with the limo at the Copacabana, to see cars pull over to the side of the road as we passed.

The fight was an absolute barn burner. In the eighth Fabrice was knocked down and I wasn't sure if he'd be able to hang on. He did, and then showed his tremendous heart by knocking Branco down in the eleventh. The knockdown was just enough to pull out the decision.

We were all in a pretty festive mood afterward. We went back to the hotel and partied it up. After a few drinks one of Fabrice's security guys, Steve (I don't think he was French), got a little mouthy. Steve is a powerful guy and he challenged me to a contest. Of course there was no way I could back down, especially after a few drinks, so I told him to bring it on.

The idea was that he would do something and then I would have to do it as well. He started off by flopping down and sticking his head on the ground. He then put his knees on his arms and then pushed up into a headstand like a gymnast. I did the same and held it for almost as long. Upon returning to an upright position my face was red and I was seeing stars, but Steve was impressed.

Then it was my turn to go first. There was a tree in the lounge and I lined up to do a spin kick at one of the leaves, did I mention the hotel personnel loved us. I then spun around and blasted the shit out of the leaf. It was as smooth as silk except for the ripping of my hamstring. Like a dummy I'd left my shoes on and my foot caught on the carpet. The pain was immediate and intense, but there was no way I could show it.

Steve shook his head in amazement and admitted that he could not do what I just did. I won and I had an injury to prove I'd been in a battle. I didn't let anybody know about my destroyed hamstring and luckily a couple hours later, about six in the morning, the party came to an end. Once I was alone in the hallway I grabbed my hamstring in serious pain.

I didn't have time to baby it though because I had to be at the airport by seven. I packed and limped out of the hotel. The plane ride back completely sucked and when I got home my hamstring was a sickening black and blue, but hey, I kicked Steve's ass so it was worth it. I never did tell any of them I was in so much pain, so I guess now Steve can smile knowing that he kind of had the last laugh.

A week later nobody was laughing, especially not Tito Ortiz.

AN ANGRY TITO AND BIG TIM

It was a huge fight and long overdue, but Chuck Liddell and Tito Ortiz were both coming off losses heading into their match up at UFC 47. Chuck had gone over to Japan and Dana had high expectations for him. He KO'd Alistair Overeem in PRIDE's open weight grand prix, but was then TKO'd by Quinton Jackson in the semifinals. I already mentioned Tito's loss. It was the one where he literally got spanked by Randy Couture.

The two met up and at the risk of being redundant, the energy was thick. Bruce Buffer stood in the center of the Octagon and talked about how the fight was on after two years of media hype.

It was hard to not get fired up after hearing that.

Moments later it truly was on and the two put together a pretty exciting first round. Chuck ended it with a flurry and Tito yelled at him after the bell then came to the corner with a small cut on the bridge of his nose. It's a tough area to work on because it is mainly just cartilage, but I got him cleaned up okay. Tito was fired up for round two. There'd been so much talk about him saying that he and Chuck were friends and they'd never fight and then Chuck basically calling bullshit. A lot of people thought Tito was scared to get in the Octagon with Chuck.

I knew better. Tito might talk a lot of shit, but it's because he's a fighter. He feels alive when he is in the Octagon and finally getting in there with Chuck was probably a relief. So after I wiped on a bit of Vaseline on his now dry nose and headed for the Octagon door, I was really looking forward to the second round, but it didn't last long.

The crowd was standing and Tito threw a nice low kick, then Chuck opened up. In a matter of seconds it was over and Tito was in a heap against the fence. I got to him as quick as I could and tried to clean him up, but he was so upset he pushed me out of the way and stormed off. I recognized that he was still in fight mode so it didn't bother me. I gave him a moment and then made my way back over to him. He calmed down some and knew that I was there to help so he let me clean up his wounds.

A couple months later I was back in the Mandalay and this time it was Tim Sylvia who wasn't so interested in stopping his fight with Frank Mir. We were at UFC 48 and Tim and Frank were fighting for the heavyweight strap. Back at UFC 44, the same event where Couture beat Ortiz and I had to fix up Jorge Rivera's head, Sylvia beat Gan McGee to retain the belt, afterward though he tested positive for steroids. I'd heard from somebody that Tim said he didn't even take them to improve performance, but because he wanted to look better on TV.

I believe it. A lot of fans like to give Tim crap, but he is actually a good guy and it seemed like it bothered him when he wasn't fully accepted. Now he was getting a chance once again to win them over against Frank Mir.

I was working in Frank's corner and the fight was barely 20 seconds old when Tim took Frank down. Tim was in Frank's guard and Frank threw his leg over Tim's head. He was working on an armbar and referee Herb Dean looked on. About the time Tim tried to power out of it and lifted Frank off the mat, Herb jumped in and stopped the action.

Now I pride myself in seeing things that a lot of others don't see. It is my job to protect the fighters first and foremost so I probably watch fights a little differently than others, but I have to admit, I didn't know why Herb stopped the fight and I was literally only five steps away from the action.

Tim didn't seem to know either. He was pissed and stomped around the Octagon. I piled in and Herb was saying that Tim's arm was broke. I then heard a collective groan from the crowd and looked up to see the replay. It showed an obvious snap in his right forearm. Tim had been protesting the stoppage, grabbing his arm, moving it back and forth, the big man still wanted to fight. It was obvious why Herb stopped it though and I have to give him a lot of credit. I didn't see the break and nobody else did either.

Minutes later I was backstage and I stuck my head into Sylvia's room to see how things were. Here was this big guy who was just protesting the stoppage, and now minutes later he had broken down. The adrenaline had worn off and reality set in. Not only did he break his arm, but he'd lost his first fight and the heavyweight belt because of it.

He was in serious pain and seemed to be at least partially in shock. The grotesqueness of having his arm snapped in such a fashion had set in and it was an ugly scene. He was carted off to the hospital and the doctors fixed him up. No doubt it sucked for Tim, but just a few weeks later he went on the TV show *Blind Date* and talked to his date about the broken arm, so it turned into something of a badge of honor I guess. But he didn't make a connection with her either.

VITOR AND RANDY PART 2

Randy's eye had healed and it was time for his rubber match with Vitor Belfort. The fight was slated for UFC 49 on August 21 at the MGM. Once again, Vitor entered the bout with a heavy heart. His sister had gone missing just a few weeks before his second fight with Randy at UFC 46 and now as the rubber match approached, he'd heard rumors, but still did not know Priscila's fate.

It wouldn't be until about three years later when a woman in Brazil went to the police and told them that she was part of a gang that kidnapped Priscila Belfort. She'd said that Priscila and her boyfriend owed money because of drugs. The Belfort family was adamant that this was not the case. Priscila was a student and not into drugs.

The gang planned the kidnapping in October of 2003 and carried it out in January. They held Priscila in one location, but moved her when other residents became suspicious. The rest of the time she was in a slum in Rio. The ransom was not paid and since she had seen their faces, apparently they debated about whether or not to kill her and even voted on it. Then sometime in June of 2004 they took her into the countryside and ended her life. It turned out though that there were many holes in the woman's story and the truth was still unclear.

It was a horribly tragic story and no doubt the disappearance of his sister had drained Vitor. Fighting is important, especially when you are competing at the top of the sport, but for three years Vitor did not know Priscila's whereabouts. He and his family did all they could to get her back, but to no avail. The whole ordeal no doubt placed a different perspective on fighting for Vitor.

I once again wrapped both Randy and Vitor's hands. Their fight came at the end of an exciting card that saw only one decision, Karo Parisyan over Nick Diaz, and it had three straight KO's when Justin Eilers dropped Mike Kyle, David Terrell stopped Matt Lindland in less than 30 seconds, and then Chuck Liddell put Vernon White to sleep.

Vitor and Randy met up at UFC 49 and it was a decent fight that was stopped by the doctor after the third round. Honestly I don't remember much about it though. I think because deep down I really felt for Vitor and knew he was going through such a tough time. He was out there in the Octagon in such extreme circumstances and I don't know, I guess it kind of gave me a different perspective as well.

Benny and Jimmy (standing), me, Michael, and Ernie – grape field in the background.

Pony League – batting .444
at the time!

And fielding pretty
slick, too.

Left: me and friends being bad asses in Thailand.

Right: me and friends still being bad asses in Thailand.

Above: Me and Mr. Wanna sparring. Below: Thailand masters – Mr. Pe, me, Mr. Wanna, and Ramiro Rossel.

Family photo: Carla, Charlotte, Dan, me, Angela, and Jacob.

Above: Me with Vitali and Wladimir Klitschko. Below: Team Klitschko (photos courtesy of John Hornewer).

Portrait of me taken by Martin McNeil prior to UFC 105.

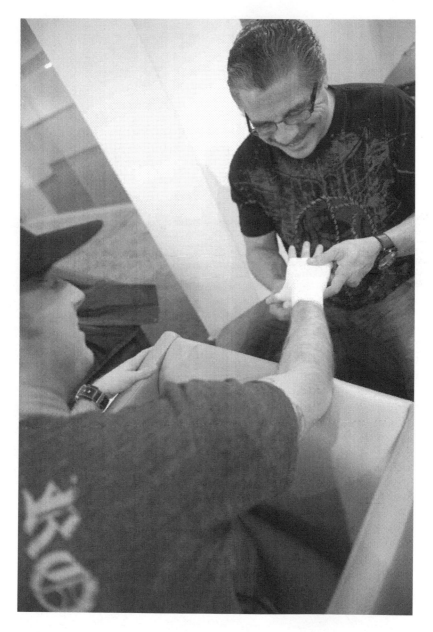

Me wrapping a fan's hand before UFC 105 (courtesy of Martin McNeil).

Deployed Marines wearing my TapoutT shirt. The wife of a Marine deployed to Afghanistan bought him my Stitch TapouT shirt. All the Marines loved it and so I told Marc Kreiner and Dan Caldwell about it. I wanted to buy 50 shirts to send downrange and they thought it was such a great idea that they sent the shirts for free.

8

THE KLITSCHKO'S
OCEAN'S ELEVEN AND WLADIMIR KLITSCHKO

IN BETWEEN FILMING *PLAY IT TO THE BONE* and beginning to work for the UFC, I was fortunate enough to be a part of *Ocean's Eleven*. They were looking for people in boxing and I fit the bill. I spent four days on the set and played the role of Wladimir Klitschko's cutman. I think you can catch a glimpse of me in the scene where he fights Lennox Lewis and the lights go out. Not a lot of airtime for four days worth of work, but Wladimir must've remembered me.

Actually I mentioned earlier, I met both Wladimir and his brother Vitali way back in 1991 when we took the team of American kickboxers and boxers to Kiev to fight the Ukrainians. The Klitschko's were there but weren't participating. They were human pillars. They towered above most everybody else and each had a body full of muscles. Years later when they were in boxing I showed them a poster from that event and they knew almost everybody on it.

So from the movie and the event in Kiev, Wladimir remembered me and it paid off. I was at an event at the MGM with my radio partner Nick Ward. I'd been co-hosting with him for a few years and we had a well-respected show called The 13th Round. Emanuel Steward was working for HBO and walked by us looking sharp in his tuxedo. He stopped and rubbed his index finger over his eye brow. "Stitch I need to talk with you about working with Wladimir," he said.

He kept on walking and I looked at Nick. "Did you see what I saw?"

He nodded, and the rest of the night I wondered about the comment.

I didn't have to wait long. The next morning Emanuel called. Wladimir had lost his last fight to Lamon Brewster and much of the blame had been placed on cutman Joe Souza for putting Vaseline on Wladimir's legs before the fight. I didn't agree with this and eventually told Wladimir as much (more on that later), but here I was with a huge opportunity to work with one of the heavyweight division's best boxers. Obviously there was no way I could say no.

I called Joe up to let him know that I'd be working with Wladimir. "Just wanted to let you know that Wladimir called me to be his cutman," I said. "Out of respect to you I wanted to pass it on to you."

"Nobody's ever done that before," he said. "Thanks Stitch, you're a good man."

I was glad to hear that he appreciated the call, and then he went on, "You know Wladimir fucked me! He called me to break the news and I said to him, 'If you were right here I'd beat the fuck out of you!'"

Now Joe goes about a buck fifty and of course Wladimir is just a tad bigger. I kind of chuckled about the comment, but Joe, being scrappy like he is, said, "I'm serious. I told him, 'If you were right here I'd kick your ass!'"

After he vented he gave me his blessings and we hung up. I thought about his comments and couldn't help but chuckle once again. A few weeks later on October 2, 2004, Wladimir was ready to take on DaVarryl Williamson and there wasn't a whole lot to laugh about, at least not at the time, instead I was thinking *what the hell did I get myself into*!

BECOMING A COMPLETE CUTMAN

We were in a tent at Caesar's Palace. Wladimir's fight with DaVarryl Williamson was outside at the New Roman Plaza Amphitheater so we had a makeshift dressing room. There were only a handful of us in it, Wladimir, Emanuel, Vitali, a photographer, myself, and somebody from the commission. It was kind of tense as Wladimir needed to answer a lot of questions after the Brewster loss.

We were only a few minutes away from going out and Wladimir was throwing punches when somehow he popped himself in the nose. It started bleeding and for the first time ever I was pressed into action before we'd even made the walk to the ring! This is the part where I was thinking *what the hell did I get myself into*. I had to get my adrenaline and my swab and go to work on his bleeding nose, and the damn thing was bleeding like a faucet. I got it stopped and just minutes later we were all making our way to the ring.

It is always a rush walking to the ring. We walked past the giant Caesar's pillars and I was a few steps behind Wladimir and feeling pretty small right next to his big brother Vitali. The fans' faces came and went in a blur, just long enough for them to register on my conscious and then we were closer to the ring and there was another face and then another. It is interesting to see their reactions to being so close to the fighter. Some reach out to touch him, others just stare, and still others cheer wildly.

Wladimir didn't look great and in round one he suffered a small cut next to his left eye. It didn't cause any problems. Rounds two and three were much of the same. Again Wladimir didn't look great, but he probably did enough to take each round.

Just 33 seconds into round four however, Williamson caught Wladimir a little off balance with a straight right. It wasn't exactly a hard punch, but it resulted in a flash knockdown. This energized everyone and the pace picked up for the rest of the round with Wladimir getting the better of Williamson.

Between rounds four and five I worked on the small cut while Emanuel was the voice of reason. He told him to take it easy and get back to working his jab and to take his time.

Wladimir did take his time and DaVarryl did as well. Not much happened until the final seconds. I was ready to climb into the ring to work on the small cut when Williamson's head crashed into Wladimir just before the bell. In an instant a fairly normal situation turned extreme. I knew it was bad and got to him quick, but the blood was already running down his face. The cut was on his forehead above his right eye and very similar to Forrest's cut against Shogun.

I quickly ran the score through my head. Most likely the judges scored the first three rounds and the fifth for Wladimir, meaning that even if the fourth was a 10-8 round (due to the flash knockdown) on all the judges' cards, he'd still win the bout. Even if Wladimir won three of five rounds, then two of the three judges would have to score round four at 10-8 just for it to end in a draw, and considering how Wladimir took it to DaVarryl after the knockdown I didn't think that would be the case.

All this happened in a split second and I made the decision. As Wladimir took the stool I leaned over to both him and Vitali. "The cut's bad and you're winning," I said. "I'm going to have the doctor stop the fight."

Dr. Margaret Goodman entered the ring and asked me what I thought. "It's a big one," I said. "He can't handle it."

"He can handle it. Come on," Emanuel said, clearly frustrated with my response because he wasn't aware of my thought process.

I replied, "No, no, no it's –"

Dr. Goodman cut me off and asked what I thought. "It's a tough one," I said and subtly opened up the cut so she could see its severity.

Emanuel was asking for a dry towel and kept urging me to work on it, but I wanted the fight stopped. Percentage wise, the best time for Wladimir to win was then and there. The gash was bad, but since being with the UFC I'd worked on a few cuts that were just as bad or worse. I figured I could keep Wladimir in the fight, but he hadn't looked great and the cut would make it that much more difficult for him.

Dr. Goodman agreed with me, and the disappointed crowd listened as referee Jay Nady stopped the fight. I continued to work on the cut. It bled through the Vaseline while we waited for the decision.

My heart jumped a bit when I heard Jimmy Lennon Jr. say, "After five rounds of action we have a split decision ... judge at ringside Chuck Giampa scores the bout 49-46 in favor of Wladimir Klitschko. Judge at ringside Doug Tucker sees the bout at 48-47 in favor of DaVarryl Williamson. Judge at ringside Jerry Roth scores the bout 49 to 46 in favor of the split technical decision winner, Wladimir Klitschko!"

First of all I don't know what the hell Doug was watching, but Chuck and Jerry had it exactly how I saw it and maybe not a lot of people were too excited for the stoppage, but I knew that it had ensured a victory for Wladimir and was a direct result of my decision regarding the cut.

Being a cutman is just like anything else. The more you do it the more you learn, and you realize that each moment can result in new understanding. On that night at Caesar's Palace underneath the Vegas stars, I felt like I became a complete cutman. That's not to say that I wouldn't continue to learn, but I saw things differently. I could truly make a difference beyond wrapping hands and fixing cuts.

The next morning the phone rang and it was Dr. Goodman. "Stitch I just wanted to let you know I already called Wladimir and I called Emanuel," she said. "The surgeon that worked on Wladimir said it was a really bad really deep cut. It was a good thing the fight was stopped when it was because it was very close to a nerve that could've created some optical damage."

I was already happy with the way things turned out, but it was great to hear this news straight from Dr. Goodman.

A couple weeks later I was at some fights at the Orleans. Referee Jay Nady was there. He waved to me. "Stitch come here," he said. I made my way over and he leaned in like he wanted to tell me a secret. "Did you do what I thought you did when Dr. Goodman came into the ring? Did you open up that cut?"

"Absolutely," I replied.

He rubbed his chin and shook his head back and forth a bit. "That was pure genius, a great move and the right move."

Again, it was great to receive the praise, especially from Jay, but I didn't have any time to rest on my laurels. A few days later I was in New Jersey at UFC 50 and after that it was back to Japan for PRIDE 28. I bet I fly more than 99.8 percent of the population, but since there's a fight at the end of each flight I guess it's worth it!

MATT HUGHES AND A LITTLE ORTIZ/MEZGER HISTORY

UFC 50 was in Atlantic City and I wrapped Trigg's hands once again. This time he didn't have 14 breaks either. I then watched Georges St. Pierre, in just his third appearance in the UFC, take on welterweight champ Matt Hughes. Obviously Hughes has a ton of fans, but kind of like Tim Sylvia, he gets crap from some fans too. I think sometimes he comes off as a little cocky because he's just a quiet country boy.

Before the fight I wrapped his hands, like I did many other times, and he was again very respectful. We talked about life on the farm. We grew up on different types of farms but many of our experiences were similar. Mark Hughes, Matt's twin brother, looked on. "So you gonna be in any more movies Stitch?" he asked.

They'd seen me in *Play it to the Bone* and always asked me about other movies. This time I told them about how I'd met Wladimir Klitschko way back at *Ocean's Eleven* and ended up working his corner a few weeks prior.

Matt met up with Georges St. Pierre and GSP gave him all he could handle early on, but with just one second remaining in the first round, the welterweight champ forced St. Pierre to tap due to an armbar. It further cemented his greatness and it also made a lot of people stand up and take notice of the French-Canadian.

Tito Ortiz was looking to snap his two-fight losing streak in the main event. He was fighting Patrick Cote who was a late replacement for Guy Mezger. That's kind of crazy story because I was about to fly out from Vegas to Atlantic City and somebody told me that Mezger was off the card. This was surprising because Mezger had wanted to fight Ortiz since he lost to him at UFC 19. Their deal really started at UFC 13 when Mezger guillotined Ortiz, but Ortiz thought Mezger had tapped earlier and then Big John stopped the action because Mezger was cut. Upon the restart Ortiz shot and Mezger guillotined him.

They met again at 19 and Ortiz won and then did a well-executed double flip off aimed at the Lion's Den and put on a shirt that read *Gay Mezger is my bitch.* This helped fuel the whole Tito vs. Ken saga and of course Mezger wanted another crack at Tito. So for sure it was surprising to hear Mezger dropped out.

Once in Atlantic City I found out why. Mezger had experienced what they were calling stroke-like symptoms. That was surprising as well. Years later he said he did have a stroke due to an anti-inflammatory he was taking.

So it was Cote, in just his fifth fight and first in the UFC, instead of Mezger. Tito got back on the winning track by claiming a unanimous decision.

A little over a week later, my man Josh Barnett was making a debut of his own. He was fighting in PRIDE for the first time and taking on none other than head kick KO master Mirko "Cro Cop" Filipovic.

Needless to say, as the plane crossed the monstrous Pacific Ocean I was excited for the fight, and excited to wrap hands at five hundred bucks a pop!

PRIDE 28

We were at the Saitama Super Arena on Halloween and I watched Josh as he made the walk down the lighted stairs to where we were standing. I'd wrapped a few extra hands and made a couple thousand dollars and now I couldn't help but think about the entrance I made with Wladimir Klitschko just four weeks earlier. It was so different than this one, and yet in many ways it was the same. That sense of impending combat leaks into the blood and with each step we are closer to questions answered.

Only this time we got an answer we didn't want. Josh waited as Mirko entered to *Wild Boys* and the crowd clapped to the beat. We hadn't seen him much during the last couple of days. Mirko was kind of a prima donna at that time. He didn't attend press conferences, stayed in a different hotel, came and got on and off the scale without speaking to anybody, that kind of stuff. I guess when you're as big a star as he was you get that special treatment, and this is not to say I don't like Cro Cop, now we have a great relationship and it shocks people how the usually subdued Croatian will give me a hug and go out of his way to visit with me every time we meet.

The fight started and Josh came out fast. Cro Cop tried a head kick, missed, and fell down in the process. Josh took advantage and ended up in his guard. This was exactly where Josh needed to be. His ground game is much better than Cro Cop's, but then the unthinkable happened.

Mirko had an overhook on Josh's left arm and Josh tried to pull it out and then started tapping frantically with his right hand. He'd dislocated his shoulder. Josh was writhing on the canvas in pain and I got to him as fast as I could. The doctors were there too and it seemed they didn't know what to do.

I considered for a moment and then I put his hands on top of my shoulder. Everybody looked on as I worked my hands up to the dislocation and used some common sense. I pulled on the arm and kind of twisted and pushed. It popped back in and Josh had instant relief from most of the pain. Everyone looked at me with a little bit of reverence so I acted like it was no big deal while thinking, *shit I can't believe that worked*!

Josh was of course horribly disappointed, as was I. He was at the top of his game and it was a huge fight for him. He'd eventually get a couple more cracks at Cro Cop, but on this night he didn't know that.

Right after Josh's fight there was a rematch of gigantic proportions. Quinton "Rampage" Jackson was getting his second shot at Wanderlei "The Axe Murder Silva" Silva. The first time they fought was almost a year earlier in a sold out Tokyo Dome and Silva won by TKO when he kneed Rampage into oblivion.

After the loss Rampage won two times, once by TKO and then once by slamming the shit out of Ricardo Arona. So there was a sickening amount of intensity around the Rampage/Silva rematch. I wasn't working in either corner, but there was no way I could miss this fight so I enjoyed it as a fan.

The two went at it until early in the second round. Silva got Jackson in Muay Thai clinch, much like he did in the first fight, and delivered some huge knees. The last landed flush on Quinton's nose and he literally fell right through the ropes, half in the ring and half out. The referee pulled him through the ropes and a trail of blood stained the white canvas.

It was hard not to run to the ring and help out. I was so used to rushing to fighters' aid. Eventually Quinton pulled himself together and on unsteady legs made his way back to his dressing room. I kept myself from heading into the ring, but I had to go check on him and I'm glad I did.

Quinton's nose was completely jacked up. It was smashed and folded to the side and he was sitting there all alone. I mean his team was there, all of them, but they were just sitting there too. It was like they were in shock and they weren't helping Quinton at all. They just left him to stew in his own pain.

I thought it was pretty sorry and was appalled by their lack of empathy. I went right up to Quinton. "Here, let me see what I can do," I said.

He looked at me and offered an almost imperceptible nod. I have those swabs or gauze, the type of thing dentists use when they work on your teeth, that I use for noses. I cleaned up the blood; it was still trickling, and went to work on getting him at least comfortable. Nobody said anything. They just looked on while I worked on Quinton. After a couple of minutes the bleeding was stopped and his mashed nose was packed to relieve the pain. I told him I was finished and he muttered. "Thanks Stitch."

At that point he was a broken man, both literally and figuratively, and I was apparently the only one willing to help him.

So PRIDE 28 was a night where I spent a lot of time fixing up fighters after the fact instead of keeping them in the action. It was a unique experience and kind of hard to stomach. I don't know if the others just weren't confident enough to help the fighters or if they just weren't educated. I mentioned earlier that I made my mark in the Japanese combat sports landscape and it probably began at this event. I loved making five hundred bucks to wrap hands, but I also recognized that I could help a lot of people by teaching them how to wrap hands and take care of fighters. Some of the PRIDE front office people must've recognized the same thing, because before long I was teaching on every trip to Japan.

VITALI KLITSCHKO AND THE ORANGE REVOLUTION

I looked at the bright orange uniform and thought *well I'm sure as hell not going to sneak up on anybody*. But I also recognized the significance of the orange color and it was obvious that this wasn't something Vitali was just doing. Both he and his brother Wladimir were very politically aware and active and it was a political time in their country of Ukraine, so we were decked out in orange.

It was my first time working with Vitali. He was fighting Danny Williams at the Mandalay. Williams had just sky rocketed in popularity as four months earlier he'd knocked out Mike Tyson. The fight happened during the aforementioned politically charged time in Ukraine. I didn't know a great deal about it until I spent a little time with the Klitschko's.

The brothers, who are about as sharp as they come and both hold doctorates in Sports Science, supported the opposition candidate Viktor Yushchenko. He was campaigning for the rights of the people and he'd been disfigured from an apparent poisoning back in September.

The first election was held on Halloween, the same day when I popped Josh's shoulder back into place and helped Quinton with his busted up nose. The vote was close but neither candidate, Viktor Yushchenko (the Klitschko's guy) or Viktor Yanukovych received fifty percent of the vote, the needed percentage to be claimed the winner.

They did it again a few weeks later and despite the polls pointing to Yushchenko, Yanukovych came out on top with a three percent margin of victory. This didn't sit too well with the Ukrainian people and allegations of voter fraud sparked massive protests. I mean we're talking 500,000 people at just one location and many of them wore orange because it was the color of Yushchenko's election campaign. This all started almost three weeks before Vitali was to fight Danny Williams and the protests became known as the Orange Revolution.

So here I was in my orange outfit complete with an ugly ass orange cap, waiting ringside for Vitali Klitschko to climb through the ropes and doing my small part for democracy in Ukraine. The fight was important to a lot of people and on more than just a sports level. The Klitschko's were, and still are, ridiculously popular figures there. For all Ukrainians, and especially those that supported the orange revolution, seeing Vitali's orange-clad team all the way over in Las Vegas, Nevada had to inspire them.

They watched along with me as Vitali, wearing orange trunks, put on a pretty awesome display. Before the fight Bob Costas spoke of the political turmoil and wondered if it would affect Vitali. Emanuel Steward, who was playing the role of commentator on this night, thought that it would motivate him.

Emanuel was right. Back when I was working with Dennis Alexio, Vitali, who was kickboxing at the time, fought on the same card. I remembered him being a giant who could kick and punch, but in the Mandalay on December 11th I gained even more respect for him. He was still a big guy, but technique-wise he did everything right. He blocked, countered, moved to his right, his left, he feinted to set up big shots. He did everything that coaches want to teach young boxers. Sure he needed a little more rhythm, but I recognized just how good of a boxer he was.

Danny Williams, who is a tough son of a gun, realized it as well. Vitali knocked him down in the first, third, seventh, and eighth round. After the last left right combo Williams answered the count, but he was on rubbery legs and referee Jay Nady stopped the fight.

I didn't have to work much on the night. I mainly sat there in my orange outfit and watched the impressive performance and I was thankful for the opportunity. It isn't very often that a man gets to take part in a cause that has the potential to change the course of an entire country, especially one that is halfway across the world. It made me think of my days back in Planada and how Cesar Chavez did so much for us through his political activism.

It was an exciting and fun night and it was the first time I'd gotten to work with Vitali and his trainer, the famous Fritz

Sdunek. I considered it and not a lot of men had gotten to do what I'd done over the last couple months. I'd worked with Wladimir and Emanuel Steward, worked in both the UFC and PRIDE, and then worked with Vitali and Fritz Sdunek!

The next day Wladimir and Vitali flew back to Kiev to take part in the Orange Revolution and I took Charlotte and the kids to dinner. It wouldn't be long however before I was much closer to Ukraine and telling Wladimir something he was surprised to hear.

THE NEXT GREAT CHAMP AND A JAPANESE RESTAURANT IN HAMBURG

There really was a time in the not too distant past when the UFC had huge breaks between shows. I'd worked UFC 50 in October, but that was it for the rest of 2004. After that event and around a little before the time I wore orange with Vitali, I did my first reality show. By the way, a couple weeks after the fight with Danny Williams, Viktor Yushchenko did win the election on the third try. The show wasn't named *The Ultimate Fighter* either. Oscar de la Hoya rushed to put out *The Next Great Champ* in an effort to compete with Mark Burnett's *The Contender.* I worked on the show.

It was fun and it prepared me for what was to come just a couple weeks later when taping for TUF season one began. Anyway, UFC 51 didn't roll around until February of 2005. It was a really good card and held on Super Bowl weekend, but honestly I don't have any good stories about it. It was at the Mandalay, sometimes the Mandalay seems like my home away from home, and it featured some big fights.

I do have a good story that took place three weeks after UFC 51. I was working with French boxer Fabrice Tiozzo again. He was fighting Dariusz Michalczewski for the WBA World Light Heavyweight title in Hamburg on February 26. This was a great match up as Dariusz had just had his 48-fight win streak snapped with a controversial split-decision loss and Fabrice was something like 46-2.

The Klitschko's had been in Hamburg for a while so Wladimir and I decided to have dinner together. We ended up at a nice Japanese restaurant and thanks to Matt Hume and my trips to Japan I knew the proper etiquette. The place was decorated beautifully with Japanese artwork, the lights were dim and at the entrance we walked by a serene pond full of Koi.

The waitress wore her black hair up and was adorned in a red and gold dress. Her movements were reserved and graceful. Wladimir and I sat at the low table eating Calamari and I couldn't help but step back and consider. Here I was a kid from a migrant camp eating in a Japanese restaurant in Hamburg, Germany with Wladimir Klitschko.

We talked and sipped on our tea from tiny glasses and then he said, "So Stitch, what'd you think of the situation with Joe Souza?"

"Look Wladimir," I said. "If you want me to be honest I'm gonna be honest with you because that's the only way I am. But putting the blame for the loss on Joe for putting Vaseline on your legs was bullshit."

Wladimir held a piece of Calamari between his chopsticks and it stayed unmoving a couple inches above his plate. His eyes widened but he didn't respond. I went on. "My personal opinion is that what happened is you fight too much like a Russian. You're very stiff and you burned yourself out."

Wladimir shook his head back and forth. "You know Stitch, you have some big balls."

"Well you asked me, so I'm gonna tell you the truth," I said. "Joe is an honorable man and a great cutman. He's there only to take care of you and for him to have gotten the blame is wrong."

Of course Wladimir took my opinion in stride. I think one of the marks of intelligence is being able to listen to others' thoughts and determine if they have something they can offer to you even if you don't like hearing them. Wladimir and his brother are both very intelligent and he seemed to appreciate what I had to say and being a true champion he accepted my criticism of the handling of the firing of Joe without arguing. Instead he ate the piece of Calamari and wanted to know how I thought he could get better. He asked what I thought he needed to do to loosen up.

"You've got to get into a rhythm and stay there," I said and moved my shoulders up and down as I talked. "I learned from the Thai kickboxers that everything has to flow."

Wladimir nodded but waited to speak because the graceful waitress was refilling our tea. "How though?" He asked once she left.

"You've got to practice it. Your movements have to transition from one to the next without effort."

Here I was coaching up Wladimir Klitschko and I could tell he wasn't quite grasping what I was saying. I figured action was better than talk so I said, "Here stand up."

He got out of his seat and I stood as well and I showed him how I thought he should move. He practiced it and the two of us shadowboxed in that dimly lit and peaceful Japanese restaurant in Hamburg, Germany.

After a few more minutes the waitress returned with our main course. We were in our own little room and I don't think she saw us. Then again she wasn't quite as graceful because she moved with a little more haste. If she did catch a glimpse she was probably thinking that she wanted to get us two psychos out of the restaurant as quickly as possible.

Wladimir really appreciated the quick lesson. I know because he wanted to train with me so we met at ten the next morning. I'd already talked to Hans, the Maritime hotel's manager and he set up a private room. But before we could get to it, the hotel guests and staff saw Wladimir and flocked to him.

We finally got down to training and I'm used to working with heavyweights so I can absorb their shots. Wladimir was a different horse. His power and speed was like no other heavyweight I'd worked with before. We worked on his balance and keeping him on his toes and mixed in a combination of body shots. I think he did loosen up some and found a little better rhythm.

After the session, Wladimir told me I trained like a Mexican trainer and I took that as a compliment. The hotel manager Hans was so excited to have Wladimir there that he asked if he could take a picture with us. It is still hanging on his office wall.

Later that night Fabrice and Dariusz hooked it up at the Color Line Arena. I worked in Fabrice's corner and he looked really sharp in route to a sixth round TKO victory, one that sent the great Dariusz Michalczewski into retirement. His rhythm was on for most of the fight and I couldn't help but think of Wladimir and me throwing our hands in the Japanese restaurant. I wondered what that waitress was telling her friends.

9

THE UFC'S EXPLOSION
THE ULTIMATE FIGHTER

IT HAD BEEN QUITE AN EXPERIENCE taping *The Ultimate Fighter*. Really the way the whole thing came about was pretty wild. Right after taping of *The Next Great Champ* I got the call about the UFC's new reality show called *The Ultimate Fighter*. Lorenzo and Frank Fertitta had let the Discovery Channel shoot a reality show at their Green Valley Ranch called *American Casino*. Because of all the exposure it gave them, they, along with Dana, came up with the idea for *The Ultimate Fighter*.

It was a make or break deal. Despite the successful live shows and a growing number of fans, the Fertitta's were hemorrhaging money. They'd bought the UFC for something like two million dollars and heading into the taping of TUF they were almost 40 million in the hole. To make matters worse, nobody wanted to put it on their network. Finally, the brothers and Dana went to Spike TV and offered to actually pay the production costs, something like ten million dollars!

I remember entering the training facility and meeting all the guys. Randy Couture was coaching one team and Chuck Liddell the other. Also Willa Ford was a host. Some of the fighters had never really had their hands wrapped, or at least not by a professional. Forrest Griffin was one of them and he reminded me of Opie from Mayberry. He seemed like just an innocent guy and really funny. He was pretty big, but it didn't look like he could fight worth a shit.

Nobody really knew what to expect. It seemed they were staying just one step ahead with each taping, kind of making it up as they went. And I sure didn't know how crazy these kids were in the house. I had heard that they got drunk a couple times and Chris Leben punched a door after Josh Koscheck and Bobby Southworth poured water on him. Forrest told me about it and said that Leben smashed the hell out of his door, so much so that he found pieces of it in his bed across the room.

So I had an idea that they were going nuts being locked away from the world during taping, but I saw much of it for the first time right along with everybody else when the show aired.

The finale was held on April 9 at the Cox Pavilion. By all accounts the show had been a success. Ratings were high and it seemed the Fertitta's and Dana's gamble had paid off, but I don't think anybody could have asked for a better ending.

The preliminary card had some exciting fights. One of them included Nate Quarry. His coach, Randy Couture, had rolled onto his ankle during a training session and he couldn't continue to fight. He did get to come back though and TKO'd Lodune Sincaid.

The main card only had three fights and it was the first time the UFC was live on cable TV. The main event was Ken Shamrock and Rich Franklin, but first it was Diego Sanchez TKO'ing Kenny Florian to win the show's middleweight title and the big contract, and then it was time for a fight that none of us could have anticipated. Forrest Griffin and Stephan Bonnar tangled for the light heavyweight contract and they put on an incredible show.

Beforehand, I wrapped Forrest's hands and then I worked his corner. At the time I never imagined that this guy from Georgia who liked to crack jokes would soon, along with a little help from Stephan, change the course of the UFC.

There is no way I can do this fight justice by describing it. It has to be seen to be believed. Both men put everything they had into it and Joe Rogan talked about the first round being the Hagler/Hearns of MMA. The second round started out at an insane pace as well and then Stephan split Forrest's nose with a jab. It opened up a huge cut and the doctor and I went into the Octagon to check it. Cuts on the nose are tough to work on because there isn't much there except skin and cartilage, but I thought it wasn't enough to stop the fight and the doctor agreed.

As soon as the round ended I got in there to work on Forrest. The doctor checked it and I told him I had it under control. After two rounds of non-stop action I desperately wanted to get the bleeding stopped so we could all see five more minutes. I did all I could and the bleeding slowed considerably. Still, by the time the round started a trickle was already running down Forrest's nose. I hadn't stopped it, but slowed it enough to where the doctor let the fight continue.

Forrest and Stephan slowed down some in the third round, but they both showed so much heart and determination. The bell sounded and I bolted through the door. I sat Forrest down and went to work cleaning the cut on his nose. The fight was over, but if it ended in a draw there was a chance for a fourth round. Somebody mentioned this and I said, "No there's no overtime on this one."

Joe Rogan and Mike Goldberg misunderstood, I wasn't saying that there wasn't the possibility of an overtime; I was saying that I didn't think it would have one. I got Forrest cleaned up and he still yelled, "Damn I'm ugly."

Then I stood behind Forrest and Stephan and pumped my hand up and down in the air. Usually I try to remain impartial, but after the amazing performance by both men I just couldn't. Everything had come together for the UFC in those 15 minutes. It was the perfect fight at the perfect time and the energy level was so high. It was just a complete victory for everybody involved. And I say everybody because Forrest claimed the unanimous decision 29-28 on all three judges' scorecards, but the fight was so great that after presenting Forrest with his trophy, Dana gave Stephan Bonnar a six-figure contract with the UFC as well!

The crowd and all of us in the Octagon went crazy. Once again I was raising my hands in the air because both men deserved it and Dana and the Fertitta's deserved it as well. A funny side note, while Forrest was getting his awards, Adam Singer, one of his trainers, was standing next to me. "Stitch, listen," he said, "I'm not gay but I've gotta give you a kiss because you did a great job on Forrest man," and then he planted one on my cheek.

I couldn't help but laugh and I also appreciated the sentiment. I was glad I could do my part to make the night play out as it did. It is things like the kiss on the cheek, I'm being figurative here, that make my job so great. It comes from these guys' hearts. They don't just tell me thank you because it is polite, but because they mean it. And on April 9, 2005 there were a whole lot of reasons for all of us to be thankful and really mean it. The UFC had just taken a huge step forward and it would reap some of the benefits just a week later.

TRIGG VS. HUGHES PART 2 AND THE END OF RANDY?

UFC 52 took place in the MGM Grand a week after the TUF finale. I'd gotten more calls from people about the sport and did an extra interview or two. The insane Griffin/Bonnar fight had an immediate impact and the city was even more energetic than usual.

I wrapped Frank Trigg's hands and he was hungry to avenge his previous loss to Matt Hughes and take the welterweight belt. We'd kind of become friends and my daughter Carla had started working as his assistant. Frank was involved in a lot and had started a clothing line called Triggonomics. There was serious bad blood between him and Hughes and the two had talked a lot of trash to each other.

After Trigg, I headed to Randy's locker room. He was fighting Chuck Liddell for the light heavyweight belt. Randy was relaxed as usual, but he also looked rundown. I of course would never have told him this at the time, but I wondered if he'd be able to perform as he had in the past. He was getting up there in age and he'd had a lot of problems recently with his marriage and a new woman in the picture. It seemed all the stress had taken its toll and going into the Octagon at anything less than one hundred percent can lead to severe consequences.

Before Randy could test himself though, Frank and Matt fought and it was almost as exciting as Griffin/Bonnar, just in a different way. The two met in the center of the Octagon and Frank just kept getting closer and closer to Matt until their faces touched. Matt pushed him away and then

Frank blew him a couple kisses. The first couple minutes were full of back and forth striking and then Frank threw a knee that must've caught Matt in the balls. I didn't really see it and neither did referee Mario Yamasaki. Matt retreated and Frank followed and started pounding on him.

Moments later Frank was working on a rear naked choke and I thought, *this is it Frank is going to be the new champ.* But Matt was almost invincible at the time and somehow he spun out of it and then picked Frank up and carried him all the way across the cage before slamming him to the mat. It happened so fast! One instant Frank was about to win, the next he was getting punched on by Matt.

From there Matt worked to a rear naked choke and Frank had to tap. A line of blood had formed on the left side of Frank's face and as the choke was applied it just squirted out. I hustled into the Octagon to clean him up. I almost had to push through Matt's brother Mark, and Pat Miletich and the rest of the group celebrating in the center of the cage just to get to Frank. I cleaned him up and he kind of shook his head in disbelief. Joe Rogan said it best, "From the brink of defeat and he pulls it out."

It really was that dramatic and a couple fights later I watched from Randy's corner as he touched gloves with Chuck. I thought my concerns for him might be unwarranted because once the bell rang Randy took the center of the Octagon and looked intent on finishing Chuck once again. The two went back and forth kind of like Matt and Frank did, until a couple minutes in when Randy backed away holding his left eye. The fight was stopped and I got off my chair ready to enter the Octagon. Of course the cut he'd received against Belfort ran through my head. I thought *there's no way lightning could strike twice.* But there Randy was holding his left eye.

Then I saw that it was not bleeding and I waited at the bottom of the steps while the doc checked him out. Randy was fine and the fight resumed, but it didn't last long.

About the time I got back to my seat, Randy was pursuing Chuck and he threw a left that missed. Chuck countered with a big right and Randy was out for the first time in his career. I raced back to the steps but this time I didn't stop. I hurried to where Randy was and bent over him. He started to come to and I said in a loud and clear voice, "Randy this is Stitch. You got knocked out."

He looked at me blankly and I repeated the words. Slowly his eyes cleared and he began to recognize that the fight was over. As I leaned over him and applied some ice I wondered if maybe his career was over as well. He'd been a great fighter, but he was over 40 years old, he was going through a lot in his personal life, and he'd just been knocked out and lost his light heavyweight belt.

The event was great, especially coming off the TUF Finale. A few days later I heard the pay-per-view numbers were through the roof, around 300,000 buys, and I knew that the UFC had really arrived.

Unfortunately, the next UFC event was still a couple months away, but the following weekend, while many celebrated the back-to-back great events for the promotion, I hopped on a plane and flew to Dortmund, Germany to work with Wladimir Klitschko for the second time. He fought Eliseo Castillo and I watched the Cuban as Wladimir took off his robe. His whole face changed when he saw the size of Wladimir. It was as if he realized for the first time that he was about to be in a serious war with a big and tough guy.

Wladimir handled Eliseo pretty easily on his way to a fourth round TKO. This was his first fight after our Japanese restaurant training session and I'm proud to say that I thought he moved with a little better rhythm.

TWO SNORERS IN ONE NIGHT

It wasn't until the beginning of summer before UFC 53 rolled around. Andrei Arlovski battered Justin Eilers for the interim heavyweight belt and afterward I heard that Eilers suffered a fracture in his right hand and his left hand had been shattered. Somebody asked me about it and I said, "I know I didn't wrap Justin's hands, wasn't me brother so don't give me credit for that one!"

In August it was a new thing as the UFC introduced Ultimate Fight Night. The inaugural UFN was in Las Vegas and I remember wrapping Ivan Salaverry. We'd become friends through Josh Barnett and Matt Hume and disappointingly Ivan didn't fight very well in dropping a decision to Nate Marquardt.

Two weeks later I watched the first fight of the night at UFC 54 in the MGM. James Irvin and Terry Martin put on a great first round. Martin kind of reminded me of a miniature Mike Tyson and at the beginning of the second round I got the distinct impression of a couple of gunslingers in an old west town. I'm not sure why that came to me, but it proved accurate. Just after the round started, Irvin got a running start and delivered a perfectly timed knee to Martin. I was working in Irvin's corner, but when the fight is over we all do our best to help the beaten man. Martin was out and his body was completely stiff when I got to him. Then I got down close and leaned over him and he was making this terrible sound, kind of like a bear. I realized he was actually snoring. It was a hard and deep snore and I thought *what the hell*?

I looked at the doc. "It's from the shock," he said. "We just need to make sure he can breathe okay and give his body a minute to relax."

Sure enough, in a few seconds the snoring softened and his body loosened up. I left the Octagon and Dana and Lorenzo flagged me down as Martin was being taken off on a stretcher. After big knockouts they often asked me how the fighter is doing. "Not good," I said. "He was stiff and snoring."

Both of them looked at me with an expression that said they were thinking the same thing I was thinking moments earlier. Fortunately, Terry ended up being okay, but it is still not exactly something Dana and the Fertitta's want the fans seeing. We all know that big knockouts can be brutal, but to see a stiffened body snoring like a bear is tough for some fans to handle.

A handful of fights later it was Tim Sylvia against Tra Telligman. The round was about over when Tim threw a head kick. It caught Tra across the neck and he dropped like a rock. Again I rushed in and his body was locked up like Terry Martin's. He was snoring too and even louder than Martin. I looked at the doc as if to say *can you believe this* and he just shook his head. We gave Tra some time and a few seconds later his jaws relaxed and his breathing returned to normal.

It was a night of big stoppages and after working thousands of fights and helping hundreds of fighters who'd been knocked out, for the first time I came across one who was completely locked up and snoring like he was struggling for oxygen. Then it happened again!

It was for sure a brutal night and as always I went home and watched the fights on TV. Both were on the pay-per-view but neither showed Terry and Tra being taken out on stretchers with oxygen masks on, and I'd say that was a good thing. The sport had experienced tremendous growth over the previous few months, but there were still a whole lot of people who would've been happy to see it fade away.

WLADIMIR AND A BLOODY MESS

Samuel Peter is a friend of mine and I try to be respectful to everyone. I'm not going to not talk to a friend just because I'm working with another one. So when I saw Peter and his trainers Cornelius Boza Edwards and Pop's Anderson, I stopped to visit with them.

As we talked Wladimir and his team walked by and he saw me with his opponent. A look of concern crossed his face and he pointed at me. I'm sure he was worried I was talking about the fight, but of course I wasn't. We were just catching up on old times. Now Wladimir understands that I'm friendly, but I'm also all business. I'd expect the fighters to expect nothing less of me.

The fight was dramatic because it's always good to work with a good corner and we had one with Vitali and Emanuel. Everything was like clockwork and Wladimir needed it because he was knocked down in the fifth and then again in the tenth.

Despite the knockdowns, he kept tagging Samuel with a brutal right cross and his face was wearing the effects. I knew Samuel didn't train as hard as he needed and could see the fight turn as he got tired. Wladimir went on to win the tough decision and afterward I watched the tape. I saw how precise our corner was and also saw that my friends in Samuel's corner were off a bit and that makes a big difference.

Sometimes though it doesn't matter how solid a corner is, and I found that out a few days later at Ultimate Fight Night 2. Jonathan Goulet was fighting Jay Hieron in the first bout of the night and I'm sure this is one that the UFC doesn't want anybody to see. Just 30 seconds into round two Goulet delivered a knee to Hieron's forehead and opened a small cut that managed to clip an artery. The blood gushed! Hieron took Goulet down and bled all over him until referee Jon Schorle stopped it so the doctor could check it out. The cut wasn't big, just bloody, so the fight continued.

Hieron spent the next couple minutes in Goulet's guard and a shower of red spilled from his head. At one point Joe Rogan talked of how they were coated in red and that a fight like this could provide fuel to critics. Goldberg kind of ignored the comments and talked about being an Ultimate Fighter. Joe and Mike are always great with their back and forth.

The blood was just running out of Jay's head and it was awful to watch.

Hieron stayed in Goulet's guard and the blood continued. Joe equated the bloodiness to a horror movie and I was amazed that the fight wasn't stopped. Finally the round came to an end and as I raced over to Jay Hieron I thought that it was the bloodiest round I'd ever seen. Joe agreed.

I guided Jay to the stool and the doctor wanted to look at the cut. NSAC commissioner Marc Ratner was standing in a dress shirt and tie with his hands in his pockets just outside the cage. "Stitch can you stop it?" he said.

"Hell yeah I can stop it," I replied.

I applied pressure and wiped the blood away. It was literally all over him, front to back and top to bottom. I put the final solution of Vaseline with adrenaline on the cut and knew I was in trouble because the blood just squirted right through it. I was thinking, *Oh shit, here it comes again!*

Incredibly they went out for the third round, but just half a minute in and the blood was raining once again. The referee stopped the fight and this time the doc decided to end it. I applied a cloth to Jay's red faucet. While I worked on it,

Georges St. Pierre, who was in Goulet's corner, entered and lifted him up, but I think Goulet was too freaked out to be excited.

It was a crazy fight, one like we'd never seen before.

I cleaned up Jay and worked on the cut. It was and still is the bloodiest fight I've ever worked and it was also the first where I became nauseated. There was just so much blood and that metallic smell was overwhelming. I got through it, but man it was stomach turning.

The last fight on that card was pretty wild too. David Loiseau, remember I like to call him my employer, was fighting Evan Tanner. It looked like Evan would finish it early when he took David's back and worked on a rear naked choke, but he was unable to sink it in.

David came out firing in round two and landed a couple high kicks, but soon Evan had him mounted again. It still looked like Evan was in complete control. Then all of a sudden David spun into Evan's guard and went to work with his elbows. After four or five the fight was stopped to examine the cuts on Evan's face.

The doctor and I cleaned him up and he already had a cut above and below his right eye and another higher up above his left eye, but hell, if all of Hieron's blood didn't stop the earlier fight, this one wasn't going to stop from a few cuts.

The action resumed with David in Evan's guard, but Evan worked it back to the feet. Then David landed another brutal elbow and the blood spilled. This time the doc stopped it almost right away and about 30 minutes after my stomach had settled I was again working on a bloody fighter.

The fight was over, but I worked just as hard on the cuts. There were five of them and each was pretty big. As I worked above Evan's eyes I was thinking, *damn this is bad*, and then like an Angel out of Heaven my partner Leon came over to help get Evan patched up. I always talk about how well us UFC cutmen work together and Leon helping me with Evan is a prime example.

On that night I realized that sometimes no matter how hard you try, you just can't win. And upon hearing that Evan Tanner had passed in 2008 I thought of those cuts. I thought of how Leon and I worked to take care of him and was glad that I got to be a part of his life.

UFN 2 was no doubt an insane event and the blood-spattered canvas can be seen at Randy Couture's gym where it now hangs on the wall. You can probably even still smell the blood.

UFC 57

It had been a few months since UFN 2. The metallic blood smell had long since left my nostrils and I'd worked a handful of events. Just days after UFN 2 I took my radio partner Nick Ward backstage and we watched Andrei Arlovski play cards and then KO Paul Buentello in 15 seconds.

A couple weeks after that I was in Japan. Remember I talked about how I started teaching over there. Well PRIDE 30 was when this really got going. I taught a couple dozen Japanese and Brazilian trainers and fighters how to wrap hands properly and before long PRIDE was using my wraps to set standards for their organization. Now Sengoku and Dream follow the same rules that I implemented back in 2005. It was a good weekend for me personally, but it sucked for Josh because in his rematch with Cro Cop he lost a decision.

In the middle of all of this I worked season two of *The Ultimate Fighter* and the finale that saw Joe Stevenson and Rashad Evans win the contracts and then a couple weeks later I helped Nate Quarry recover after he got knocked absolutely stiff by Rich Franklin at UFC 56.

I got some time off over Christmas, but in January I was back cageside with Jonathan Goulet. I couldn't help but think of the blood bath he caused at UFN 2, but he didn't get a chance for a repeat performance at UFN 3. Duane Ludwig knocked him out in like four seconds. The official time is 11 seconds, but trust me, it was closer to four.

That brings us to UFC 57 at the Mandalay. Again the building was electric as Randy Couture and Chuck Liddell started trading punches for a third time. Randy won the first bout, Chuck the second. I was in Randy's corner and earlier in the night I'd wrapped his hands. I sat down next to him. "Let's get you suited up," I said. "You want the knockout wrap or the tapout wrap?"

"The knockout wrap," Randy said and winked.

They almost always go for the knockout wrap and something cool about this moment is that Randy later mentioned it in his book, *Becoming the Natural*.

Now with around a minute left in the first round Chuck landed a few clean shots. Randy shot and took him down, but Chuck popped back up. They were in a standing position and Randy's head was against Chuck's back. From where I was I couldn't see it, but as they turned I noticed blood was streaming from Randy's face.

The round ended and I got to work. It was his nose and I could tell it was broke. "You're alright," I said to Randy, and then to his corner, "I need to sit him down. Where's the stool?"

He never did get to sit down, but I got the bleeding stopped fairly easily. Round two got underway and the men exchanged punches for the first minute. Then Randy pressed forward and looked to slip as he threw a left hook. Chuck countered with a right and it was over in an instant.

I got to Randy and he seemed clear headed. His nose was bleeding again and I went to work on it. Dana came up behind Randy and asked him to stay and say a few words. Chuck talked and I wiped the blood off Randy and helped his corner pull off his gloves. With his gloves in his hands he waited for his turn to speak.

I stood behind him a little ways and listened to what Randy had to say. I glanced at the big screen and noticed a tiny trickle of blood coming from his nose. Then Randy kind of raised the gloves in front of him and announced that he was done fighting, that it was time to move on.

The crowd literally gasped at the announcement. Hell I might've gasped too. I half expected Randy to retire after his last loss to Chuck at UFC 52, but this one caught me, and everybody else, by surprise. I thought *wow, what an honor to be part of Randy's history and get to work his last fight*. Of course we now know that he had a little bit more fight left in him.

Something else that was surprising, or maybe not so surprising knowing my man Nick Diaz, after he lost a tough decision to Joe Riggs both of them got hauled off to the hospital. Not long after the Couture/Liddell fight I was back in the locker room and Burt Watson, the event coordinator, burst in even more worked up than usual. "They got in a fight at the hospital," he said.

"Who did?" I asked.

"Nick Diaz and Joe Riggs," Burt said. "They were all beat up and getting stitches and while waiting for the doctors to come in they started jawing at each other and all a sudden they were fighting! Can you believe that? They already fought for three rounds but didn't get enough."

I just kind of shook my head. It had once again been an exciting and even historical night as Chuck and Randy were really the first big name UFC guys to fight each other three times and then Randy retired. It was also a wild night as one fight ended in the Octagon and resumed in the hospital.

FERNANDO VARGAS, BEST DAMN, AND CANNES

Fernando had been very accommodating back when John and I were filming *Boxer's Nightmare* and now a few weeks after UFC 57 I was back in the Mandalay working with him for his first fight with Shane Mosley. In the second round Fernando received a headbutt. He returned to the corner and it looked like somebody had planted a marble underneath his left eyebrow.

The fight was back and forth and between each round I used my enswell, a flat cold piece of metal, to keep direct pressure on the swelling to try to keep it away from the eyelid.

It worked until the seventh when the swelling started to blow up. By the end of the round it had doubled in size and it looked like somebody had placed a lemon underneath his eyebrow. Pictures of the swelling are all over the Internet and a lot of people said it looked like Fernando had a second head.

I was afraid the doctor would stop it after the eighth, but he gave me a chance to work. The swelling had all but closed Fernando's eye. I kept pressure on it and did my best to keep his eye open. He went out for the ninth and despite the lemon on his eye the round was competitive.

Heading into the tenth the eye was basically closed and the swelling was too much to control. The doctor, referee Joe Cortez, and Marc Ratner talked while I applied some Vaseline and it was obvious that they were close to stopping the fight.

A little over a minute into the tenth Fernando took a barrage of punches from Mosley and Cortez jumped in to end it.

A couple interesting things happened afterward. A few days later I was on *The Best Damn Sports Show Period* with Chris Rose and John Salley. The lead in said I was there to *separate the cutmen from the cutboys.*

John was my protégé and he helped me fix up Rod Dibble. The former hard-throwing major league pitcher came out with a serious make-up job and his face looked jacked. I showed how I worked on the cuts and Chris asked if I sewed in between rounds. He was obviously confused about what I do.

They also showed a photo of me with Sylvester Stallone. I was in Rocky VI with him. "I remember in Rocky one," John said, "Rocky's eyes are all messed up and he goes, 'You gotta cut me.' They cut him so he could see. Tell me, that's how they do it right?"

I answered by explaining why this was not a good idea. It actually creates more problems because you have to deal with the cut and the swelling. I also brought up the Vargas fight that had just happened the previous weekend and they showed photos of Vargas' head.

"First of all, how did you know which head to work on?" Chris said. "What do you tell him?"

"You tell him to go beat the hell out of Shane Mosley because the fights gonna be ending!" I said.

This got a laugh and overall it was a really good time. I got to put my name on *The Initiator Wall of Flame*. I wasn't sure what the hell it was, but it was cool anyway to put my name up there with the likes of Eric Chavez, John Daly, Vince Young, Willie McGinist, and others, especially because my flame just read *Stitch*.

The other interesting development after the fight wasn't near as fun. I got a call from Fernando. I thought I'd done a good job keeping him in the fight as long as I did. After the swelling grew to monstrous proportions I kept him in for two more rounds. He didn't agree and told me he thought I didn't do all I could have. I don't know, maybe he wanted me to cut him like in Rocky. Anyway, I told him that I wasn't sure if Jesus Christ himself could've done any better with that swelling.

The call was definitely frustrating, but I also understood it. Often when a fighter loses he has to deflect some of the blame. Fernando was just doing that in this case. We just didn't see eye to eye (no pun intended) on this issue.

I didn't work his rematch some five months later, but that was fine by me. On that same day, July 15, I was in Cannes, France working Fabrice Tiozzo's last fight. I took Charlotte to this one and we spent the week as tourists. We had a great time and I'd promised her a gift from Christian Dior. She saw a crocodile purse that she liked and it was fifty percent off so I figured what the hell. The lady rang it up and it was $3,000 *after* the discount! I nearly choked, but for sure Charlotte deserved it. She's been a wonderful and supportive wife for over 15 years.

She also got a little air time during the event. I was warming up Fabrice in the dressing room and I heard Charlotte's name in French. I looked up at the monitor and there she was sitting ringside with Fabrice's wife. It was a great week and it ended on a high note when Fabrice won by TKO in the fifth.

APPRECIATING THOSE WHO FIGHT

UFC 58 at the Mandalay had some interesting fights. Rich Franklin destroyed David Loiseau for five rounds and the middleweight belt and Georges St. Pierre withstood a poke in the eye from B.J. Penn to win a controversial split decision. The fight however that I remember the most is Spencer Fisher and Sam Stout.

It was incredible and the story leading up to it is good too. Spencer always wants me to wrap his hands and this time was no exception. We sat down across from each other and I'd heard that he had to cut a crap load of weight for the fight in just a couple days because he was a late replacement for Kenny Florian.

"How you feeling after the cut?" I asked.

"Good," Spencer said, "Twenty pounds in two days was hard." I agreed with him and he went on, "Monte [manager Monte Cox] called a couple days ago. I was drinking a Dr. Pepper and I put it down and headed to the gym."

"No shit," I said.

"Yeah and I fought just two weeks earlier too."

It was hard to imagine what he was going through. Fighting, recovering, fighting and having to cut to 155 in a couple days. It takes a strong body and mind to come out successful after a couple weeks like that.

On top of Spencer's weight cutting, if I remember right this was the first fight in the lightweight division since it had been put on hold a couple years before and it was Sam Stout's debut with the UFC.

It was just the third fight of the night and in Las Vegas this meant that the arena was about half full. Anywhere else it would mean a packed house because unlike boxing, UFC fans arrive early and cheer loudly from the first fight on. Vegas is different, the crowd arrives a little later.

Matt Hughes was working Spencer's corner and he climbed down the steps as the fight was about to get underway. I sat right behind him and we watched a tremendous scrap. One of the best I've ever seen. Spencer and Sam went at it for three rounds and the circumstances leading up to it made it that much more amazing.

That fight will always stick with me for what it took for Spencer to put himself in that position and then to fight all out for 15 minutes like he did. I also remember how they beat the crap out of each other and then had no ill feelings afterward. That is one of the great things about this sport. These guys will do everything they can to beat their opponent and then go have a beer with him afterward.

About six weeks later I was in a completely different venue with a different sport as Wladimir was fighting Chris Byrd in Mannheim, Germany. Chris is a really nice guy and Wladimir beat the shit out of him until the fight was stopped in the seventh. Still though, Chris hung in as long as he could and got up after being dropped by a right in the fifth.

Everyone on team Klitschko celebrated in the ring, as boxers do after wins. I made my way over to Chris. He had a nice sized cut above his eye and his mom, dad, and sister, Tracy (she also boxes) worked his corner and none of them are really able to fix cuts, at least not in the same way I can.

I wiped Chris down and asked Tracy, "You want me to take care of Chris real quick?"

"Yeah if you could do that, that'd be great," she replied.

I made sure the bleeding was stopped and covered it with Vaseline. I do this with all the guys I work with and try to get it done before the cameras are on them. I figure that they deserve it after going out there and fighting as hard as they can and it might protect their pride a bit.

Now I wasn't working with Chris, but he is a friend and taking care of fighters is what I do. That's what I would have told Wladimir too if he would have said something. He didn't, I'm sure he recognized why I was doing it and it wasn't going to change the course of the fight. Wladimir had already won.

I've been involved in and influenced the outcome of more MMA and boxing matches than probably any other man on the face of the earth. I'm up close and in the cage or ring with the guys and I know what they go through. I hear the strikes. I see and fix the effects of those strikes. I understand what mental and physical challenges they must face just to give themselves a chance to win, whether it is cutting weight on short notice, battling through a tough situation, continuing to throw hands and take shots beyond exhaustion, or holding on to their pride and desire to continue to compete after a devastating loss.

Because of all this I truly appreciate each man who does all that it takes to fight professionally.

10

BACK AND FORTH: UFC AND PRIDE
FREQUENT FLYER MILES AND LEGENDS

FROM MANNHEIM I FLEW BACK HOME TO VEGAS and then I was on a plane crossing the Pacific to work with Josh in Osaka at PRIDE Total Elimination, the first round of a tournament. It was a busy week as I got there early and did seminars on how to wrap hands and fix cuts and then worked with Josh for a couple days by wrapping his hands and padding him out in his final training sessions. I think I brought him a lot of confidence and I love doing pads with him.

He fought Aleksander Emelianenko and did a tremendous job. This performance was one of the best I've seen from him. He controlled Aleksander and subbed him with a keylock in the second round.

With the win I knew I'd be back in Japan soon for the second round, but first I was closer to home at the Staples Center in Los Angeles for UFC 60. This event featured the return of Royce Gracie, the "Godfather" of the UFC. Royce really is a legend. He turned the United States on to the importance of the ground game and now he was coming back to fight another legend in welterweight champ Matt Hughes.

Before this fight happened though, I wrapped Spencer Fisher's hands once again and then worked as he fought Matt Wiman. This time it was Wiman who was the late replacement. He took Leonard Garcia's place after Garcia broke his leg while training.

It turned out to be another great fight, not quite like Spencer's last fight with Sam Stout, but still exciting. The ending was really crazy. After Matt looked great for most of round one, Spencer cut him with an elbow. Then in round two he rocked him with a right. Matt shook his head and even kind of raised his finger up in the air as to say "I'm fine." Then Spencer took off with a flying knee. Matt ducked right into it and it was lights out. It was one of those crazy KO's where you watch it once and then want to watch it over and over again.

The main event was being billed as the old meeting the new and that was an appropriate way of looking at it. I worked in Matt's corner and backstage he was pretty fired up about Spencer's flying knee KO (they trained together with Pat Miletich at the time).

As Big John got the fight underway, we all wondered if Royce really was the ultimate legend and if he could somehow submit the unstoppable train that was Matt Hughes.

It quickly became apparent that he was not. Matt just had his way with Royce and took him down about a minute in. He worked from side control and locked in a Kimura on Royce's left arm. I watched as the arm kept bending and bending and knew Royce wouldn't tap, but kept saying in my head anyway *tap Royce, tap.*

Matt realized he wasn't going to tap either and after it looked like the elbow popped he let go of the submission. He then worked to Royce's back, flattened him out, and beat him up with elbows and punches until Big John stopped it.

It was an amazing performance, but at the time we'd all grown to expect nothing less from Matt. I congratulated him after the fight and made my way to the back. I was packing up my bag when Burt Watson came in the room. "Stitch, can you go in with Royce and work on some of the swelling?" he asked.

Talk about a great honor. I went into the dressing room and his father and the rest of his team were there. "I'm here to see if we can take care of some of the swelling," I said to Royce.

He nodded and I went to work. This was really my first time ever meeting Royce. Maybe he knew who I was and I certainly knew who he was, but we'd never talked. He was quiet and humble and of course disappointed with how the fight turned out. In a few minutes I had done what I could do and I left.

Now when I see Royce Gracie he always approaches and says hi. I think he appreciated what I brought to the table and this is a great example of how what we do for the fighters creates a certain bond with them.

UFC 60 was a night that showed the world a lot. We all saw that Royce Gracie, the same man who dominated those early UFC's, was much older and couldn't compete with the ever-evolving top fighters in the game at the time. It also gave me a chance to work with that legend for a brief period of time and I was honored to get to do so.

JOSH AND EVAN AND ANDERSON'S DEBUT

In all walks of life there are a select few who are able to do things that others don't think they can. When we see them accomplish something despite the odds, it inspires. Mixed Martial Arts is no different and Josh Haynes, a contestant on season three of *The Ultimate Fighter*, accomplished more than a lot of people thought he would.

He lost a lot of weight and made his way onto the show where he fought as a light heavyweight. He'd had a rough few years as his second son, Thor, had a brain tumor and if I remember right wasn't expected to live. He pulled through after multiple surgeries and chemotherapy, but in talking about the trying time it choked Josh up and who could blame him.

Something that a lot of people probably don't know, but this shows what kind of guy the late Evan Tanner was. Back in February of 2003 right in the middle of a stretch where Evan was working his way toward another middleweight title shot, he fought on a card called *Fighting Against Cancer* for free in an effort to help raise funds for Josh's son.

On TUF 3 I don't think anybody expected Josh to make it to the finals. He did, and faced Michael Bisping. Mike has a strong personality and people either like him or hate him. I liked him from the get go. He is so full of energy and he's another one that after I wrapped his hands once he requests me every time.

Mike beat Josh up pretty good and even now it is easy for me to visualize Josh's face so full of blood. He fell just short of the big prize, but I give Josh a ton of credit. He lost all that weight, persevered through tough times, and became an Ultimate Fighter. He did much more than anybody expected.

A few days later Anderson Silva made his UFC debut at Ultimate Fight Night 5 and I don't think anybody expected that he'd go on to do what he has done. He was meeting up with Chris Leben on this night and I remember Chris talked about knocking him out and sending him back to Japan where the competition was easier.

There was quite a bit of intrigue around this fight as Anderson was making his debut and Leben was a hard-charging brawler. Leben was 5-0 in the UFC, but Anderson moved so smoothly and stuck him with a few jabs. Then about 30 seconds in he landed a high kick and followed it up with right-left-right and Chris went down. Anderson held up thinking it was over, but Big John let it continue, so he jumped on Chris and continued the barrage until a big knee ended it.

It was then that I think everybody realized that Anderson was amazing seeing him destroy Chris as he did. I also don't think anybody could have expected him to do what he did over the next few years though.

"I THINK YOU LOST A TOOTH"

The next morning, just eight or so hours after Anderson's debut, I was on a plane for Japan. Josh was fighting Mark Hunt at PRIDE *Critical Countdown* in Saitama and it was a busy couple days for me. I did a seminar and showed a number of Japanese and Brazilian fighters and trainers how I wrapped hands. Then I worked with Josh during his final session and the fight was almost an afterthought. I wasn't worried because he was on the top of his game and I knew he was better than Mark. He proved it by subbing him with a Kimura in just over two minutes.

Upon returning to Las Vegas I learned that I would be unable to attend UFC 61 so I missed Tito Ortiz and Ken Shamrock's second fight. It was a monster event and was the first to break one million pay per view buys, but Charlotte and I were on our way to Cannes, France so I could work with Fabrice Tiozzo once again. As I mentioned before I bought her the purse and worked with Fabrice for his final fight and it was a great trip.

I was back in the Octagon for UFC Fight Night 6 at the Red Rock in August. Every now and then we have an odd fight and this time it was Forrest Petz and Sam Morgan providing the oddness. Morgan dominated, but couldn't finish and it led to one judge scoring the fight 30-23 for Morgan. There was one fight that was much closer and sticks out in my mind, Diego Sanchez vs. Karo Parisyan. I was working in Karo's corner and he and Diego went at it. Karo got cut with an uppercut early, but it wasn't bad. I went in between rounds and worked on it while Tito Ortiz coached Karo.

Round two was back and forth as well and I cleaned up Karo's cut and stopped his bleeding nose in between rounds. Then in the third Karo took a knee while in the clinch. I saw something fly through the air and thought; *damn he just lost a tooth*.

The fight ended and while cleaning Karo's face up I said, "I think you lost a tooth."

He looked at me through his swollen eyes and cheeks. "No it's alright, it was just a veneer."

At the time I didn't know what the hell a veneer was. I just nodded and thought that he'd been punched one too many times and was loopy. Later I found out that it's a thin layer of material that goes over a tooth.

It was a hell of a fight and the veneer comment still cracks me up to this day.

A little over a week later, at UFC 62 in the Mandalay, Forrest Griffin and Stephan Bonnar were back in the Octagon as well. I was in Forrest's corner and thanks to the first fight the hype was huge, like any world title fight in boxing. During the fight I was waiting for it to kick in and them to go at it toe to toe. And finally they were going at it toe to toe. It was a good fight and Forrest won a decision again, but it wasn't like the first one. Of course how could we have expected it to compare. Everything came together so perfectly on the first go.

Still it was a fun fight, most of them are. Then again, sometimes they are just real damn hard.

PRIDE FINAL CONFLICT ABSOLUTE

Erik Paulson and I hustled Josh back to the dressing room after the decision was announced. He'd just gone the distance against Antonio Rodrigo Nogueira in a really close fight. We'd hoped he'd finish Big Nog in a hurry but it didn't happen. Now he had a handful of fights before he'd be back in the ring to take on Mirko "Cro Cop" Filipovic for a third time. Josh really wanted this fight, especially after the decision loss from almost a year ago.

We headed up the ramp and all I could think of was Mirko landing that head kick on Wanderlei Silva. It ended the fight after a little more than five minutes and it came just before Josh's win. No doubt Mirko would be the fresher man.

We had a handful of fights before the finals so once in the locker room I cut Josh's wraps off and Erik and Matt Hume got bags of ice to place on his legs. He also ate a couple of bananas, rehydrated, and tried to relax while lying on the floor.

Our only focus was getting Josh physically ready to go out there and face Cro Cop after a grueling 15 minute battle with Big Nog. Fighting twice on one night, especially against such high level competition is exhausting. Josh's adrenaline was so high for the first fight and then he had to contend with the adrenaline dump and try to get going once again. He was determined. He wanted another shot at Cro Cop, but what a difficult situation!

After about an hour I re-wrapped Josh's hands and held the pads while he hit them a bit. He tried to conserve as much energy as possible while still getting warmed up enough to fight.

Mirko looked sharp and much fresher and he landed a number of punishing combos. Josh hung tough and stayed in the fight for a while, but Mirko was just too much. He landed a barrage of strikes almost eight minutes in and one of them resulted in an accidental eye poke. Josh submitted and it put an end to a challenging night.

I guess Cro Cop was Josh's kryptonite because he beat him three times in the span of a couple years, but now the two are pretty good friends.

I mentioned Matt Hume earlier. He deserves a lot of credit because he's the one that introduced me to all the PRIDE people. He was like the American representative for PRIDE and he told them about what I did. This led to the seminars on how to wrap hands and fix cuts. These seminars were needed too because they did some crazy stuff over there. They'd get tape and roll it up and put it on the knuckles, wrap hands down to almost the fingertips, all kinds of craziness in the hopes of finding an advantage. So I worked with everybody: fighters, officials, trainers, doctors, with the goal of better protecting the fighters.

The groups really enjoyed it and learned a lot. It was at one of these seminars for the fighters that I wrapped Murilo "Ninja" Rua's hands. Mauricio (his brother), Wanderlei Silva, all the Brazilians were there and I think it was Wanderlei who first said it, but they decided I looked like Carlos Santana, the famous musician. I don't know I guess I kind of do look like him and after that all the Brazilians started calling me Santana. It's funny to hear coming from them with their accents.

A couple years later, at UFC 104, Mauricio reminded me that I had wrapped his brother's hands and he wanted me to wrap his. I thought it was cool that he remembered and I did in fact wrap his hands at 104, but well before that I took on a much bigger role at PRIDE 32, the promotion's first event in the United States. That was still six weeks away though and in MMA a lot can happen in six weeks.

PULVER, PENN, AND KEN

Jens Pulver was so excited to be back in the UFC. He was the second MMA guy I'd ever wrapped and now almost exactly five years later at UFC 63 we were in the locker room and I was wrapping him again. He'd spent a lot of time in PRIDE, but now he was back with the UFC. His energy was through the roof and he fought a young kid named Joe Lauzon.

The energy and excitement didn't translate to a victory. I felt for Jens as he got knocked out in under a minute. It was a huge win for Joe and worked as a catapult for his career.

A few fights later I was feeling for B.J. Penn too. He was taking on Matt Hughes for the welterweight title and I was in his corner. Back at UFC 46 Penn subbed Hughes, but Matt had won five straight since.

B.J. was doing great for the first two rounds, but in the third things fell apart. It looked like he just gassed and Matt got him in a crucifix and beat the hell out of him until the fight was stopped.

I went to work on B.J. and he was so drained, more so than maybe any fighter I've ever worked on. I kind of put my arm under him to give him balance because he literally could not stand on his own. I told his trainer, Rudy Valentino, "Hold on to B.J. or he'll fall."

Rudy held him up and B.J. was like a wet noodle. He couldn't even really talk and at that point I knew it had to be more than him just getting pummeled while in the crucifix. Sure enough, soon after we figured out that his ribs were jacked up.

It was pretty wild because here we had the guys that I worked with and knew from my start with the UFC back in 2001 and now at UFC 63 the two former champs had suffered tough losses.

Another case of old meets new, at least figuratively, happened a couple weeks later in Hollywood, Florida when Ken Shamrock and Tito Ortiz fought for a third time. Tito beat Ken up pretty bad once again and I don't have much to tell about this one, but for some reason this event reminded me of something that made me feel kind of like an ass a few years earlier.

At one of my first UFC events, I can't remember which one exactly, I was wrapping hands and this guy comes in. I glanced at him, but I was focused on my job so I didn't pay much attention. A moment later I glanced again and thought that he looked familiar. Finally I said, "Man you look familiar, do I know you?"

"You might," he said with a smile. "I've been around the game a little bit."

I introduced myself and he said, "I'm Ken Shamrock."

No wonder he looked familiar and I felt like a dummy, especially because I realized he was messing with me by saying "I've been around the game a bit." Guess it goes to show how little I knew at the time and now I think it's funny that I made such a stupid comment. You can learn a lot in five years though. Actually in MMA you can learn a lot in just one night!

BLOOD AND BREAKS

UFC 64 took place at the Mandalay on October 14, 2006. The card featured two title fights, first Kenny Florian and Sean Sherk met for the lightweight belt and then Rich Franklin attempted to defend his middleweight title against Anderson Silva.

Right from the get-go Sean took Kenny down and Kenny spent much of the fight on his back. This was a really bad spot because just seconds into round two Kenny cut Sean with a short elbow. Referee Steve Mazzagatti halted the action so Dr. Davidson could take a look at the cut. While he was doing so Kenny kept looking over at us (I was in his corner) and saying he couldn't see.

Sean's blood had drained into his eye and he needed it cleaned out. Dr. Davidson obliged and Sean shook his head like *are you kidding me.*

After the second round Kenny came back to the corner and I wiped him down. There was so much blood on his face it looked like he was the one who'd been cut. I cleaned him up and he complained of blood in his eyes so I flushed them out with some water.

Sean bled all over Kenny for about four minutes in round three and this time when Kenny came back I wiped him down and he said the blood was getting in both his eyes and his mouth. It was so bad that one of the officials from the athletic commission was checking to see if Kenny could keep fighting!

Of course he could and they went back out for rounds four and five and it was more of the same. I watched closely after Kenny talked of the blood getting into his mouth and sure enough I could literally see it spilling into his mouth. In between rounds I wiped blood out of his left ear, his mouth, and both eyes before applying Vaseline.

Ten seconds into the fifth and Sean dumped Kenny again and then bled on him some more. This is the only time I've ever seen somebody bleed on another person for twenty minutes and it was nuts.

Sean won the decision and this fight showed me that an advantage could become a disadvantage. Kenny cut Sean above his right temple and then suffered the consequence for a long time.

There were some serious consequences for the next fight too. With Sean's blood smeared all over the canvas and Kenny probably back scrubbing himself vigorously in the shower, Anderson Silva and Rich Franklin hooked it up. Anderson was fresh off his destruction of Leben and getting a crack at the belt in just his second fight in the UFC. He obviously deserved the opportunity.

The fight started off pretty even until Anderson got Rich in a Muay Thai clinch. He kneed Rich's body until he dropped his hands and then battered his face with more knees. In a matter of minutes it was all over and Anderson Silva was the new middleweight champ.

I got to Rich as fast as I could. We hauled him up and sat him on the stool. His nose was completely bent out of whack, probably even worse than Quinton's back at PRIDE. I put pressure on it and could feel where it was broken and separated. There was a jagged point right on the bridge and when I moved it everything moved back and forth.

I was still working on him as we were standing with Big John for the official announcement. Anderson leaned over to check on him. "I'm alright," Rich said. "I'm okay."

I was thinking *I don't know if you are Rich*, because he was busted up. I hated to see it too because Rich is such a humble and classy guy.

I was back at home later on that night. It was almost one in the morning and Charlotte and I were watching TV. I'd just got finished telling her about feeling that jagged point on Rich's busted nose when the phone rang.

It was Dana's right-hand person Donna Marconi. "Stitch, do you know where we can get some permabond?"

Permabond is an adhesive used for cuts. "No I don't, but what do you need?" I asked.

"Well we need permabond," she said.

"What for Donna?"

"Well here, I'll just let you talk to Rich's doctor."

A man got on the phone and introduced himself. Turned out he was a chiropractor, "You know where we can get some permabond?" he asked.

Donna is awesome, but I was kind of getting frustrated. Here it was in the middle of the night and they wouldn't tell me what the hell was going on. Finally he said, "Well Rich has some cuts and we're trying to close them up."

I wasn't so sure why that was so hard to say or why they didn't just go to the hospital, but now I understood. I still didn't have any permabond though.

Donna got back on the phone. "Stitch I hate to ask this, but can you come over here."

I thought, *why not.* "Sure Donna," I said. "I'll be there in a few," and gathered up my bag and headed back to the Mandalay. I figured it was to help Rich out and he deserved it.

I got to the Mandalay and headed through the luxurious lobby. Even though it was the middle of the night the place was packed and the slot machines were ringing. As I crossed toward the hotel elevators I bumped into some familiar faces, my daughters Carla and Angela. They were out partying after the fights. "Dad what are you doing here?" Angela said.

I told them about the phone call. It was funny seeing them out and they were shocked to see me. But I was working, not drinking red bull and Vodka's.

I got up to Rich's room and he was in pretty good spirits for a guy who'd just lost his belt and in brutal fashion. His doctor was there, as was Donna Marconi and Rich's wife Beth. They'd already worked on his nose and it had what looked like duct tape over it. He had a couple small cuts that nobody had addressed. They weren't that big of deal and I took care of them and then put a butterfly on them to keep them closed, no permabond necessary.

So I learned a bit on that night. It isn't so good to cut a guy who's going to spend much of the fight on top of you, Anderson Silva was a complete bad ass, and I'll make house calls if you are as nice as Rich Franklin.

I guess a few days later he had surgery on the nose, probably about the same time I was busting my ass to get ready for PRIDE 32. It was set for the following weekend in Las Vegas and as I mentioned before, I played a large role in this event.

A BUSY WEEKEND AND TWO SAD GIRLS

Since I'd been working with PRIDE and doing seminars, I took on the job of organizing cutmen for PRIDE 32. By now the UFC had four cutmen, Leon Tabbs, Don House, Rudy Hernandez, and me. I brought them on board for the event and basically did what Burt Watson did for the UFC in determining who needed hands wrapped by us and then designing a plan to ensure that process went as it should.

That's a tougher job than most would expect. We had 16 fighters on the card and you can't be too sure how everything will unfold. Sometimes you get two or three quick finishes in a row, other times two or three decisions and it changes the pace of everything.

Frank Trigg was commentating for the event and at one point he said something like, "Stitch is like American Express, I don't leave home without him." I thought that was pretty funny and it was actually a nice compliment.

I basically ran all over the place the entire night between being there for Josh (I still worked his corner) making sure everyone was assigned and organized, and wrapping hands (this was another time in which I got to wrap Fedor). It was really fun and exciting to see PRIDE in Las Vegas and to get to be such a big part of it.

In Japan, PRIDE had never let us put Vaseline on the fighters. I tried and tried to get them to change this rule, but for whatever reason they wouldn't. Since this one was in the U.S. though and we were following a different rule set we were able to apply Vaseline and I think this is really important. The Vaseline helps to keep them from getting cut.

Josh handled Pawel Nastula fairly easily and subbed him with a toe hold in the second round. Then Mauricio Rua and Kevin Randleman fought. Randleman took Rua down in a hurry and Rua started working on a submission on Randleman's left leg and foot. As Rua tried for the sub he cranked on Randleman's foot and the big wrestler screamed repeatedly but didn't tap.

After a couple minutes though he was twisted like a pretzel with his left leg bent up over him while he was on his back and Rua forcing his knee to go the wrong way. Finally he tapped.

The next fight and main event featured Fedor against Mark Coleman in a rematch. The first time around Fedor subbed Mark with an armbar. This time Mark kept looking for the takedown and Fedor kept pounding him.

In the second round Fedor secured an armbar and Mark, bloody face and all, tapped. I headed into the ring and Don House and I worked to clean him up. His face was all distorted with a huge mouse under his left eye and swelling all over.

During the post-fight interview Mark started talking to his daughters who were in the crowd. "Daddy loves you," he said. "I'm okay."

Then all a sudden they lifted Morgan and Mackenzie into the ring. These girls were like eight and six years old at the time and their dad's face was seriously jacked up. Of course they were crying like crazy and he hugged them and told them he was alright, but it was a really odd moment. It got odder when Mark picked them up and carried them over to meet Fedor. He told them that Fedor was really a nice guy (who just happened to beat his face in).

That moment stirred up a little controversy as a lot of people thought he shouldn't have brought them into the ring and some even said it was all choreographed. Something else that brought a little controversy was all the positive tests for steroids. Pawel Nastula and Vitor Belfort tested positive and Kevin Randleman had a suspect urine sample. All three of them lost, but I think these results gave fuel to the argument made by a lot of fans on the Internet forums that many PRIDE fighters were on steroids.

I was asked about each incident, Coleman and his daughters and the steroids, a little bit later. "I don't get into the politics. My job is to take care of the fighters and that's what I do," I said.

It's true. I stay out of the political stuff unless it involves the Klitschko's and the rise of democracy in the Ukraine! Speaking of the Klitschko's, a few weeks later I was working with Wladimir once again and this time, unlike my last trip to New York City with Johnny Tapia, I actually worked at The Garden.

MADISON SQUARE GARDEN

It may seem strange to some that getting to work in Madison Square Garden was my measuring stick for success. The truth is, even though Don King and Bob Arum moved most of the big title fights to Las Vegas, The Garden is the Mecca of boxing. Its history is so rich and so many huge fights happened in its famous ring.

As I sat in my hotel room on November 10, 2006, the night before Wladimir was scheduled to fight Calvin Brock, I considered The Garden's history. Sure it wasn't the same building, but way back in the 1880s John L. Sullivan beat Joe Wilson in the first fight ever at the venue, and since it has hosted a laundry list of huge fights: Joe Louis vs. Rocky Marciano, Sugar Ray Robinson vs. Gene Fullmer, "The Fight of the Century" between Joe Frazier and Muhammad Ali, the Frazier/Ali rematch, Marvin Hagler vs. Felix Trinidad, Evander Holyfield vs. Lennox Lewis, the list goes on and on.

Plain and simple, The Garden is steeped with boxing history and I'd made the transition to the UFC and MMA, but I grew up with boxing. That's why I saw working in The Garden as the one symbol of my success.

I could actually see the building from my hotel room and I kept looking out the window at the curved facade lit up under the New York City lights. It was late, but I was on west coast time so I started flipping through the TV channels. I couldn't believe it when I found *Play it to the Bone* and Antonio Banderas was talking about how he didn't take a dive in The Garden.

Here I was across the street from Madison Square Garden and watching myself on TV, not bad for a guy from a migrant camp in central California. I had to call Charlotte to tell her about it and she laughed because I sounded like a little kid, but I didn't care.

The next day I was in the dressing room bent over getting my bag together to start wrapping when this old Puerto Rican guy came out of nowhere. He stood over me. "LA's your town, but New York's my town," he said.

I looked up at him. "I'm from Las Vegas," I said and kind of laughed while thinking *what is this all about.*

This didn't deter the old cutman. He went on about how New York was his town, blah, blah, blah. I found it comical that he felt he needed to be like a puppy and piss on his territory. To this day I don't know his name, but I guess in a round about way he was complimenting me.

Wladimir was getting the best of Calvin but Calvin was making a fight of it. Then in the sixth Wladimir got cut above the left eye due to an accidental headbutt. Jim Lampley said, "So there will be work for Klitschko's cutman Jacob Duran to do between rounds ..."

I didn't want to see Wladimir get cut, but at the same time I was glad to get a chance to work. Lennox Lewis, who was also commentating, had said during the sixth that he thought it was a pretty big cut. The cameras zoomed in between rounds and it was decent sized, just above the left eye, but I'd seen way worse in the Octagon.

I had just finished closing it up perfectly when Emanuel Steward said, "Hold on hold on the doctor wants to see it."

Then the damn doctor reached in and wiped everything away. All a sudden I had to start all over. I only had seconds left between rounds so I did my best to form the cotton candy-like Avitene and get it into the cut once again, but there wasn't enough time and it didn't go in quite right.

I was pissed because now Wladimir had to go out in the seventh with the cut not fixed like it should have been.

I watched the seventh round and Wladimir's face intently. He landed a couple big shots and got Calvin in trouble and then dropped him with a huge right. My son Daniel talked about one of those big punches. "Dad it looked like a ripple effect," he said. "His body just rippled all the way down."

This was a great way to explain it and Wladimir can hit real hard. I was glad for that too because by him ending the fight when he did, the cut that the doctor screwed up didn't come into play. I met Wladimir once it was over and started cleaning him up. I was happy to see that despite what had happened the cut was still mostly dry.

UFN 7

A month later I was at a completely different, but equally as cool, venue as The Garden. I'd worked UFC 65 in Sacramento. The card had a lot of good fights and Georges St. Pierre TKO'd Matt Hughes in their rematch for the welterweight belt, but now I was at Marine Corps Air Station Miramar in San Diego.

This was the UFC's first trip to a military base and it was amazing. The hangar was filled with Marines in their uniforms, and all but like ten seats was reserved for military members. The few that were available were auctioned off. I looked out the open hangar door and there were jets and helicopters sitting on the tarmac. I got chills at the sight.

The fight I remember most from this card was between Karo Parisyan and Drew Fickett. I was in Karo's corner and about a minute into round two he was in Drew's guard and took a short elbow that opened him up just below his right eye.

I've talked about fixing up a lot of cuts, but this one was a little different. Karo made the mistake of looking up at the big screen and opening the cut with his fingers as soon as the round ended. He saw how big it was and kind of freaked out. I went to work and wasn't having much of a problem getting it closed, but Karo kept saying, "I can't see, I can't see," and he was ready to quit.

Manny Gamburyan was in the corner and if I remember right Neil Melanson was as well. Manny looked at me and said, "What do we do?"

"I can't tell you what to do," I said. "My job isn't to give instructions. My job is to work on the cuts."

It's true. I very seldom talk in a corner unless it is to give instructions to the fighter to help me fix a cut better. A corner should have one person designated to talk, or at the very least should only have one person talking at a time. One minute goes by fast when you're trying to coach a fighter so everything needs to run as smooth as possible.

In this case though, I noticed a real sense of urgency. They weren't sure what to do and Karo, despite having a cut that wasn't really affecting his vision and a one that I could fix, was ready to call it a night.

I took it upon myself to be cutman and coach at the same time. It just wasn't fair for Karo to stop when he was most likely winning a really tough fight. "Karo, don't worry about the cut. I'm gonna handle that," I said. "Listen, you're doing real well on the stand up. Stay on your stand up this last round and you'll be fine."

He really was doing fine with the stand up and I also recognized that while on his feet the cut, which was below his right eye, would not cause problems. Karo did keep the fight on the feet. With a little over a minute left he even threw Drew to the canvas, but let him get back up. It wasn't until about half a minute remained before Karo took Drew down.

The fight ended and I cleaned Karo up and stopped the bleeding again. "Stitch, I want you to work all my fights from now on, all my corners," he said.

"Okay, Karo, I'll try my best," I said, and I really would try to work in his corner. If he felt most comfortable with me then I wanted to be there for him. Not because he was a close friend of mine or anything, but because I recognized that me being there might give him the mental edge he needed to fight at his best.

All three judges gave Karo the nod and of course he and his corner were ecstatic.

A couple weeks later at the UFC's year-end show at the MGM I was walking toward the Octagon and I saw Karo sitting there on the first row of the lower tier. "How's the cut healing?" I asked.

"It's healing well," he said as he touched his scarred cheek.

"Good, it looks good," I said.

"Hey Stitch I want you to meet my dad," Karo said and introduced me to his father who was sitting next to him.

Karo's dad and I shook hands. "Thank you so much for taking care of my son," he said. "I would like to invite you to my house for dinner."

I thanked him for the offer and my heart swelled because of it. I love being in the trenches, but to receive an offer like this meant just as much to me. These fighters are some of the best and toughest athletes in the world, but a lot of them are also young guys with moms, dads, wives, and kids who worry about them. And to think that by being in there taking care of them I am easing the fears of their loved ones is very important and it's one of the reasons why I have the best job in the world.

CRO COP TO THE UFC AND PRIDE 33

It was at the UFC 66 post-fight press conference when the announcement was made that Mirko "Cro Cop" Filipovic had signed with the UFC. This spawned a great deal of excitement, as he was fresh off beating Josh Barnett in PRIDE's 2006 open weight grand prix finals.

As I've mentioned before, Mirko was sometimes seen as a prima donna in Japan. I don't know if that is the best word, he did his own thing and everybody catered to him. I also mentioned that now the two of us are friends. It was not long after UFC 66 when this friendship began.

Prior to fighting, Mirko had sent Nevada State Athletic Commissioner Keith Kizer one of the wraps that he used in Japan. It was taped all the way around to include the knuckles and all (obviously Mirko hadn't been to one of my seminars). Now most commissions ensure that the tape is off the knuckles and Keith came up to me and asked what I thought about the wrap. "It goes against everything that your rules state," I told him.

He knew I was right so he didn't let Mirko use them.

I didn't plan it this way, but soon thereafter I was the one designated by Burt to wrap Cro Cop's hands. Having him in the UFC really was a big deal and Burt told me that I'd take care of him well in advance. After the weigh in Mirko and I went into a room in the Mandalay and Carla just happened to be with me.

I did a test run for him while a photographer snapped a bunch of photos. He really liked the wraps and the photographer ended up putting together a really cool montage of the whole process and down the road Mirko autographed them for Carla.

I thought that was nice and I cut the wraps off carefully in order to preserve them and then asked him to sign them for Carla. He was more than happy to do so. Mirko is a seemingly serious and quiet guy, but in reality he is very nice and has a great sense of humor. There are even some videos floating around of him pulling pranks on others.

He fought Eddie Sanchez in his UFC debut on February 3, 2007 and made quick work of him with a TKO late in the first round. Unfortunately for Mirko this fight would be overshadowed by his next.

Something else that kind of overshadowed UFC 67 came a few weeks later and down the street from the Mandalay at the Thomas & Mack Center. It was PRIDE's second effort in the U.S. and once again I ensured that everything was set up as far as assigning cutmen.

After PRIDE 32 I realized I needed reliable glove runners. I mentioned earlier that Carla was working with Frank Trigg. Angela was working in the MMA industry as well for Xyience. They both grew up around the game so I naturally thought of them. They did a terrific job ensuring that the gloves got to the fighters on time and this gave them an opportunity to be backstage during the show.

There were a couple big knockouts on the card. Rameau Thierry Sokoudjou shocked everyone by dropping

Antonio Rogerio Nogueira in a matter of seconds. The main event saw PRIDE's welterweight champ Dan Henderson pull off an amazing spinning back fist and then stop middleweight champ Wanderlei Silva with a left hook. Both stoppages were memorable, but the fight that really sticks in my mind came right before the main event.

Lightweight champ Takanori Gomi met up with Nick Diaz and it was all fireworks with a spectacular ending. I was working in Gomi's corner and he swarmed all over Nick at the start. A couple minutes in it looked like Nick was finding his range when Gomi blasted him with a right. Nick is as tough as they come though and he survived. Then the fight returned to the feet, and all a sudden it was Nick blasting away at Gomi.

Nick got cut above his left eye and below the right eye, but Gomi was completely exhausted. He couldn't lift his arms and Nick just peppered him with shots for the final minute. The round ended and I had to run across the ring to get Gomi. He was slumped against the ropes and hell he might still be there if I didn't haul him back to the corner.

While Leon did a great job stopping Nick's cut from bleeding, I did all I could to help Gomi recover. I massaged ice on his neck and shoulders and tried to get his breathing back to normal. Then with the ice on the top of his head I rubbed Vaseline on his face and it was time for round two.

Diaz came across the ring and started firing shots and Gomi answered. After a minute the referee stopped the action so the doc could check on Nick's cut. It seemed this was a huge break for Gomi who was still sucking air.

The fight resumed and each man continued punching the other. Gomi implored the ref to stop it because Nick's face was so swollen, but he wasn't hurting him enough for it to be stopped.

After a minute and a half Gomi shot and Nick immediately transitioned into a Gogoplata and with his shin across Gomi's throat he pulled his head down with both hands. Gomi was forced to tap and the crowd was going nuts.

Gomi's corner rushed to him, but I could tell that other than being exhausted he was fine. I headed over to help Leon fix up Nick's battered face and while Leon worked on the cut on the cheek I worked on the one above the left eye. It was an amazing fight and both Leon and I congratulated Nick as we worked.

Later, the amazing win was changed to a no contest because Nick tested positive for Marijuana, but man it was still a hell of a fight and a hell of a comeback on Nick's part.

Another big comeback was right around the corner at UFC 68.

11

THE UFC (AND RANDY) MARCHES ON
RANDY'S RETURN AND SERRA'S GOOD LUCK CHARM

I COULDN'T HELP BUT THINK OF THE TIME I asked Randy, "How is it that you're so relaxed, but once they put that pin in the gate you're whole personality changes."

He just kind of shrugged. "Well Stitch, that's just the way I am."

His response was so laid-back and it fit his pre-fight demeanor perfectly. Now here I was sitting across from Randy Couture as he returned to take on heavyweight champ Tim Sylvia at UFC 68. Despite the 13 month layoff he was the same as before, all smiles and cordial and we visited as if we were catching up over dinner.

Randy decided to return after commentating Tim's fight against Jeff Monson at UFC 65. He thought he could compete and Dana and Lorenzo were happy to give him a chance. Tim wasn't too happy about it because years earlier he'd helped Randy renovate a house up in Oregon. In his book *Becoming the Natural*, Randy said that Tim called him and said, "I thought we were friends?"

"We are. This is just a fight. It's nothing personal," Randy replied.

This fight was in the middle of a madhouse weekend in Columbus, Ohio. It was during the Arnold Classic (named after Arnold Schwarzenegger) and the weekend has turned into a sports bonanza. I'd never seen more huge biceps, rounded traps, and shredded pecs as I did that weekend, and that was just on the chicks!

There wasn't any madness (or muscled up chicks) inside the locker room though. I wrapped Randy and it was so quiet you could hear the tape as it came off the roll and formed a cast on his hand. Once again I marveled at his calmness and knew that in no time at all, that demeanor would change.

The crowd inside the Nationwide Arena was going absolutely crazy as the fight got started and Randy wasted no time. They touched gloves and Mike Goldberg welcomed back Randy and started to push the movie *Shooter* with Mark Wahlberg.

Randy didn't give him a chance to finish. He threw an inside low kick and then blasted Tim with an overhand right. The crowd erupted, it was maybe the loudest I'd ever heard, and in a split second Randy had Tim's back. He was unable to finish him, but the course of the fight had been set.

I thought of my question to Randy about when he entered the Octagon and how easy going his response had been. Here we were seeing that personality change and in dramatic fashion in the first ten seconds of the fight.

Randy went on to dominate Tim for five rounds and as soon as the fight was over he was right back to his composed self.

Somebody who wasn't so composed (at least not until he got his good luck charm) was my buddy Matt Serra. I was cageside at UFC 69 in Houston and Burt Watson came up to me. "Serra wants you to wrap his hands," he said.

"Burt, I'm working this fight. I can't," I said.

A lot of times I'll go back and forth, but when I'm already in the middle of working a fight I think it is best that I stay with it. Burt could appreciate that, but Matt could not.

A few minutes later Burt was back by my side. "Look, Serra says he wants you to wrap his hands. He's not gonna come out until you wrap his hands!"

I had a flashback to the time when I wrapped Ray Lovato's hands and Trinidad wouldn't come out because of the tape. This was definitely different circumstances though. "Alright," I said, "but who is gonna take my place?"

About that time Don House came hustling up to the cage so I headed back to wrap Matt so we could have a welterweight title fight. He saw me and thrust his hands in the air with his palms up. "Stitch, come on man. You know you're like my good luck charm. I depend on you!"

I laughed. "I know, I know. I realize that," I said.

I really like Matt. He has such a boisterous personality and he isn't afraid to say what he thinks. I wrapped him up and told him good luck then headed back to the cage.

A little bit later I watched as he and Georges St. Pierre shook hands and bowed and then started punching each other. Neither man had the advantage for the first few minutes. Then Matt caught GSP with an overhand right behind the ear. Just like that his legs were gone and Matt caught him with another right. GSP tried to scramble away but Matt got him with a right-left and I was sitting there thinking *I can't believe this. Maybe I am his good luck charm*.

Seconds later Matt got the mount and punched Georges until Big John stopped it. Matt did a cartwheel and everyone was in shock. He was a huge underdog, but he'd just claimed the belt. He put his arm around me and leaned up to my ear. With all the noise it was hard to hear, but he said, "Stitch man thanks. I told you I needed you."

A moment later, Joe Rogan interviewed Matt and said, "Matt Serra, welterweight champion of the world."

You can see me in the background clapping and smiling. It wasn't that I had anything against GSP. It's just that the circumstances surrounding the fight, not coming out until I wrapped him and then the big knockout, were just so wild. It was a fun night, for everybody except GSP, but he'd have a lot more good times than bad.

UFC 70 was just around the corner, and somebody else was about to have a really bad time.

BACK TO ENGLAND

It had been almost five years since the UFC's first venture across the Atlantic for UFC 38. That was the event where I wrapped Ian Freeman's hands and he beat Frank Mir and then the UFC bought drinks at the club and Lee Murray, Tito Ortiz, Chuck Liddell, Pat Miletich, and a bunch of other guys got in the crazy back alley brawl.

Guess it made sense that we waited so long to make a return trip, especially considering the reception we got on the first go. This time it was a lot different. There were still some detractors, but there was also a lot more media coverage and the fans were much more numerous.

We were in Manchester and I was excited because Master Sken's, remember Mr. Ken from my days in Thailand, gym was in the town of Stockport, just twenty minutes away from the Manchester Evening News Arena. The last time I'd seen him was back in the early 90s when I attended his wedding and the only other time was when I bumped into him in Los Angeles. I was at a kickboxing event and my brother Ernie came up to me. "You have to see this. Some guy is throwing amazing kicks," he said.

I checked it out and my brother wasn't lying. I told the guy how good his kicks were and he looked at me funny. "Jacob, it's me Mr. Ken!" he said.

I had invited him to UFC 70 and he invited me to his gym so the morning of the event Leon and I headed out and it was a really special moment. We watched his students work out and it immediately threw me back into those days in Thailand when I trained day and night with Mr. Ken (now Master Sken), Mr. Kit, Mr. Wanna, and Mr. Pe.

Master Sken's students finished up and they gathered around. He then gave me the official paperwork making me a Kru (master trainer) in Muay Thai and he dated it back to 1976. I bowed deeply as he handed me the certificate and was blown away. It was such an honor and something I didn't expect thirty years after the fact.

Master Sken told his students that I had been an instructor and good for combat sports for many years. He also told a few stories of those days so long ago and I remembered every one of them.

A little after noon Leon and I headed back to the hotel to get ready for the event and Master Sken said he'd be there.

As UFC 70 got going I scanned the crowd and sure enough there he was. I was so happy that he'd get a chance to see the fights and see me work, and man did he see some craziness.

Crowd favorite Michael Bisping TKO'd Elvis Sinosic in a spirited fight and Andrei Arlovski decisioned Fabricio

Werdum, but everything was overshadowed by the main event, Gabriel Gonzaga and Mirko Cro Cop. Mirko was coming off his destruction of Eddie Sanchez while Gonzaga had quietly won his first three bouts in the UFC.

Everyone expected Mirko to dominate and figured there was a good chance he'd kick Gabriel in the head at some point. Turned out it was the other way around and I just thought I was surprised after Matt Serra beat GSP.

It had been a decent first round, but with just about ten seconds to go Gabriel whipped a high kick toward Mirko's head. It landed perfectly, shin to the side of the melon and Mirko dropped like he'd been shot.

Referee Herb Dean took a couple hard steps and dove to save Mirko. I didn't remember getting up, but I noticed I was at the bottom of the steps and on my way into the Octagon. Exactly five seconds after Herb had stopped it, I was bent over Mirko. He was snoring much like Terry Martin and Tra Telligman only it was harder and faster. I knew, thanks to the previous snorers and Dr. Watson and Dr. Davidson, to give him a little bit of time and started wiping him down. The doctor got there a few seconds after me and heard Mirko. I'm sure he had the same thoughts I had back at UFC 54.

He immediately reached in to pull the mouthpiece out but Mirko's jaws were locked. "Give it a second, give it a second," I said. "He'll relax."

Then another doctor arrived. I wiped Mirko's forehead and the second doc tried to pull the mouthpiece out too. I told him the same thing I told the first and he looked at me like *you're crazy, he can't breathe.*

"His body will relax in a few seconds," I said.

Now there were four or five of us around Mirko and after about twenty seconds the snoring slowed and his body relaxed. I was by his head and kept wiping him down as he came to. "Mirko this is Stitch," I said in a loud voice. "You're okay. You got knocked out."

I don't think it registered and I said it a couple more times. Slowly he came back and the doctor was able to remove the mouthpiece. He looked at me like *I'm glad you knew what to do.*

Later I watched the tape and I have to give credit to Herb. He not only dove in to save Mirko, but he also noticed that his right leg was bent under him and his ankle was twisted in gruesome fashion and he quickly straightened it out. When I enter the cage I'm focused on the face. I never did see the leg.

I'm not a doctor, but experience goes a long ways. I've helped so many fighters come back after a vicious KO. It's an important part of the job and it wouldn't be too long before I'd have to help another huge-name fighter recover after being put to sleep.

THE ICEMAN, RAMPAGE, AND TYSON GRIFFIN

It'd been a little over a month since Mirko had been knocked out by the head kick. Now I was running into the cage again. This one was almost as surprising as the last one. Chuck Liddell had been ripping through one opponent after another since losing to Quinton Jackson at PRIDE back in 2003. UFC 71 was his chance at redemption, but Rampage caught him with a right and then pounded on him until Big John stopped it.

I got there and Chuck was on his feet. Big John had his arm around him and Chuck didn't think he'd been knocked out. This happens often because the fighter is out, loses time, and recovers pretty quickly, but they're disoriented. Dr. Davidson was trying to check him, but Chuck turned to me. "What happened? Did I get knocked out?" he said.

I nodded my head. "Yeah, you got knocked out."

"What happened?" he asked again.

"You got knocked out Chuck," I said.

He was having a hard time understanding. It happened so fast. He'd won his last seven fights by TKO or KO and defended his title four times. He'd trained hard to avenge his loss to Rampage and then he threw a left to the body and bam! He was staring at the ceiling with Rampage punching his face. It happens that fast in MMA and the fighters have a hard time processing.

Chuck actually ask me one more time (seems they usually ask in three's) and I rubbed ice on his neck and told him, "You got knocked out."

I put ice on the guys who've just been knocked out for a couple reasons. I want to give them a different temperature on their skin to kind of pull them back into reality, and also just in case they end up having any swelling on the brain it makes sense to start applying ice right away.

Chuck's trainer, John Hackleman, came in. "Keep an eye on Chuck," I told him. "He's still unsteady."

Hack nodded and did just that and in his book, *My Fighting Life*, Chuck talks about asking Hack what happened. "You went to the fucking body," Hack said.

Apparently he'd been telling Chuck not to go to the body unless he first threw a combination to protect himself. It goes to show that the difference between winning and losing can be extremely tight at such a high level of fighting and nobody is immune to being stopped.

Something else that is extremely tight is the wraps on Tyson Griffin's hands. I'm not kidding, that kid likes his hands wrapped way tighter than any other fighter I know. I wrapped his hands at UFC 72 in Belfast, Northern Ireland as I did a few times before. "Remember, I don't like the tape next to the pinky," he said.

I nodded. Normally I put tape between each of the fingers. He doesn't like it between the pinky and ring finger. "I remember," I said. "You still want the wrap tight?"

He did, so I started cranking away. "You want it tighter?" I said.

"Yeah, tighter," he said. "I like the way it feels."

I pulled harder and the tape actually ripped as I circled his wrist. I think it's interesting that he likes the wraps that tight, just as others like it a little looser or some like it with less tape while others like it with more. Wrapping the hands is really an organic and fluid process. I make tiny adjustments as I go to ensure each fighter has exactly what they want and need before entering the Octagon.

Tyson went out and won a razor thin decision over Clay Guida in an unbelievable fight. The two fought on their feet, grappled, scrambled, almost subbed each other, it was great. As a matter of fact, Big John has called it one of his favorite fights of all time to referee.

The 209 and Cologne

I've talked a lot about fights in which one man was trying to avenge a loss to another. Really I don't think avenge is the best word for rematches. Often it isn't that a man has to seek payback in the form of punching, kicking, or submitting a guy who beat him. Instead it seems to be more a desire to gain feedback. A fighter has information (he lost to this guy before) and he wants to see if he has gotten better to the point of now being able to win. The rematch is a measuring stick for improvement.

Don't get me wrong, there are still those fights where one guy has to knock the other's teeth down his throat or cut off his circulation because he just can't stand him. This was the case at the TUF 5 Finale. B.J. Penn had lost to Jens Pulver years earlier and they'd gone back and forth as coaches during the season. When they finally fought, B.J. was ready to rip Jens' head off. He looked really sharp and battered Jens for much of the first round. Then in the second he submitted him with a rear naked choke and made sure everyone knew he had earned his revenge by squeezing the choke for as long as he could.

All this talk of fighting to test oneself or fighting to avenge a loss is one side of the house. Then there's the other side, the guy who doesn't give a shit about avenging losses or finding out where he belongs in his division, he's fighting because he just loves punching and getting punched.

The fight just before Penn and Pulver featured one of these guys. The younger Diaz brother, Nate (he looks like a kid but can beat the crap out of most), was fighting Manny Gamburyan for the season five title and his brother Nick was in his corner. Both men came to scrap and unfortunately the fight ended when Manny shot in and dislocated his shoulder in the second round.

It was a disappointing ending to what was shaping up to be a hell of a fight, but the point is that the Diaz brothers are real fighters. They show up to bang and don't care what people think of them. Nick, even more so than Nate will say what he wants and he doesn't care about repercussions. In Mixed Martial Arts this is often a good thing. It's important to have that bravado that says *you want to fight me? Okay then let's fight!* But at the same time it can get you in a little bit of trouble (remember Nick's hospital fight with Joe Riggs).

I always enjoy working with Nick and Nate. You never know what's going to happen, but as crazy and as streetwise as they are they always show me a lot of respect. It might be easy to gather that Nick isn't much of a hugger, but often after working with Nate, Nick will come in and give me a hug. We're both from the 209 area code. They're from Stockton and I guess guys from the 209 have to look out for each other.

A couple weeks later I was a long ways away from the 209, but it was a familiar theme of avenging a loss. I was with Wladimir Klitschko in Cologne, Germany for his rematch with Lamon Brewster.

Wladimir wanted to make up for his loss to Lamon. I could feel it as I stood next to him holding his mouthpiece while Michael Buffer made the introductions. This fight meant a lot to him. It was the loss to Brewster and the thoughts that the Vaseline on the legs had affected Wladimir's stamina that led to the release of Joe Souza and the hiring of me as the Klitschko's cutman.

Wladimir was a different man than he was in that first fight though. He'd grown a lot in his last few outings and had won six fights in a row. During the staredown he kept his eyes focused on Lamon while Lamon stared at the ground.

Wladimir looked relaxed and confident as he peppered Lamon with jabs and sharp rights for much of the fight. After the sixth round Lamon's trainer, Buddy McGirt, decided he'd seen enough. Unlike the first fight, Lamon had no answer for Wladimir.

It was such a matter-of-fact performance. Wladimir had wanted to erase some of the sting from the first fight against Lamon and he did so.

Whether it is in MMA or boxing, there are a number of reasons why these guys are motivated to fight and sometimes avenging a loss is one of them. Another reason is to be the best. Over the next couple UFC events I worked with the best as Randy Couture defended his title against Gabriel Gonzaga at UFC 74 and then Dan Henderson and Quinton Jackson fought at

UFC 75 in London to unify the UFC and PRIDE light heavyweight belts. It was a great scrap that ended in a decision victory for Jackson.

Before both of those events though, I worked with Vernon Forrest. He won a unanimous decision over Carlos Manuel Baldomir in Tacoma, Washington. I mention this not because anything spectacular happened, but because Vernon was always such a class act and I loved working with him. Almost exactly two years to the day of this win Vernon was at a gas station putting air in the tire of his Jaguar when a couple of thugs tried to rob him. They took his wallet and other items and fled. He gave chase and was shot seven or eight times.

I heard the news the morning after it happened. I thought of that fight two years earlier in Tacoma and his senseless death was hard to stomach. Vernon truly was a great guy and he is missed.

ONE MORE ROUND AND THE BEGINNINGS OF A DVD

Originally, I'm talking years earlier, the *Giving the Fighter One More Round* DVD was going to be *Cuts, Cornermen, and Confidence* and that was going to be the DVD I was going to do before I met John Barnthouse and we ended up doing *Boxer's Nightmare*.

Education has always been part of my plan. So I'd just been waiting for the right time to do a DVD. Around the time of UFC 74 and 75 and I guess a little before that, I decided I needed to put together *Giving the Fighter One More Round*. I called up Mark Zacher and Jim Baltutis at One More Round and asked them if they'd sponsor it. They said they would so I got busy.

First, a little background about how I got hooked up with OMR. I'd started out doing stuff with TapouT. It wasn't formal. They were giving me t-shirts and I'd wear them when I could, then I had the idea for them to make me a cornerman jacket and I'd give it to a fan after each event. Mask designed it and we did that, and every so often they'd give me some money. We had a great relationship and I loved Mask, Punkass, and Skrape, but then I got a call from Matt Hughes' wife Audra.

He was the first fighter sponsored by OMR and Matt had told Mark Zacher that I was the perfect guy for One More Round. Audra asked if I'd be willing to talk to him and I agreed.

Charlotte and I met Mark in a little bar area at the Gold Nugget and talked about a partnership. During the course of our conversation I asked, "How'd you come up with the idea for One More Round anyway?"

"Well you know I have BC Ethics so I've been in the business," Mark said. "One day I was watching Rocky VI and there's a part where Rocky is telling his son, 'I gotta go one more round,' and it hit me that that is what life is about. It's about going that one more round whether you're a fighter or not, you've got to go that one more round."

I just shook my head. It was crazy that the idea for OMR came about because of the very same Rocky movie that I was in. We ended the meeting with a handshake deal and I started wearing One More Round clothing.

It was tough. Even though I didn't have a formal deal with TapouT, it broke their hearts that I went with One More Round. Carla was good friends with Dan (Punkass) and the TapouT guys were great. For the longest time every time I'd see Mask at an event he'd say, "Stitch, we've got to get you back man."

"I'd love to get back with you guys," I'd say, "you know I love you guys, but I'm a man of my word and I told Mark that I'd be with him as long as I could."

Mask understood. He didn't really like it, but understood. It got to a point where I really became synonymous with OMR. People routinely asked me if it was my own company. I had a great relationship with One More Round at it led to my DVD, but in the summer of 2009 I ended up back with TapouT, tragically Mask was not alive for my return, and I'll talk more about Charles "Mask" Lewis a little later.

GIVING THE FIGHTER ONE MORE ROUND

Back to the *Giving the Fighter One More Round* DVD, with the blessings of OMR I started taking my video camera everywhere. Anytime I came across an opportunity to interview somebody about the importance of a good wrap I whipped out the camera and started asking questions.

I was sitting with Roger Mayweather in the River Rock Casino hotel lobby in Richmond, B.C. Canada. The sun was streaming in and people strolled by as we sat in cushioned chairs and talked boxing. Roger is a great boxing historian. As a matter of fact probably he and Mike Tyson are the two best boxing historians I've ever met. Roger was a champion and future hall of famer, and here he was spitting out all kinds of great facts and figures. Sometimes he is a little hard to understand, but not this time. He was speaking so eloquently and with such knowledge that I decided to pull out my video camera. "Roger," I said, "I'm putting together a video. Do you mind if I record this?"

"No, no, let's do it," he said.

He did a tremendous job and getting his perspective was really important for the boxing aspect of the video. Roger wasn't the only one I interviewed though. I got boxer Ishe Smith in the dressing room while I was wrapping his hands, another spur-of-the-moment deal and I realized that I didn't need to set anything up to get great interviews.

Right before the weigh in at UFC 75 I was considering asking Mike Bisping for a few words. I knew it wasn't the best time and somebody said that he didn't seem in the best mood. After all, he was dehydrated and hungry. I decided to ask anyway and he was happy to do it even though it was during one of his most stressful times.

After UFC 75 I caught up with Mark DellaGrotte at the airport. I call Mark the grasshopper. He has worked hard to learn as much as he can from me because he knows the importance of having a working knowledge of what I do. Josh Barnett is the same way and he talks about it on the DVD. I also caught up with Kenny Florian and Greg Jackson while waiting for a plane.

One of my favorite parts came when I interviewed Frank Mir in our dressing room before a fight and he said, "... I put my hands out, I feel Stitch massaging my hands getting ready asking me if I have any injuries, and my stomach just drops out the bottom. Here we go again."

Frank really explained what that moment is like. It is the time when the fighters realize that it is here. All the training, all the hype, all the excitement is gone and it's time to fight. It's an important moment for the fighter. A good hand wrap gives them confidence when they need it most.

When it was all said and done I had a ton of great interviews with everyone I mentioned and more, including Ronald Hearns, Don House and even my man Leon Tabbs even though he isn't always real fired up about getting publicity.

I didn't have Barnthouse to help me out with the technical side of the editing on this one, so I made my way over to Media Underground on Harmon Street in Las Vegas. Paul Remo does some work with the UFC and he was willing to help out. I remember getting out of my car and heading through the glass doors excited about how the video was going to turn out.

I'd helped educate people for so many years just by answering their questions and showing them what I know, but now I was going to get to take it to a whole new level.

I'd done a seminar with Isham Harris at Fighters Warehouse. Carla and Angela knew Isham through Triggonomics and Xyience. He asked Angela if she thought I'd be interested in doing a commercial for him. We worked out a deal where I did the commercial for cheaper and then filmed a seminar I did at his store in Tampa, Florida. I added this to *Giving the Fighter One More Round* and the segment I did for *The Best Damn Sports Show Period*.

The final piece was with my co-host Nick Ward on our radio show The 13th Round. We had Dr. Davidson and Dr. Watson on and talked about the role of a cutman and answered questions from callers.

In the end we had a great product and it wouldn't have been possible without everyone's cooperation. They were all so willing to step forward and I think that shows just how much they appreciate what I do. They wanted to help me out because they know that I do my best to take care of the fighters.

With the release of the DVD in June of 2008 I could now educate others on how to take care of fighters even if I never met them, and that is really important to me. I hope it shows in *Giving the Fighter One More Round.*

JAMIE VARNER, THE WEC, AND BACK TO UFC 76

In mentioning my buddy Isham Harris at Fighters Warehouse it reminds me of Jamie Varner. I've been wrapping his hands since he started in the WEC and Jamie get some crap from some fans, but he's always been great around me. I wrapped his hands in his first WEC and he won, so like so many other guys he wants me to wrap him each time. Also, a lot of people might not know this, but he, along with Trevor and Todd Lally, also played an important role in helping Representative Jonathan Paton bring MMA under its current rules to Arizona.

The reason Isham reminded me of Jamie is because it was at the seminar where I filmed for *Giving the Fighter One More Round* that he absolutely cracked me up. The next day we were scheduled for an autograph signing at the store and Jamie was one of the guys hired for the event. We were staying at one of the Embassy Suites in Tampa and Jamie had gone out to party it up. He showed up to the signing and I noticed something was written on his arm. "What the hell you got all over yourself Jamie?" I asked.

He turned his hand over so I could read his arm. In Sharpie marker it read *Hi, my name is Jamie Varner. If lost, I am staying at the Embassy Suites.* Below that it listed the address, and all I could do was shake my head and laugh.

I did a lot of head shaking at my first WEC event too. Zuffa (the owners of the UFC) had purchased the promotion around late 2006 and Burt Watson called me to say all the cutmen would work the WEC shows as well.

That was fine. I wasn't exactly excited about it, I mean it was work, but I didn't expect too much from Zuffa's new promotion. I showed up at the Hard Rock, did my usual thing, and then watched as a bunch of these younger and smaller guys (there were some big guys on the card too) just scrapped. I was like, *wow*! Those guys strike and roll around the cage like a couple of snakes and really get after it. After that first show in

January of 2007 I looked forward to every WEC event and it is very rare when one disappoints.

I started the book with the story of Forrest Griffin's win over Mauricio Rua back at UFC 76. That was also the event where Chuck Liddell and Keith Jardine fought, actually right after Forrest's fight. Keith did a great job and really had Chuck struggling to get his timing throughout. It was a close fight, but Keith blasted him with some brutal kicks to the legs and side that I think helped him score the decision win. It was no doubt the biggest of his career.

As I was heading back to the locker rooms I saw Keith's dad. We all know Keith is a big guy and looks pretty dang mean with his long goatee and bald head. Well his dad is a little bit bigger and looks a little bit meaner. He is just a lumberjack of a guy. There he was standing on the other side of the railing on the first row of the stadium seats and I stopped to congratulate him. Then I noticed that tears were running out of the corners of his eyes and down his cheeks. He was so proud to see his son perform as he did in such a big event. I realized that more than a quick congratulations was in order. I stopped and shook his hand. "I know you're proud of your son and you should be," I said.

He nodded just as you'd picture a proud father would. "I am," he said.

It was such an awesome moment. Imagine being a mom or dad and watching your son climb into the Octagon. They hang on every little movement and pray that their son will be the one moving in the right place at the right time. And then to see him perform at his best, it has to be a relief and provide a sense of tremendous pride. I walked away from Keith's dad and had a lump in my throat. I was happy that he was able to be so proud of his son.

About a week after UFC 76 I returned from working in New York and Charlotte handed me a letter from Forrest. It was a card that read, *Thanks for everything. I appreciate it!* And there was a gift certificate to a really nice restaurant.

For some reason I thought of Keith's dad. I guess it was because this card came from Forrest's heart and it kind of made me proud to receive it, but even more it made me proud just to be a part of the sport.

I still have the card to this day.

"I CAN SEE HIS SKULL" AND DÉJÀ VU

I make it a habit to head to the Octagon about 30 minutes before each event to visit with the doctors. It's important for us to work closely with them and it's especially important when it is the UFC's first time in a new area. We'd been to Ohio of course for UFC 68, but this was the promotion's first time in Cincinnati. I told the doctors what we do and what to expect from us and I ask them to give us a chance to do our jobs, but at the same time we understand that it's there call as to whether or not a fight continues.

Everyone was fired up for the first fight on the pay-per-view card between Alan Belcher and Kalib Starnes. The fight was less than a minute old when Kalib was bleeding badly over his right eye. I prepared to go to work and Alan looked to be in control. Then two minutes in Kalib turned it around and started blasting away. Next it was Alan's turn in what was shaping up to be a great back and forth fight. With about a minute and a half left, referee Yves Lavigne yelled for the doctor to get ready.

The round ended and I beat the doc into the Octagon. Yves brought Kalib right to me.

I went to work on the cut and Yves told the doc, who was squatted down next to me, "You let him work and after that you tell me."

The cut was bad, but I felt I had it under control.

I removed the q-tip and many, including Joe Rogan, thought the cut was too bad. I heard he referred to it as a hole in Kalib's head.

Again, it was a nasty cut, but you know what, when the round started there wasn't a drop of blood above Kalib's right eye.

For the first minute and a half of round two Kalib was definitely in the fight. Alan was probably getting the best of it, but there was no guarantee it would stay that way. Then Yves stopped the action and the doctor checked the cut. It looked as if Kalib wanted to continue and the cut was still dry, but the fight was stopped anyway.

I entered the Octagon and Kalib was screaming at his own corner. "I told them I wanted to fight. He told me he saw my skull. Fuck you!"

Don House wiped Kalib down and I didn't even have to really work on him because the cut was still dry. The crowd seemed just a little less pissed than Kalib was about the stoppage and I was frustrated as well, but at the same time I have to respect the doctor's decision.

Not long after the fight I made my way over to him. "Doctor, why'd you stop the fight?" I said.

"Well I could see his skull," he replied.

"Yeah," I said, "but it's not going to bleed much more. It's not going to get much worse than that."

He looked at me like I was a lunatic, but it was the truth. The cut wasn't affecting Kalib's ability to fight and there wasn't any nerve or optical damage. It's not like Alan was going to start borrowing into his skull next, so let the fight continue!

That's one of the issues we have though as the UFC expands across the globe. When we go into new areas we have doctors who haven't worked many fights or are working them for the first time. They haven't seen all the different types of cuts like Leon, Rudy, Don, or I have. They sometimes stop a fight based on how the cut looks, and that isn't the best barometer.

A little later I asked Yves, "What happened?"

"Well it looked pretty bad. I just wanted the doctor to take a look at it," he said.

He did what he had to do and the doctor did what he had to do as well. Our number one job is fighter safety, but in this case I was perturbed with the outcome. Kalib should have had the opportunity to continue.

A few fights later it was Rich Franklin's chance to get the belt back from Anderson Silva. The event was named *Hostile Territory* because Anderson was coming to Rich's hometown, the mayor, or somebody important, even named a Rich Franklin day.

The fight was so much like the first time Anderson and Rich met. It lasted a little longer and round one ended with Rich almost knocked out. Then in round two Anderson locked him up in the Muay Thai plum and delivered knees to end it. I got to Rich and it was the same broken nose and all, serious déjà vu. This time though I didn't have to go to his room in the middle of the night.

However, I did get Anderson Silva's shirt for a fan. My buddy Ben Thompson runs Fighthype.com and lives in Cincinnati. He was at UFC 77 and brought his friend Brian Peterson along. They came up to my room and I wrapped his hand because it was his first UFC. I like doing that because I then sign it and cut it off so the wrap is preserved. It's a unique souvenir.

During the process Brian mentioned how much he liked Anderson Silva's walkout shirt. "I know his manager Ed Soares. I'll ask him when I get a chance," I said.

After the fight we were in the hotel lobby when Anderson came in. Even though he'd just beaten the hometown boy the fans went crazy. They were snapping photos and asking for autographs and once Anderson saw me (I always wrap his hands) he came over and gave me a hug. I congratulated him and said, "Anderson, look, my friend here loves your shirt. Where's Eddie (that's what I call Ed Soares) so I can get one?"

Anderson was wearing the sweatshirt we were talking about and it was the very same one he'd walked to the Octagon in just a little over an hour earlier. He smiled and started peeling it off right there in the hotel lobby. He gave it to Brian and bowed as he did it. What a class act and in that moment he truly made Brian's night. It was his first UFC and he got his hand wrapped in the exact same way that Anderson got his hand wrapped and then Anderson gave him the very same shirt that he walked to the Octagon in.

Brian and all the fans that were circled around us were in awe. It was such a cool thing to do and it illustrates the bond between fighters and fans in the UFC. The way the fighters and the rest of us interact with the fans is very important. The sport is still new and we understand that all of us, fighters, coaches, cutmen, commentators, fans, and even new doctors, are all in it together.

Two Great Fights, a Good Bye, and a Happy Birthday

The Ultimate Fighter Season Six finale featured a main event of Roger Huerta and Clay Guida. I was working Roger's corner and the two got after it with Roger coming close to being stopped at least a couple times. After the second I went in with Dave Menne, who was working Roger's corner. "You have to knock him out Roger!" Dave said.

Roger didn't knock him out, but within the first minute of round three he sunk in a rear naked choke to defeat Clay. It was a memorable fight for just about everybody ... except Roger. I got to him after the win and started wiping him down and working on him. "Man I don't remember much," he said. "For a while I just went blank."

The shots he'd taken from Clay had knocked the memory out of him, but not his will to fight. Dave Menne knew this and knew that Roger would have to finish it in the final round to get the win. It was such a great fight and it showed so much heart on Roger's part. You've got to love Clay Guida too. He always puts it all on the line.

The fight also happened to be the last (at least for a while) Big John McCarthy worked in the UFC. We cutmen often shared a room with the referees and Big John is cool and he's done as much for the sport as anybody.

The month of December in 2007 held another great fight. It was my birthday, December 29, when UFC 79 took place. This was a huge event with Rich Clementi subbing Melvin Guillard in a serious grudge match and GSP showing how great he is in subbing Matt Hughes in round two, but the fight that I will forever remember was between Chuck Liddell and Wanderlei Silva.

People had been waiting a long time for these two to meet and the hype was phenomenal. I went into the locker room to wrap Wand's hands. He was seated on a wooden bench, arms folded. He looked relaxed, but ready to unleash. We gave our greetings and I got busy. During the process he told me he'd try to put on a good fight for me. Earlier in the week I'd mentioned to him that it was my birthday.

I finished and he nodded his approval. Wanderlei is always an intense guy before a fight, but this time I could feel it. I wished him luck and headed out. I didn't have to tell him, he knew I'd be working the red corner, across the Octagon from him.

That's just part of the game, sometimes I'll wrap a guy's hands and work the other guy's corner, sometimes I'll wrap both their hands. I have a growing list of fighters I always wrap, so often the latter is the case.

Like a dense fog, the anticipation sank over the Mandalay Bay when Chuck climbed through the door to meet Wanderlei. These two are MMA legends and here they were finally squaring off.

Wanderlei moved his head back and forth and Chuck's eyes followed him as Herb Dean gave them their instructions. The fight started slow, then Wanderlei tried to bait Chuck by acting like the first exchange hurt him, and it was on. The second half of the second round was insane and afterward both Leon and I entered the Octagon because both Chuck and Wanderlei were bleeding.

So often, fans asked me which fights are most memorable. This one has to be at the top. I sat cageside and could hear, even feel the shots as they landed, thump ... thump ... thump. I was thinking, *shit, these guys are in a fucking battle!* Every strike was a potential fight ender, even more so than usual, and it was so exciting.

The third round came to an end and I took care of Chuck. He was in the better shape of the two and it didn't take me long to get him cleaned up. As he was pulling on his t-shirt I headed over to Wanderlei. Leon was pressing his enswell on his bruised and distorted face and Wanderlei looked completely exhausted. He even had a hard time pulling on his sponsor jacket because his arms were so blasted.

I leaned over and placed my hand on his shoulder. "Awesome fight Wanderlei," I said.

He nodded and his swollen lips formed into a smile. Then he said something I'll never forget, "Happy Birthday."

"WHERE WAS STITCH?" AND BROCK LESNAR

Dr. Davidson and another Doctor from Newcastle walked up to me in the dressing room. It was a few hours until UFC 80 was to kick off at the Metro Radio Arena. Paul Kelly was in tow and he kind of nodded sheepishly as he approached. It was his first time in the UFC and he was fighting fellow-Brit Paul Taylor in a fight that marked the first time two Brits ever fought each other in the Octagon.

"Hey Stitch," Dr. D said, "Can you do anything with Paul's hand?"

As he talked he grabbed Paul's wrist and turned his hand over. He had a line of stitches that stretched across all four fingers. Apparently he was horsing around and got cut somehow. I pulled his hand a little closer and ran my thumb over the area. It looked as if the section of his fingers closest to the palm had been slashed with a knife. "I can position some tape over the cuts so they won't be a problem. They'll probably open up again, but we can probably control the bleeding pretty well."

It was obviously too late for a replacement and the doctors didn't think the cut would hinder Paul in any way, so they were glad I could help and I was honored that they'd come to me with the odd situation. I wrapped Paul's hand that night and did what I could for the stitches. He then went out and had an absolute crazy slugfest with Paul Taylor. I mean these guys went nuts, especially at the start of the fight, one of the best starts I've ever seen.

Taylor and Kelly won fight of the night, but it was B.J. Penn who walked away with submission of the night. He met up with Joe Stevenson for the lightweight belt because Sean Sherk was stripped of the title. Sean was in attendance too and that ramped up the energy as the fight grew near.

B.J. rocked Joe early and really set the tone. Then he cut Joe with an elbow and the blood gushed. In round two both Joe and B.J. were covered in Joe's blood. I mean it was all over the place and it was hard to watch Joe struggle with B.J. wrapped around him and his face and shoulders painted in red. Finally he tapped to a rear naked choke and blood squirted a good two or three feet into the air, like a damn horror movie.

It's these kinds of cuts when I go up to Leon and jokingly say, "Better you than me!"

Afterward I was walking back to the hotel with Irvin Bounds, Joe's corner. "You know," he said, "as soon as we got back to the locker room Joe said, 'Where was Stitch, where was Stitch?'"

I felt honored for the second time on the day. It meant a lot to think that Joe was asking where I was. I wish I could've been there. I don't know if I could've made a difference, and even though I joke with Leon about it being better him than me when he gets a nasty cut like that, the truth is I would love to work on them all. I guess you could say it's in my blood.

A few weeks later I was back in the Mandalay. The weigh in had just finished and I went to a back room to meet Brock Lesnar. The humongous former pro wrestler (and former NCAA wrestling champ) was making his UFC debut and nobody really knew what to expect. I was assigned to wrap his hands so we were doing a trial run.

The room was almost empty, just a couple tables and a handful of folding chairs sitting on plush carpet and six or seven men standing around, Marc Ratner, Kirk Hendrick and Brock Lesnar included. I wrapped his hands and he was pretty quiet throughout. Once finished, I told him that was how I do it, but I could make adjustments if he wanted. "No this is great," he said.

Carla just happened to be with me again, and I cut the tape off so the wraps held their form and Brock signed them for her. It just happened to be almost a year to the day that she got Cro Cop's wraps after the first trial run with him. Surprised she doesn't have an account with eBay!

The actual event saw Big Nog come from behind to sub Tim Sylvia in the third round and it also saw Brock Lesnar pound the hell out of Frank Mir for the first minute and then referee Steve Mazzagatti stopped the action and penalized Brock for hitting Frank in the back of the head.

After the re-start Frank quickly subbed Brock with a kneebar and it was over just like that. I entered the Octagon and saw a fury in Brock's eyes. Usually I clean up the fighters and get them ready for the camera, but I thought, *shit, I'm not messing with this guy!* It turned out that he wasn't real happy, but he was gracious in defeat. "You win some you lose some," Brock said. "I'd like to win them all, but you can't."

A SERIOUS FAN AND A SERIOUS STAR

Panama Lewis had started working with Sultan Ibragimov and he called me because they were in Vegas to train. He asked if I wanted to do some pad work and I said sure. I hadn't done pads for a while and it's nice to get out there and break a sweat. I met Sultan, a highly-touted Russian heavyweight, and worked the pads with him. He gave me a nice compliment afterward saying of all the people that he's done pads with, I was the best. It was a good time and we sparked a friendship.

Now months later in February of 2008 I was in Wladimir's corner and Sultan was standing across the ring from him. We were in Madison Square Garden and I couldn't help but think of my other trips here, from the Copacabana to the cutman pissing on his territory to getting to work on Wladimir's cut against Calvin Brock. This fight wasn't so memorable and Wladimir handled Sultan easily in route to a unanimous decision.

What was memorable was my buddy Rick. Rick and his wife are huge, and I mean huge Klitschko fans. The first time I worked his fight in Vegas they drove all the way from Michigan or somewhere a long ways away (this is where I first met Rick), and they were at this one too. They were in the hotel lobby before the weigh in and I got a chance to introduce them to Wladimir. I told him how they were huge fans and then Rick lifted up his sleeve. He literally had the Klitschko "KO" logo tattooed on his arm! Neither Wladimir nor I could believe it and Wladimir got him one of the team jackets. Rick was stoked about it and I can only hope he doesn't use it as a blanket at night.

A week after working with Wladimir I was in Ohio at the Arnold Classic amongst all the big muscles. The card, UFC

82, was good and Anderson defeated Dan Henderson, but other than that I don't have much, at least right now.

Montreal was the UFC's first time in Canada and the fans were going absolutely ballistic well before the fights. The event sold out in something like one minute! I wasn't so sure I was going to get to see those fans. For whatever reason, customs screened just about everybody that was UFC affiliated. They asked if we owed child support, if we had any DUI's, have we been arrested, all kinds of stuff like that. A few of the people on the production side answered yes and they didn't let them into the country.

They pulled me aside and went through my bag. I had all my equipment and they asked me what everything was. As we were going through the process I'm thinking, *shit we're neighbors and they're scrutinizing me more than any other country and I travel all over the world.*

I made it through the Fort Knox of customs and headed to the hotel. Montreal is such a beautiful city and it hit me just how big a star Georges St. Pierre is there. There were signs everywhere, even on the windows of the high rise buildings downtown, *Good Luck Georges, Georges St. Pierre this, GSP that* ... they were everywhere. I can easily see how he keeps winning Canadian Sportsman of the year awards.

It was a high-energy weekend and come fight time the fans were like no other fans. The card had like eight Canadians and one odd fight between Nate Quarry and Kalib Starnes where Kalib back peddled for much of it. Then Rich Franklin TKO'd Travis Lutter and next it was Georges and Matt Serra in the rematch. I was Matt's good luck charm when he upset GSP in Houston, but this time I didn't give him enough luck.

The atmosphere was bordering on the edge of hysteria as Georges beat Matt up pretty good in route to a second round TKO. It was such a great environment and I was glad to be a part of the UFC's first trip to Canada. As we flew over Michigan on our way home, I thought of Rick and his Klitschko tattoo. I wonder just how many Quebecers are running around with GSP tattoos on their arms.

UFC 84 WITH B.J., TITO, AND WAND

UFC 84 at the MGM was named *Ill Will* and it fit. The event had a number of story lines as it was Tito Ortiz's last fight (we thought) in the UFC. He and Dana White had been involved in a much publicized feud. Tito even wore a shirt to the weigh in that read "Dana is my bitch!" Talk about trying to burn all your bridges.

There was also the match between Sean Sherk and B.J. Penn. They'd gone at each other and right after he subbed Joe Stevenson at UFC 80, B.J. yelled into the microphone, "Sean Sherk, you're dead!"

I was standing not too far behind B.J. when he yelled it and then Sean came into the Octagon. I was thinking, *oh shit, I might have to work overtime tonight.*

Sean claimed that B.J. really didn't have the lightweight belt until he beat him and it seemed both were ready to kick the crap out of the other. Before they could fight though, Tito met up with Lyoto Machida.

I'm usually in Tito's corner, but for this one I was with Lyoto. I kind of felt bad because I like working with Tito and this was thought to be his last fight in the UFC. Some people aren't too fond of him, but like I say, "Whether you love him or hate him, you've got to love him."

B.J. looked tremendous in the main event and out boxed Sean before stopping him with a brutal knee and punches. Then he went Bruce Lee on us and licked his bloody gloves.

There were definitely some stars on the card, but what I remember most is Wanderlei Silva and Keith Jardine. It had been just under five months since Wanderlei fought Chuck and then wished me happy birthday. I entered his locker room to wrap his hands and he was standing on a red mat that was stretched across the floor. I noticed his ankles were wrapped. I'm not sure if he did it on his own or if one of his trainers did, but the wrap looked kind of shitty. "Wanderlei," I said, "you want me to give you a Muay Thai wrap?"

He looked down at his feet, looked up at me, then smiled. "Would you please?" he said.

I cut the tape off and wrapped his ankles then his hands. Wanderlei is an intense guy right before a fight, after all he's nicknamed "The Axe Murderer," but he was even more intense for this one. He'd lost his last three fights to Mirko, Dan Henderson, and Chuck. I was at all of them and they were exciting, but still he needed a win and Keith was coming off his huge win over Chuck.

Keith looked clown mad during the stare down and then the fight was on. It didn't last because Wanderlei caught him with a short right and then a left and jumped on Keith to finish it. He knocked him out cold in just 36 seconds. It was a big win for Wanderlei and it came in dramatic fashion. I was happy for him, but at the same time I thought of Keith's dad and those tears of pride after he beat Chuck Liddell. I wondered what was going through his head as his son lay on the canvas.

That's the nature of the game I guess. One minute your hands are raised and the next you wake up looking at the rafters. Or it's like Greg Jackson says, "Sometimes you're the bug, and other times you're the windshield." Every fighter knows this going in, and I'm sure their loved ones do as well, but talk about riding an emotional roller coaster.

EVAN TANNER AND ANOTHER CARD FROM FORREST

I haven't even talked about Andre Ward, but I've been working with him since he turned pro. I've known him since he was a kid because he trained at King's Gym in Oakland (the one I was the first member of). I mention Andre because I was in the Cayman Islands for his fight with Jerson Ravelo on June 20 so I missed The Ultimate Fighter 7 Finale on the following day. Andre did as he normally does and looked sharp in stopping Jerson in the eighth.

I did watch TUF 7 and noticed that Evan Tanner looked a little out of sync against Kendall Grove. It was Evan's last fight before he tragically passed away in the California desert. He was such a unique personality and such a thinker. One day he'd speak so profoundly and then the next you'd hear that he was crashing a boat or getting drunk in the mountains or flying off to help build a playground. He wrote so eloquently and put his life out there for the world to see. He was definitely loved by many.

I wish I could have been there for his last fight. I worked his corner at UFC 82 when he made his return against Yushin Okami a few months earlier. It was tough because in an instant I saw him get old. He just couldn't get off against Yushin, and in between rounds he kept asking what he needed to do, what he needed to change.

He's the same guy who way back at UFC 34, one of my first events, kept trying to sub Homer Moore with a triangle. In between rounds Nate Quarry was in his corner and told him to fake the triangle and go for an armbar. Evan told him he didn't know how to do that and Nate said, "Just do it anyway." I am not kidding, less than a minute into round two Evan had his first armbar win and it came after faking a triangle. How great is that? And it absolutely illustrates the type of person Evan was. Once a seed was planted, he made it grow in a hurry, whether it was good or bad. I know I said it before, but he really is missed.

A couple weeks after TUF 7 I was back at the Mandalay for UFC 86 and Forrest Griffin, another guy who shoots from the hip, was fighting Quinton Jackson for the light heavyweight belt. It was a great fight and I could tell Forrest's leg kicks were hurting Quinton, but at the same time Quinton was the harder and more dangerous puncher.

Of course Forrest got cut. I love guys like Forrest, they keep me working! I kept the bleeding under control and the fight went to the cards with Forrest getting the nod. It was a really close decision and I don't think a lot of people expected Forrest to be able to fight Quinton as he did. Forrest is the proverbial underdog though and he finds ways to win or at least be competitive most of the time.

A little over a week after UFC 86 I was returning from Hamburg and on my way to Anaheim. Wladimir fought Tony Thompson and I've got to give Tony credit. He didn't seem intimidated by Wladimir as he stood across the ring from him. He also looked like he was taking an afternoon nap on the couch when Wladimir knocked him out in the eleventh. He was lying on his arm and he looked to be in a comfortable sleep, and I guess he was.

Upon arriving back at my house, Charlotte and I were sitting at the kitchen table drinking iced tea. I told her about my few days in Hamburg and that Tom Loeffler sent his regards. Tom promotes the Klitschko's and he's first class and a good friend. We visited a little longer and then she said, "Oh, I forgot, an envelope from Forrest came for you the other day."

She got up and plucked it off the kitchen counter. Forrest had given me the card and gift certificate after he beat Mauricio Rua so I guessed it was something similar. I opened it and found a card that read *Stitch, thanks so much for being there for me.* Then I noticed another piece of paper. I pulled it out and did a double take. It was a check for a thousand dollars.

I showed it to Charlotte and her reaction matched mine. It was such a considerate gesture and I thought *shit, I kind of like this!* But really it wasn't the dollar amount that was important. It was the fact that he thought highly enough of me to send me a card, the money was nice, don't get me wrong, but it reminded me of the time a couple years earlier when I wrapped Joe Stevenson's hands. He reached into his pocket and pulled out a wad of money as a tip. I think it came out to $86, but I was really moved by the fact that he wanted to show his appreciation beyond just saying thanks.

Forrest Griffin and Joe Stevenson are two perfect examples of what is right in MMA, there are many more as well. And sure there are some assholes too, but hey, that's how it is in all walks of life.

AFFLICTION BANNED AND MORE ON TUF SEASON SEVEN

Tom Atencio with Affliction had called a month or so earlier to ask if I'd help get cutmen lined up for their first event. Josh Barnett was on the card and at the time the UFC didn't have an event scheduled, so I told him I'd be happy to help.

Not long after that though, the UFC announced a card on the same day in an effort to counter Affliction. I was stuck in between because I didn't want to go back on my word with

Tom, but I also hated missing a UFC event. I talked with Donna Marconi and she understood, so I did what I felt was right and kept my word to work the Affliction show.

I headed to LA almost right after getting the thank you from Forrest. Since Josh was on the card and I needed to ensure cutmen were lined up (my job was a little harder with the UFC event on the same day) I got there early. I spent a couple days at Erik Paulson's gym, CSW, padding Josh out before he fought Pedro Rizzo. Paulson's gym is really nice and upon entering the foyer he's got a ton of photos on the wall of great fighters and wrestlers, and then one of Elvis Pressley.

I worked with Josh and he was sharp. I felt confident he'd handle Rizzo and he did with a KO in the second round. It was a busy night for me as I wrapped a lot of hands, including Fedor's and Vitor Belfort. Ever since I went to Vitor's hotel room before UFC 46, he asked for me to wrap him. Vitor KO'd Terry Martin in round two and Fedor fought Tim Sylvia. He dropped him in a matter of seconds and subbed him with a rear naked choke. It was a stunning performance.

I also saw Juanito Ibarra there. Juanito has been training boxers for years and has worked with some MMA fighters. He is well known in the combat sports world, but unfortunately he and I had a little bit of a run in on TUF 7 a few months earlier.

Before I can get into it I have to go back to years earlier. Juanito came to the cutmen, trainers, and fighters when I first started working with the UFC and talked about creating a union. I thought it sounded like a good idea as he talked of how it would advocate for jobs and such. Nothing ever came of it though, despite his passion.

Now fast forward to TUF 7, Don House and I had been the cutmen for every season of the reality show. Juanito was Quinton Jackson's trainer and Quinton was a coach, so I knew he'd be on the show as a trainer. "Don't be surprised if Juanito wraps the fighters' hands," I told Don.

He understood and it made sense. What I didn't expect was him wanting to be the cutman. They called me about the schedule and said, "Juanito is going to be the other cutman."

"Whoa ... okay," I said, and it was obvious I wasn't happy.

The first day of shooting I walked in and saw Juanito. "I need to talk to you," I said.

We went into a room and sat down. "I just want to let you know that I understand you're going to be the cutman," I said. "But you know Don House and I have been the cutmen for all the reality shows and you've talked in the past about wanting to create a union and give guys job opportunities, but you're doing exactly what the union would be trying to fight in taking a job away from a cutman."

He hadn't considered this. I mean I don't think he was gunning for Don's position. "Well I am a cutman," he said.

"I understand you're a cutman, but you're here in the capacity as a trainer and in working as the cutman you're taking the job away from Don," I said.

"Oh man I didn't know that," he said. "Well how much are you guys getting paid?"

"It's not about the money. It's just that you're taking his job," I said.

We left the discussion and I hoped everything would work out, but it ended up that Juanito worked the cuts and wrapped hands, and Don wasn't a part of TUF 7.

Back to Affliction Banned, after Josh fought I was walking down the stairs and Juanito was there. He called me aside. "Hey man, let's start all over again," he said.

"Okay, sure," I replied, but I kept walking.

I look back on the whole deal and feel bad it went down that way. Maybe there will be a time when we will make amends and laugh about it, but just a few months after it all happened, at the Affliction event, was too early for me.

In some ways Juanito and I are cut from the same cloth. We've been in combat sports for our entire lives and it pumps through our veins. Sometimes veterans of the game will meet and swap stories over beer, and other times they will rub each other the wrong way. This time happened to be the latter. All that aside, I was glad to be a part of the event. It is nice to be part of somebody's history, even if it doesn't turn out as they hoped.

LESNAR'S LUNCH PAILS

The hometown crowd inside the Target Center in Minneapolis was going nuts as I pushed through the Octagon door. I got to Heath Herring and his face was already swollen. Just seconds into the fight Brock blasted him with a straight right and then beat him up for much of the round. I used my enswell and Heath kept making noises as if he was in pain. This is usually an indicator of some kind of fracture and I brought that up to the doctor. Sure enough, later we learned that the first punch had broken Heath's orbital bone.

Brock dominated Heath for the next two rounds as well and it showed his savageness. Heath is a veteran and damn tough, but Brock was all over him all night. After wrapping his hands for a second time, it didn't surprise me that Brock was able to break Heath up. He's got lunch pails for hands and because of those hands the fight almost didn't take place.

Before the fight I'd wrapped Brock's hands. Then we worked to get the gloves on over the tape. It's not easy, especially with hands the size of Brock's. He's trying to jam his hand into the glove and I'm trying to force it over the tape when we heard a rip and the glove slid on. We kind of looked at each other like *oh shit!* But at the same time I'm thinking *damn that's awesome, hands like the Hulk.*

It turned out not to be so awesome because the same thing happened with the other glove. Burt Watson had to get the second pair of gloves. He had a worried look on his face as he handed them to me. "Stitch, be careful. This is our only other pair because they are specially made at four X."

It hit me that if we ripped one of these gloves we'd be screwed. I remembered a technique I'd picked up from Wladimir. When he puts his gloves on he puts a little Vaseline on the knuckles of the wrap so they'll slide on easier. I put a little Vaseline on Brock's knuckles and we held our breath as we worked his hands into the gloves. This time they went on with out falling apart.

I ended up with the pair that ripped, they were useless after all, and Brock signed them for me.

Also during the hand wrapping and glove trouble, I'd noticed Brock's Death Clutch shirt and commented that I liked it.

"Well I have one for you," he said.

"Yeah?" I said.

"Yeah, I packed one for you. Well not me, my wife did. As she was packing the stuff she asked, 'Do we get one for Stitch?' and I told her yes."

Once the gloves were on he reached in his bag and pulled out a shirt, my size and all. It was a really nice gesture and I thought *that's pretty cool, Brock Lesnar is thinking about me outside of the dressing room.*

Brock catches a lot of shit from some fans thanks to his pro wrestling background and sure he doesn't mind playing the bad guy, but in knowing Brock Lesnar as a person I can tell you he's okay in my book. And if he wasn't I wouldn't say so, I don't want to get hit by those lunch pails!

CAJUN FOOD AND A WHOLE LOT OF TRAVELING

Chuck Liddell started to come around. "What happened? He said.

"Chuck, you got knocked out." I said in a clear voice. As usual after KO's, I then had to say it two more times before it started to register. We were in the middle of the Octagon at UFC 88 and Chuck's uppercut had been a fraction of a second slower than Rashad Evans' overhand right.

It was a brutal KO and I was in the Octagon about four seconds after it happened. It's a weird thing because the crowd is at its loudest yet once at the side of a downed fighter I don't hear it. Fighters talk about not hearing or even forgetting the crowd is there during the fight, and that's how it is for me at the moment right after a knockout. The world gives way and my focus is solely on helping the man who was put to sleep, in this case Chuck.

A little less than two weeks later I was in Omaha for UFN 15. It was a good card, they almost always are, but what was better was the Cajun restaurant Don House and I ate at three days in a row. It was named *Jazz, A Louisiana Kitchen* and it was damn good!

With the Cajun restaurant still on my mind, two weeks later I was eating Bratwurst and working with Vitali Klitschko for just the second time. After he beat Danny Williams back in 2004 in the "Orange Revolution" bout, he retired. It wasn't until 2008 when he decided to return so here I was in Germany.

Berlin is a beautiful city and right across from the O2 Arena is the last still-standing piece of the Berlin Wall. I stood in front of it and stared at the slab of concrete, I thought of how it changed so many lives for so many people and it made me consider its historical significance.

One of the great things about my job is getting to travel all over the world and see places that I never would have seen otherwise. As a kid in Planada I often thought about what the world was like and dreamed about seeing it. Now I'm getting to see it and learn about it firsthand.

We all learned on that trip that Vitali Klitschko was back in a big way. He was fighting Samuel Peter and many people thought it would be a tough fight. Samuel had a contingency of Nigerian politicians ready to see him beat a Klitschko (remember Wladimir already beat Samuel). Unfortunately for them it didn't work out that way. Vitali peppered him with solid shots throughout. I could see his eyes turn bloodshot red and the disappointment at not being able to penetrate the offense of Vitali.

By the sixth or seventh round I was thinking *they gotta stop this fight because he's getting the shit beat out of him.* Samuel's corner was in desperation mode and nothing was working.

After the eighth he retired on the stool and I went in his corner to give him my condolences, or congratulations, depending on how you look at it.

With his eyes bloodshot and his face battered, Samuel said, "Stitch, you always beat me."

"Well Samuel, you got my number," I replied.

His comment meant a lot and he is a friend so I wasn't kidding when I told him he had my number. I'd love to be in his corner. I remember the Nigerian politicians were pissed because he quit. Even the German media asked me if I thought it showed an uncharacteristic side of Samuel when he quit on the stool.

I told them that from my perspective as a cutman that the answer was no. He was getting the shit (don't think I used the word shit) beat out of him and sometimes you know when you're going to win and when you're going to lose, and there was almost no way Samuel was going to win this fight. Also, nobody wants to see a guy get damaged long term. For him to call it quits was the smart and right thing to do, but the media couldn't appreciate that.

After the flight back home to Vegas I spent a few days with Charlotte and the kids and then it was back across the Atlantic to Birmingham, England. It was the UFC's first time in Birmingham and the one fight I remember was the barn burner between Chris Lytle and Paul Taylor. It earned fight of the night and I was glad to see them earn some extra money.

And guess what, seven days later I was in Chicago for UFC 90. I'd come almost full circle in the five-week stretch as I criss-crossed from Omaha to Berlin to Birmingham to Chicago with a few stops back home in between.

If only Chicago and Omaha were a little closer, Don House and I might have made a quick road trip for some more Cajun, after all, I'm pretty used to traveling and it was that good.

TRUE WARRIORS

Things slowed down a bit in November. Mike Brown stunned everybody when he knocked out Urijah Faber to take the Featherweight belt, and then Randy Couture returned after a lengthy absence due to a contract dispute with the UFC. Brock took the heavyweight belt from him with a second round TKO and this time we didn't rip any gloves before the fight.

I guess the slow month was needed to prepare me for December 10. The UFC event was called *Fight for the Troops* and it helped raise around four million dollars for the Intrepid Fallen Heroes Fund.

Prior to the fights, all us cutmen went to the chow hall on base. We ate with and visited with the troops and it was a great time. A young Texan, Sgt Gonzalez, was sitting across from us and decided to give us the pins off his uniform. It was such an honor so I told all the other cutmen that we should wear them during the event. They thought it was a great idea so we all wore our pins.

Later, I was sitting cageside as the event was about to start. The arena was full of GI's and we'd been taking photos with them almost nonstop and loved every minute of it. A guy from behind me said, "Stitch, can I take a picture with you?"

"Sure, I'd love to," I said as I turned around.

"Can you hold my prosthetic leg?" he said.

Right off the bat I was in a little bit of shock, but not wanting to skip a beat I immediately said, "Yeah sure!"

So there I was with my right arm over the guy's shoulder. He was smiling from ear to ear and in my left hand I'm holding his leg. It was a surreal moment and it made me think. He wasn't much older than a kid and he had to go through some serious battles in either Iraq or Afghanistan to end up losing his leg. And after that he had to go through many more battles as he dealt with rehabilitation and learning to live with the prosthetic leg I was holding. It took a lot for him to end up next to me at a UFC event and here he was kind of making light of it.

That moment was heroic, and I wasn't the hero. I had such a reverence for him and for all the men and women who fight for their country. I also recognized that it was great for him because he was so happy to be at the UFC and during that night he was able to put all those battles and pain out of his mind and have fun enjoying the fights.

It helped me recognize what these guys and girls do. You see them having a good time as they cheer for the fighters, but you also see the injuries. They are the true warriors and we owe them a lot.

Speaking of injuries, the event was full of crazy injuries, but nothing compared to Corey Hill's leg break. It happened at the beginning of round two and it is probably the freakiest injury I've ever been a part of.

Corey threw a leg kick and Dale Hartt checked it. We all heard the crack, but it didn't sound too different from any other leg kick. Then Corey fell down. I didn't notice that his leg was collapsed as he fell, not many others did either. Then I heard Joe Rogan. "Stop the fight! Stop the fight! Stop the fight!" he kept screaming.

Dale got up, he was in side control, and I saw that Corey's leg was literally in an L shape just above his right ankle. I jumped into the Octagon as fast as I could. I had my ice bag which is kind of funny because it wasn't going to do any damn good.

I got on my knees behind his shoulders and cradled his head in my hands and his shoulders were on my knees. He was in such pain and he looked up at me. "Stitch, what happened, what happened," he said.

"Corey look," I said. "You broke your leg and it's pretty serious so scream all you want. I'm here to take care of you."

I decided it was best to let him know exactly what happened and that it was okay to show that it hurt; nobody would call him a pussy for it. As we talked I glanced at his leg and I could see the gruesome separation. It was in two and going the wrong direction. The doctor was there working to get it in a position where Corey could be moved and he said to me, "Stitch pull on his shoulders."

I did and Corey was going through so much pain. Then thankfully they started giving him morphine. This was all still in the cage, and about the time the morphine started to flow Joe was standing three steps away and interviewing Dale. I heard him say that it was, "Probably the most serious injury we've ever had in the Octagon."

He asked Dale about it and Dale talked about how he wanted to win, but didn't want to see Corey like this. I didn't want to see him that way either. It was such a brutal break and we were on the canvas for probably close to ten minutes. After the shot of morphine Corey said, "My father's here."

He wanted to let his dad know that he was thinking about him and I asked Don House to go find him to let him know. They gave him a second shot of morphine and he was starting to relax as the pain dulled. I stayed right there holding his head in my hands and talking to him as the doctors got him on the stretcher.

Just before they took him out of the Octagon, Corey looked up at me. "Stitch, I almost had him," he said.

I thought that was great and it shows the heart of a warrior. Here he was with his leg basically severed above the ankle, concerned about his father and knowing that he was royally screwed, and he says, "Stitch, I almost had him."

There was only one way I could reply, "Yeah, you're right. You almost had him Corey."

MARK COLEMAN KICKING MY ASS

Just three days after Corey Hill's leg break I was in a hotel in Mannheim telling Tom Loeffler and Vitali Klitschko about it. We were there for Wladimir Klitschko's bout with Hasim Rahman, who was another guy I'd padded out and was friends with. Wladimir stopped him in the seventh and then I returned to Vegas for UFC 92.

It was a star-studded event and Quinton finally got revenge on Wanderlei when he KO'd him with a left hook. It made me think of that time when I worked on his nose after Wanderlei had rearranged it for the second time in PRIDE. Greg Jackson's statement also came to my mind, "Sometimes you're the bug, and other times you're the windshield."

Don House and I then watched Frank Mir out box Antonio Rodrigo Nogueira and it showed what kind of fighter Frank is. He showed a dimension that I didn't think he had. Then I watched as Forrest got beat by Rashad and again Greg's saying came to mind.

I kicked off 2009 in a new location and the fans were fired up. UFC 93 was in Dublin. The crowd was small because the 02 only held around 9,000 fans, but they were a loud group. It was a great event and Chris Lytle and Marcus Davis lived up to the hype by putting on a super fight.

I was in Marcus' corner and he wasn't cut, but I had a feeling I needed to get my shit together. With a little bit left in the round I got my swab and my mixture of Adrenaline and Vaseline ready and put some Vaseline on my hand. I was prepared even though Marcus hadn't been opened up. Then with about ten seconds left in the round he got cut.

It was like clockwork, Mark DellaGrotte said, "Stitch, he got cut," and boom I was right there ready to go even though the cut just happened. That moment was much like the one back when I first worked with Wladimir. I knew that I was progressing, getting better.

A few fights later I was waiting outside the Octagon as the music blared and Mark Coleman walked toward me. The last time he fought was at PRIDE 32 when he got beat by Fedor and then brought his daughters into the ring. He got to what they are now calling the *Harley Davidson Prep Point* and started pulling off his shirt and shoes and then stumbled backwards. I reached with my right hand to help keep him from falling and he pushed me aside. Then he realized that he didn't have a reason to go psycho on me and kind of apologized.

I put the Vaseline on and then he lost to Mauricio Rua. He was beat up pretty good and I tried to clean him up and he shoved me again! I realized that he was emotional and not thinking logically at the moment so it wasn't a big deal. However, a bunch of fans were pissed. A month or so later we were in Columbus and I was walking into the hotel. Mark was in his car at the valet. He jumped out. "Stitch, I want to apologize to you," he said. "I'm sorry that I pushed you. You know man I love you."

I laughed and told him no problem. He went on, "I got a lot of shit from the fans, but I was just embarrassed that I was stumbling. I know you were trying to help me."

"Well you know what," I said. "I felt kind of honored getting beat up by Mark Coleman. That's not a bad thing."

He laughed, and now every time I see him he gives me a hug and tells me he loves me.

One more thing about UFC 93, it was about six months before the UFC debuted in Germany and Oliver Copp and Tobias Drews are well-known German commentators. Oliver is a big part of the UFC and MMA in Europe and does a tremendous job. Tobias though wasn't sold on the sport and this was his first live event. Every time in Germany with the

Klitschko's he'd tell me how it was too brutal and would never work.

About halfway through 93 I walked by him and said, "Tobias, what do you think?"

"This is tremendous," he said. "I didn't expect it to be as good as it is."

But that's what the UFC live events do to people. It changes their perspective on what type of game MMA is with the fighters being tremendous warriors and sportsmen, even if they do push their cutman around before their fight.

AFFLICTION DAY OF RECKONING

It was a week after Dublin and I was in a hotel elevator in Anaheim with Charlotte and Daniel. Gilbert Yvel had just fought Josh Barnett and Josh had beat on him for much of three rounds. Gilbert's face was swollen horribly. I mean he looked like the elephant man.

He tried to smile and nodded politely even though he knew I was in Josh's corner, and I introduced him to Charlotte and Daniel. Charlotte didn't say it at the time, but she was stunned at how beat up he was. Then almost a year later when ho debuted in the UFC he saw me and asked, "How's your wife and son doing?"

"They're doing great," I said. "You know I pointed you out to my wife and told her you were the guy on the elevator last year and she said, 'Well I don't recognize him.' I told her that it was because now this is the way you normally look."

Really Gilbert was so nice after taking the beating to Josh. He's had his fair share of trouble, but what a lot of people probably don't know is he also once donated his purse to victims of a fire in his hometown of Rotterdam.

That whole night at Affliction was crazy. First I saw Doug Crosby, one of the UFC judges and he brought up the Corey Hill leg break. "Stitch, I just want to let you know that I've always respected you," he said. "But I really respect you now after how you took care of Corey. I saw how much attention you were giving him and how you were cradling him.

That just showed the kind of character you have. You have a lot of compassion and you're a man's man."

I really appreciated his comments, but I was doing what comes natural, taking care of the fighters.

Later on, after Fedor literally knocked Andrei Arlovski out of the air, I went by his dressing room. I'd wrapped his hands once again and wanted to congratulate him. The media was outside his room and they weren't letting anybody in. I poked my head in the door to congratulate him and was welcomed in. I told him I had my wife and son with me and he told me to bring them in too.

Fedor gave me a hug and once again I was drinking Vodka with him and his team. They took a team photo and he made sure I was in it and then he let Daniel hold the belt and we took some shots of Charlotte, Daniel, Fedor, and me. It was just a super moment not only hanging out with possibly the best fighter in the world after a huge victory, but also being able to have Charlotte and Daniel share in the moment.

"GREASE GATE"

In the middle of the thumping music and screaming crowd, I lean over to each fighter as they get to me just outside of the Octagon and say, "Hug your team. I'll put the Vaseline on you. Then the referee will check you out."

At UFC 94, and all the events before it, I did not make this statement, but then "Grease Gate" happened. We all remember the craziness, first Georges St. Pierre destroyed B.J. Penn and then B.J. said that Georges was slippery and it was realized that Phil Nurse had touched Georges' back in between a couple rounds after applying Vaseline to his face.

All hell broke loose afterward and whether it was intentional or not, it happened, Vaseline got on GSP's back. I'm not going to go into the whole story, I'd have to write another damn book to do so, but it did change the way we as cutmen and referees work with fighters before they enter the Octagon.

After the event, everybody was going crazy. Speculation and accusations were flying and Burt Watson told me that he wanted to sit down with all the cutmen to work out a solution.

We did just that and quickly, because the next UFC event was in Florida just two weeks later. Interestingly enough, it was the Florida Commission that got credit for coming up with the new rules, but actually Leon, Rudy, Don, me, and Burt sat around on folding chairs not long after UFC 94 and came up with the plan.

Burt cut right to the chase. "We got a problem. How do we make it better?" he said.

We kicked around ideas and it didn't take long for us to agree that the best solution was to have the fighters hug the team first, we put the Vaseline on them, the referee checks them, and then they go straight into the Octagon. Once the Vaseline was applied, nobody could touch them. And then only the cutman could apply Vaseline in between rounds.

This made sense and the UFC informed the commissions of the changes to ensure we didn't have another "Grease Gate." Really the rules should have already been in place, but sometimes things have to happen to instigate change. I'd seen it in Japan in one form or another and I'm sure it happened in the UFC and other organizations as well. Guys hug their fighters with Vaseline on their hands and just like that they have an advantage over an opponent who is great off his back.

I'll make an admission here, when Josh fought in PRIDE I'd pull him into the dressing room and blend in a little of the Adrenaline chloride and Vaseline mix to his brow even though it was illegal. I wasn't doing it for an advantage, but because it helped eliminate unnecessary injuries.

Getting back to GSP and B.J., I know Georges is a class act and even though he did get Vaseline on him, I don't believe it was his intent. It was just an unfortunate thing that happened and out of a negative we got a positive in the rule change. We tend to forget just how young modern MMA is. The NFL, MLB, and NBA make small rule changes almost every year. I expect there will be slight alterations to MMA rules for many years to come. Hopefully they'll continue to make the sport better.

On February 7, 2009 at the USF Sun Dome in Florida I started saying, "Hug your team. I'll put the Vaseline on you. Then the referee will check you out." And the B.J. Penn vs. Georges St. Pierre welterweight title fight of two weeks earlier had an impact on the sport, just not one that any of us expected.

12

SAD TIMES
A LEGEND CASHES IN HIS CHIPS AND BELIEVE

I HAD A HEAVY HEART during the weekend of UFN 17 in Florida. During the first event with the new rules regarding Vaseline, I learned that Chuck Bodak, a legend in the game and the only man I can truly call my mentor, passed away at the age of 92.

Chuck had a stroke in 2007 and complications led to his death in February of 2009. I'll always remember the advice he gave me and his wacky ways. We often throw around the word legend as if it defines somebody who was better than average, but a legend is much more. Chuck Bodak was a legend in the world of boxing and upon hearing of his passing I thought of what he said to everyone during his birthday while on the set of *Play it to the Bone*, "When I cash in my chips, Stitch will be the next, best cutman in the business."

I don't care about being the best, but I do hope that Chuck knows that I'm doing my best and I hope I'm making him proud.

A month later at UFC 96 in Columbus, Ohio, I watched as Matt Brown dismantled Pete Sell. Yves Lavigne is a top-notch referee, but on this night he started to stop the fight too early and then let it go too long. He admitted that he made a mistake and he's a man for doing so. We all screw up from time to time. As long as we use those mistakes to get better, then so be it.

Of course this didn't help Pete as he was beat to hell in about 90 seconds. Finally, Yves waved it off and I was a few steps behind the doctors. I got to Pete and applied ice to the back of his head and the left side of his face. He was kind of in a seated position. Blood was running from his right nostril and he didn't believe the doctors as they tried to tell him that he got knocked out. "No, no, no," he said, "what happened?"

They tried to explain it again, but he wasn't buying it. I intervened. "Drago, look, this is Stitch. You got knocked out."

He looked at me through glossy eyes. "Stitch, you ... I believe."

Later on as Pete talked with Joe Rogan about the fight he said, "Stitch told me I got knocked out."

I think it is hilarious that Pete said, "Stitch, you, I believe," but it also shows that these guys need to hear it from somebody they know and trust. First there's the fact that their head got rattled, but the confusion also probably comes from the inability to fully recognize that they were capable of being knocked out after all the preparation. Think about it, fighters have to go into a fight confident that they will end the night with their hand raised, not with their toes pointed to the ceiling. All the physical preparation and mental rehearsal leads to one conclusion, victory. Then suddenly people are around them trying to tell them they got knocked out. It's hard to comprehend, but if the news comes from me they are going to absorb it much more easily.

It still sucks though.

UFC 96 was also the last event TapouT co-founder Charles "Mask" Lewis attended. I just talked about Chuck Bodak being a legend. Well Mask was a legend for different reasons. He was and still is an inspiration to so many and his energy and personality was infectious.

I didn't really talk to him at UFC 96, but as I mentioned earlier, just about every time I saw him he'd say, "Stitch, we got to get you back man."

I always told him that I was with One More Round because I told them I would be, and Mark Zacher and Jim Baltutis are stand up guys. Mask appreciated this, but he kept trying. It was at WEC 38 in San Diego about six weeks before UFC 96 when backstage Mask and I talked at length. He kept telling me how important I was for TapouT and his attitude was so positive. I told him then that I'd love to come back to TapouT if the opportunity arose. It did during the summer because the UFC and One More Round had issues, but by then Mask was already gone.

During the early morning of March 11th, just a few days after he attended UFC 96 in Columbus, a drunk driver slammed into his Ferrari. It hit a tree and was literally cut it in half. Mask wasn't out partying. He wasn't street racing either as was the popular opinion. Instead he was coming home from the gym because it was the only time he could find to workout in his busy day.

It was so heartbreaking to find out what had happened and how. The cornerman jackets we wear today were designed by Mask and there is a tribute to him on the right side of our chest. It reads, *Mask Believe*.

He believed, and he inspired others to do the same. It's sad when legends pass and even sadder when the good die young.

JORGE RIVERA

I headed over to Stuttgart, Germany to work with Vitali Klitschko. He TKO'd Juan Carlos Gomez in the ninth round and I mention this event because it is actually where the deal to do this book was sealed. I'd had a handful of people mention the idea of doing a book, but this was the first time I'd taken the next steps with a writer and on March 21, 2009 we decided we'd collaborate on it.

A couple weeks later I was in Nashville, Tennessee for UFC Fight Night 18. It was the UFC's first event since Mask was killed and they did a nice tribute for him. Punkass and Skrape left a chair open for him and it definitely hit home seeing that empty space. It normally would have been filled with such life.

Sadly, the emotional evening wasn't over. Earlier I'd wrapped Jorge Rivera's hands. He wasn't on my list, but he is one of the guys that I make a point to wrap no matter what. We sat facing each other in folding chairs and I wrapped the tape around his wrist and hand while somebody popped the pads behind me. The locker room was quiet aside from the intermittent popping sound and I noticed a certain tightness in

Jorge that I hadn't seen before. We didn't talk about it and really didn't talk much at all.

He went out and fought Nissen Osterneck and it was a close battle. Afterward he pulled on what I thought was his sponsor-covered shirt, but I caught a glimpse of it and noticed a photo of a girl. It made me think of the time Vitor wore a shirt with his sister's photo on it and I got a sinking feeling.

Dan Miragliotta stood between Jorge and Nissen and Mark DellaGrotte stood a couple steps behind Jorge. I was a couple steps behind Mark. Bruce Buffer made the announcement, "... declaring the winner by split decision, Jorge "El Conquistador" Rivera!"

I stood on the top of the Octagon steps talking with Dan as Joe Rogan interviewed Jorge. Joe asked about Jorge's thoughts after losing his daughter.

I was stunned. For whatever reason I didn't know about the death of his daughter. I later found out it happened in the summer of 2008 and he lost his teenage daughter Janessa. The reason for Jorge's tightness during the hand wrapping came crashing on top of me. I couldn't even get my head around the thought of losing one of my own daughters and I felt deeply for him.

Jorge thanked God and started to choke up. He talked about how difficult the year had been.

He ducked his head and started to break down. "It's alright brother," Joe said.

Jorge wiped his face on his shirt, the one with a photo of his daughter, and went on to thank his mom and dad and family. Then he said, "And to Janessa Marie Rivera who I love and I miss dearly."

As I listened to him tears almost came to my eyes and I thought about how much pain he was going through, yet here he was. There wasn't much media around the fight and it was on the under card. I don't think too many people knew of how courageous Jorge was to climb back in the Octagon after losing his daughter. Shortly after the interview we gave each other a hug and he thanked me. Really though I was the one who needed to be telling him thank you.

UFN 18 was the last of a very emotional stretch for me. It had been a tough couple months, but at the same time inspiring. I'd seen how much the fans care and I'd witnessed courage up close and personal. Still it was a tough couple of months.

13

OUTSIDE THE RING AND CAGE
ANDRE WARD WITH A CUT AND SMALL GLOVES

I'VE KNOWN ANDRE WARD since he was a kid. His trainer Virgil Hunter and I have been friends for years. I used to sell him M and M boxing equipment. I also had custom shoes made for Andre and his younger brother.

Virgil and I always talked about how once Andre became a professional I'd be his cutman. I loved watching him progress during his amateur career and to see him do so well in the 2004 Olympics was awesome. Andre was actually a super middleweight, but his close friend Andre Dirrell was also a super middleweight, so he decided to go up to the light heavyweight division.

The move up in weight didn't slow Andre down and he won the gold medal. His final fight was against Belarusian Magomed Arlpgadjiev who had quite a bit of size on him, but Andre beat him 20-13 to bring home the medal.

Shortly thereafter I started working with him and have been ever since. On May 16, 2009 I was in my old stomping grounds of Oakland with Andre as he fought Edison Miranda at the Oracle Arena. It was a special fight for both of us.

Since it was something of a homecoming for me I got to see the guys from King's gym and a lot of them came to the fight. They saw me work my ass off because Edison cut Andre wide open with a head butt in the first round.

I jumped into the ring between rounds and went to work on the cut. It was above his left eye, not very long, but deep. Nothing I couldn't handle, but at the same time there were still a lot of rounds left in the fight. It's funny because a bunch of the old trainers and cutmen from the area, most of whom I knew, were sitting ringside. As I'm working the cut I hear people yelling advice on how to take care of it and then as the minute was coming to an end, a guy in the second row said, "Stitch, Stitch, use Thrombin, apply Thrombin on it."

On my way out of the ring I kind of acknowledged him with a nod because I didn't want to seem like an asshole, and thought *damn, I'm getting coached on how to work a cut.*

The second round wasn't so good for Andre. Edison roughed him up a bit and I headed in to work on the cut once again. And once again the old guy from the second row started coaching me up. "Stitch, Stitch, apply pressure, apply pressure."

Normally I wouldn't have been able to hear him, but he was only twenty feet away, and of course for the most part I was already doing what he was saying. Andre did what Virgil told him too and the fight really turned in the third. Still though, the cut was a factor and it would be for the rest of the night. My new coach was with me for the rest of the night too. After the third he hollered more advice about Thrombin and applying pressure.

I kept the cut dry during the next couple rounds and after the sixth I ducked between the ropes and now the guy was yelling, "Stitch, Stitch, great job man, great job!"

I don't know if he feels he should get some of the credit for the work that I did, but I'm proud of the job I did. It was such an important fight for Andre, his first real test against an experienced fighter and hard puncher in Edison Miranda. The cut, being Andre's worst at the time and in such a serious fight, could have changed the course of the game.

Andre dominated the rest of the way and won the decision. He acknowledged me afterward and it was a great way to end the homecoming, but there's a little more to the story. Before the fight Virgil approached me. "Andre likes to get gloves that are extra large," he said. "But they sent him larges instead and he's starting to freak out. Can you go talk to him and give him some encouragement?"

"No problem," I said.

So before the fights I knocked on Andre's dressing room door. When he answered I said, "I understand you're having a bit of a problem with the gloves. What is it?

"Well, you know Stitch I like them big and they don't have any," he said.

"Don't worry my man. I'll make some adjustments on the wraps and you're going to love them," I said. "You're not going to have any problems at all."

Andre was visibly relieved and I had some tape created by my friend Ian Dixon called WAR WRAP. It really is great stuff and I said, "I got a special tape that I'm going to use on you and everything will be okay."

I started wrapping his hands and he saw the tape complete with the word WAR embossed on it and I knew the smaller gloves weren't going to be an issue, especially when he pulled them on and they fit perfectly and he gave the little shy smile that he does when he feels comfortable.

Like I said, it's a great tape, but it wasn't like it really changed the way I wrapped Andre's hands. It did wonders for him psychologically though.

I was glad I played such an active role in helping Andre in a really tough fight, and in Oakland with friends looking on. I'm sure if you ask a guy from the second row he'll tell you I never would have been able to stop the bleeding if it wasn't for his advice, even though I've kept a few cuts dry in my day, and a week later it was Mike Pyle who was dry, but not in a good way.

MAKING WEIGHT

I had just arrived at the MGM and went to take a leak before going behind the curtain for the weigh in at UFC 98. The weigh in has become an event in and of itself with thousands of rabid fans attending. A stage is set up with a huge curtain for a backdrop. Behind that curtain are the Octagon and the area where the fighters hang out and do final checks before weighing in.

I noticed Mike Pyle was a few steps in front of me. "Hey Mike. How you doing?" I said.

He kept walking though and that's not like him. He turned into the restroom and headed for the sink. I went to the urinal and noticed he wasn't right. About the time I finished peeing he started dry heaving. We've all been drunk to the point where we've had the dry heaves, and they hurt. "Mike what's going on, what's wrong? I said.

He looked at me and his eyes were sunk in, his skin looked thin liked it had been draped over his bones and then pulled tight. "My stomach hurts," he said in a raspy voice. "Gotta make weight."

"Bullshit Mike," I said. "This is pretty serious."

I got some water and had him put it in his mouth and swish it around. "I gotta make weight, can't have any water," he said.

The sink area was kind of in the open. Some people had noticed what was happening and they were standing around watching. "Look man, you've got to drink a little bit of water," I said.

"Just dehydrated," he said. "I'll be alright."

I could tell though that he wasn't alright. Fighters are experts at cutting weight and over in Japan I remember seeing Frank Trigg stay in a sauna until he couldn't stand and dropping 18 pounds in the process. He then won his fight the next day. Mike was the worst I'd seen though. It's hard to even describe just how dried out he was.

"Mike, forget this," I said. "You look terrible. You've got to drink some water."

He knew he was in bad shape, but still wasn't convinced so I reached over to his forearm and pinched his skin. I let go and we both watched as the skin just stayed there. It looked like a camel's hump. This really freaked Mike out and one of the ushers said, "Should we get a medic?"

"Yeah, we definitely need a medic," I said. "And if you can maybe find a banana we can get a little potassium in him along with the water."

Marc Ratner came over and as I dabbed a wet paper towel on Mike and gave him some water. I filled Marc in on what was going on. The medics came and loaded Mike on a stretcher. They took him to a room in the arena and the doctors checked him out. They decided they could give him an IV to get him healthy and he could still probably make weight, but at that point Mike was already spent.

The story leading up to why Mike had to crash diet to cut weight and ended up dry heaving in the bathroom with rigid skin is crazy as well. Josh Koscheck was going to fight Chris Wilson, but dropped out due to injury. Brock Larson took his place, but then Chris Wilson was mugged in Brazil. His family was basically held hostage while he helped the criminals load up his stuff. Despite the robbery he was still going to fight, but then there was trouble with his paperwork. This resulted in Mike taking the fight (his UFC debut) on just a few days notice.

After the incident in the bathroom and due to the short time to cut weight, Mike was given an extra pound allowance and weighed in at 172. The next morning he called me. "Stitch, I just want to thank you for taking care of me. It means a lot," he said.

"No problem," I said. "How do you feel?"

"I feel great now."

Dr. Davidson wasn't as happy with me though. He didn't think I should have gotten involved and I should have let the doctors make an assessment on Mike's condition. They weren't in the restroom at the time though and they didn't see how Mike was. I took it upon myself to take care of Mike and I'd do it again in a heartbeat. We have to recognize that the fighter's health is more important than the actual fight and weight cutting was something John and I covered extensively in *Boxer's Nightmare*.

I'm sure if Dr. Davidson would have seen Mike at that moment, he would have done the same as me. He's an outstanding doctor and does what's best for the fighters. I can see where he was coming from, but again, he didn't see Mike dry heaving in the restroom or his paper-thin skin dried and folded like a camel's hump.

Mike might've felt great after getting fluids in him, but I have to think it affected his ability to fight. Brock Larson subbed him with a triangle choke in just over three minutes.

The other memorable moment of UFC 98 came when Lyoto Machida KO'd Rashad Evans. With a flurry of punches the belt changed hands and afterward I was in the dressing room to congratulate Lyoto as I'd wrapped his hands many times. With his father, the great Yoshizo Machida looking on, Lyoto bowed to me and said, "In the ring, you are my father."

Compliments can't get any bigger than that.

UFC 99 AND THE KO SWELL

The arena and hotel were just a few blocks from each other. Everyone loaded up on the same bus for the short drive to the weigh in. I stood outside waiting to board when Mirko came up to me. He smiled and gave me a big hug. He is usually kind of a quite guy and I noticed some of the fighters were looking out the bus window at us. I'm sure they were surprised he was so enthusiastic to see me, but I'd wrapped his hands a few times and we'd become friends. At the time Josh Barnett was scheduled to fight Fedor so Mirko was giving me information about what he thought Josh would need to do to beat Fedor. It meant a lot to me that he was giving me the information to give to Josh.

I finally piled on the bus and Wanderlei was leaned over in the front seat looking like death. The cut had been tough on him but he didn't show it during his fight with Rich Franklin. He lost, but it was a great scrap and controversial decision.

Before Wanderlei and Rich fought, a couple other things happened outside the cage. Mike Swick TKO'd Ben Saunders and then returned to the Octagon to watch his friend Cain Velasquez fight Cheick Kongo. I was in Cain's corner and Mike sat down next to me. "What do you think of this fight?" I asked.

"Cain is great at what he does. I see him dominating Cheick," Mike said.

Cheick is about as intimidating as they come and I looked through the fence at him as he waited for the fight to start and thought *Mike must be a little crazy*, but all I did was nod in response.

Early on Cheick rocked Cain a couple times. I glanced at Mike and he still seemed confident. Then Cain slammed Cheick to the mat and controlled him the rest of the round. Cain had taken a few big shots so Javier Mendez asked me to go in with him between rounds.

"Listen, keep doing what you're doing. Keep your composure," Javier said to Cain. "You're overpowering him and you're breaking him mentally."

Javier is a great coach and his advice was spot on and interesting. Cain doesn't show a lot of emotion and the talk of breaking him mentally seemed that it'd be better for a more emotional fighter. Cain absorbed the words though and followed Javier's advice flawlessly and he dominated Cheick for three rounds. I was impressed all the way around and I have to give it up to Mike, he was spot on.

Dale Hartt had fought earlier and was subbed by Dennis Siver. Not long before Cain fought, Dale came up to me outside of the Octagon. Remember he was the one involved in the horrific Corey Hill leg break and he handled it well. His eye looked pretty messed up and he asked me to help with the swelling. I pulled out my KO Swell and touched it to his face. It hurt him bad, but he started laughing. I was thinking *this guy's freaking crazy* and as I applied more pressure he laughed harder despite the pain. Some guys express pain in different ways, for Dale it is by laughing his ass off and I guess it makes sense because he's a funny kid.

After Dale left I found Dr. Davidson, "Dale's cheek bone is really sensitive," I said. "It might be broken."

He checked it out and sure enough the orbital bone was broken.

Earlier I talked about the enswell, the cold metal piece that cutmen apply to swelling, and here I just called it the KO Swell. The new name is thanks to an idea I had and my wife Charlotte coming up with a name for it.

The KO Swell came about a couple years before UFC 99. I was at the airport with Mark DellaGrotte. We were talking about how to improve the game for the fighters. I had a water bottle and I took the bottom of it, where it is kind of concave, and placed it against his cheek. "This is what I want to create," I said. "It makes it where the metal will cover more of the face and reduce more swelling."

"That's a great idea," Mark said.

I had ideas for either a round one or a rectangular one, but being as busy as I am it wasn't until a few months later, at UFC 77 in Cincinnati when I woke up in the middle of the night and the design hit me. I sketched out what I wanted on three or four sheets of paper. After that we did a prototype that is shaped to fit the contours of the face and now I'm using my very own KO Swell. It works much better than the traditional enswells.

It's seems like such a simple thing and it's surprising that it hadn't already been done, but I think it shows how I'm always thinking about how to make it better for the fighters. I've talked about the importance of education and I try hard to educate everyone I can because if it wasn't for my education through experience as a cutman something like this seemingly basic innovation might've never developed. TapouT is now making the KO Swell available to cornermen everywhere.

SEVEN MORE DAYS IN GERMANY

After UFC 99 I didn't fly back to the States. I was working with Wladimir the following weekend in Gelsenkirchen so I made a three hour drive south to Kaiserslautern to visit U.S Troops stationed there. I got to spend time with wounded service members at Landstuhl and One More Round provided about fifty shirts that I handed out at the Landstuhl USO.

The following day, Heather, the prevention coordinator who organized everything, had it set up for me to do a meet and greet with 212th CSH HHD. That's the Combat Support Hospital stationed at Miesau. They had a podium set up for me and I talked about what I did and then gave away some of my DVD's and wrapped amateur boxer SPC Ronald Grant's hands. Then CSM Mendoza shook my hand and placed a coin in it. It was such an honor to receive a coin from him.

He then took us to the chow hall. It'd won a bunch of awards for its food and I could see why, it was damn good. I got to visit with more soldiers and CSM Mendoza is a big boxing fan and we talked at length about the sport. I know he enjoyed it, but I probably had more fun than he did.

Later, I sat down with my co-author on this book and we interviewed for a few hours outside of the hotel Christine, where I was treated to the suite. It was a busy couple of days and here's something funny about the visit, we went out to a village about 15 to 20 minutes from base to a Schnapps House. We ate German food and had a few shots and a group of guys across the room kept looking our way. Finally one of them walked over. "Anybody ever told you that you look just like Stitch, the cutman for the UFC," he said.

"Yeah people have told me that before," I said.

I didn't tell him I actually was Stitch and everyone at the table thought it was pretty funny. I'm sure he figured there was no reason for me to be in a small village in Germany so he didn't think it was actually me. I felt kind of bad though so I finally told him.

I left on Wednesday morning and took the train back up north to Gelsenkirchen to work with Wladimir. It was my first time on a European train and it only added to the experience. Wladimir met up with Ruslan Chagaev and handled him pretty easy. What was crazy about this fight was the venue. It was in the Veltins-Arena and over 60,000 people were in attendance. It was wild standing in the corner and looking out over the sea of faces.

My ten days in Germany was a blast. I did so much and got to be a part of the first UFC event in the country, got to visit the troops, drink at a traditional German Schnapps House, and then was part of what I believe was the largest crowd ever at an indoor boxing event.

Once again, as I boarded the plane to fly back to the States I couldn't help but think of my days in Planada and all those times when I wondered about the world. No need to wonder anymore, I was getting to experience it.

TapouT and UFC 100

I hated it, but handing out the OMR shirts to the troops was the last thing I did with One More Round. I was unable to wear OMR clothing into the Octagon so it only made sense that we parted ways.

Once back in the States, Dan Caldwell (Punkass) and I texted back and forth. He of course knew how hard Mask tried to get me back before he passed. I told him I was available and he jumped at the chance.

TapouT president Marc Kreiner's secretary called and said he wanted to set me up in the Mission Inn hotel so about a week before UFC 100 Charlotte, Daniel, and I made the drive to Riverside. We were in the Presidential Suite and it was an amazing hotel. The next day I headed to the TapouT offices and was again blown away.

Marc gave me a tour of the whole complex and it is impressive. When I'd left TapouT to go with One More Round a few years earlier, they were growing, but what they'd done was amazing. He also showed me the room dedicated to Mask and it was hard to not get teary-eyed knowing that this was his vision and it had done so well, but he wasn't around to enjoy it.

We finished in Marc's office, complete with his mish-mash of items on the wall from gold records to a letter from Oprah to UFC gloves and shorts. Marc and I negotiated a deal and I was negotiating for the other UFC cutmen as well. He talked about doing my own shirt and we decided to create a new vest for all of us to wear in the Octagon.

Marc commented that I was like family and I felt like it. I always did, but even more so now. We made a long-term commitment to each other and I plan on slipping on my TapouT vest for many years to come.

The Friday after meeting with Marc, I was in the Mandalay for the fan expo. It was an enormous success with the convention center packed with booths and fans filling every aisle. I got to set out my Stitch Duran Gear at the Xyience booth and signed autographs alongside Wanderlei. It was nuts to see so many fans in one place and all of them so excited. It captured just how important the UFC was to the MMA fans and showed how big the sport had grown.

I was out doing stuff until past midnight on Friday and up by about six the next morning to get ready for interviews and appearances. I then signed autographs for about four hours at the Xyience booth until I had to head over to the arena to start preparing for the event.

UFC 100 was a momentous event and the card was stacked. A couple things really stand out. I was in Dan Henderson's corner, but when he KO'd Mike Bisping, Mike landed closer to me (plus no offense to my man Leon, but I'm faster than him). I got to Mike and he was in another world. Like so many other guys, he said, "What happened?"

I told him, "You got knocked out Mike."

Of course it didn't register at first and we went through the exchange a couple more times. Finally he looked at me and said, "I got knocked out," and it was a statement, not a question.

GSP dominated Thiago Alves and then Brock Lesnar put on quite a display against Frank Mir. We all know he beat Frank up good and then went a little crazy afterward. I went over to congratulate him, but Brock headed toward Frank like he was going after him again! I remember the Nevada inspectors were trying to separate them and Brock was like a gorilla gone rampant. I said to one of them, "Shit you'd better leave him alone. Better just let him vent because there's no way you're going to control him."

They took my advice and stood by as Brock yelled at Frank. Then he got on the microphone and made his now infamous speech about Bud Light and Coors Light and all. It was kind of insane being in the Octagon during all that, but putting it all aside it was a hell of a performance by Brock.

About twenty minutes later I went into his locker room to congratulate him and it was hilarious. Brock and his wife were in one corner and everybody else in the room was in the far opposite corner. It was like they were trying to get as far away from him as possible and they were kind of all huddled together. I don't know if Dana White had just been in to get onto Brock about his after-fight antics or if they all just decided to give him his space, but I thought it was funny. They were like kids who just got scolded by the principal. They didn't want to mess with Brock.

Brock had just gotten out of the shower and he sat on the bench in his shorts. I headed over to him and as I crossed the room I thought *shit I hope those guys don't know something*

I don't know. Then Brock smiled real big. "Stitch, what'd you think man?" He said.

"That was pretty awesome. You looked great," I said.

"That felt great," he said.

We talked for another minute and everybody else stayed huddled in their corner. I guess they were just letting Brock be himself. A little later though he wanted to take a group photo and wanted me in it. I thought it was cool to be included and it shows the kind of relationship that I have with Brock. Not that we are good buddies and spend time hunting together, but he appreciates what I can do for him and I can for sure appreciate how incredible of a fighter he is, and sure he let off a little steam after getting revenge on Frank Mir, but emotions run high right after a fight.

FIRST TIME TO PHILLY AND ROCKY BALBOA

Believe it or not, UFC 101 was my first trip to the famous fight town of Philadelphia. Leon Tabbs and Burt Watson are both from there, and I'd flown through with them a lot of times but we always parted ways at the airport.

Philadelphia made me think of Rocky. I had a part in *Rocky Balboa*, the sixth and final installment in the legendary series. Crazily, I turned down the offer at first. I was scheduled to work with Fabrice Tiozzo in Paris and the following week I was to work with Audley Harrison in London. Audley is a well-known Brit fighter and for good reason. He won the gold medal in the 2000 Olympics at super heavyweight.

They called about doing the movie and I hated it, but said, "I'd love to, but I can't because I'm already working these fights."

They understood and despite not taking the offer I was excited. I called Charlotte at work and told her about it. She was excited as well. "But I can't go," I said. "I've got to go to France and England."

"Are you crazy!" she said. "You've got to take it. Rocky's an American icon. You're always thinking about others. You need to think about yourself sometimes too."

I had been negotiating with Audley's manager about fees, hotel, and travel and the email was on the screen. I sat there for about 30 minutes considering what Charlotte said. Finally, I decided she was right and sent an email to Audley's manager explaining the situation. He understood and then I called up the casting agent to ask if the role was still available. It was, but she said they'd need to audition people to help me in the corner.

"Wait, wait, wait," I said, "If you need boxing people, let me get some to help out."

She thought it was a great idea so I called up Livingstone Bramble. He'd just moved from Las Vegas to New York like two weeks before. "Bramble, you want to do the Rocky movie," I said.

He thought I was bullshitting, but finally I convinced him and he flew back. Next I called Don House and he was up for it as well.

It was a fantastic time. Antonio Tarver played Mason "The Line" Dixon and I wrapped his hands each day. We built a good relationship while on the set. I remember thinking Ron Shelton was a great director, and he is, but it was awesome watching Sylvester Stallone work. It was funny because he would direct with a robe on over his boxing shorts and shoes. Then when the fight scenes would come he'd pull his robe off and get into action.

The fight scenes weren't that heavily scripted and really realistic because the prop master, who I worked closely with, used a pretty unique trick. First, he used 12 ounce instead of 10 ounce gloves and then he took the padding out and put in a much softer material. It made it where Antonio and Sylvester could really punch each other without as much of the consequences. They did such a good job that when Antonio goes to the body and hurts his hand, I was thinking his hand was really hurt! I didn't know the script. I was just there doing my thing and I was relieved when I realized that his hand wasn't really jacked up because I was the one that wrapped it.

Paulie (Burt Young) gave me one of his cigars, Sylvester was cordial and respectful and I got to be a part of history. How many people can say they were in one of the Rocky movies? And now people usually recognize me from two things, the UFC and Rocky.

Speaking of history and the UFC, 101 was historical as it was the promotion's first event in Pennsylvania. The commission had just approved MMA months earlier so we headed to the city of Brotherly Love.

While there I met up with Junior Seau. The star football player had started doing a show on Versus called *Sports Jobs*. It was my job to show him how to be a cutman. The morning of UFC 101 we went to a gym in Philadelphia and filmed the segment. I also brought him his very own TapouT vest. On the back it read *Seau* and on the front it read *Junior* with *Stitch* just below it.

It was really fun and Junior made it better by signing a photo for my son Daniel. He's a high school linebacker and big fan. Unfortunately, the outcome of the Forrest Griffin/Anderson Silva fight put a damper on the show. Junior of course wasn't going to work cuts, but he was ready to shadow me. He didn't get much of a chance because Anderson put on an awe-inspiring performance and stopped Forrest early. It was tough because of my friendship with Forrest, especially seeing him so upset that he left the Octagon right away, but all fighters know that sometimes it just isn't their night.

The next fight saw B.J. dominate Kenny Florian. It was another incredible performance that showed once again just how good B.J. is.

It was a good event, but I didn't have much time to consider it. We had a WEC event on the other side of the country about 16 hours later.

WEC 42

After a late night in Philadelphia I was at the airport while the sun was still somewhere over the Atlantic. WEC 42 was scheduled for later in the day at the Hard Rock. I didn't sleep well on the early morning flight. I never sleep well on flights, and was pretty tired upon arriving in Vegas. After a quick stop at the house I headed back to work.

The tiredness wore off in a hurry once we start prepping for the event. The energy doesn't really let you feel tired. As always with the WEC, it was a great show and the featured fight saw bantamweight champ Miguel Torres taking on Brian Bowles.

Brian was coming off a couple big wins, but Miguel is a monster and was 37-1 coming into the fight. From the start I thought Miguel looked off a bit. A little over a minute in he got hit with an overhand right that wobbled him. Then just when it seemed he was getting his rhythm he moved forward with a flurry and Brian caught him with a right hook and finished the fight in a matter of seconds.

The doctors and I got to Miguel at about the same time. He started coming around and I had to tell him the three times, the standard number, that he was knocked out. When it registered he looked at me. "I gotta go. I gotta get out of here," he said.

"No, no, no, you've got to stay Miguel," I said. "Whether you're a champion or not you've got to give Brian respect and stay here."

Thoughts of Forrest leaving the Octagon flashed in my head. I'd heard in transit from Philadelphia that he was getting shit for leaving so fast. Losing like Miguel did was already painful enough. I didn't want him to get shit for taking off too.

"You're right," he said and stayed put.

Afterward, I went to the dressing room to check on him. His mom was there and her cheeks were wet with tears. "I'm just glad he's okay," she said to me. "I know this happens and I expect this from the game, but I just hope he's okay."

I was applying the KO Swell and ice to his face. "He's fine," I said for both her and Miguel's benefit. "You should be proud of your son."

She was relieved and definitely proud of him. Miguel is a tough kid, but that's one of the things that make this game so good. It just takes one shot for an underdog to claim victory and a champion to fall, or to steal from Greg Jackson once again, "Sometimes you're the bug, and other times you're the windshield."

A few weeks later at UFC 102 in Portland neither Randy Couture nor Antonio Rodrigo Nogueira were too keen on being the bug. You just never know when Randy's going to get old, but this time certainly wasn't it. He fought another legend in Big Nog, you know he's like Timex; he takes a licking and keeps on ticking. Once you think you can count him out, don't count.

Big Nog got the best of Randy, but Randy showed major heart. It was just a good old fashion fight and we all love those.

SOUTH ON I-35

UFC Fight Night 19 was in Oklahoma City on Wednesday September 16. It was the UFC's first time in Oklahoma since way back at UFC 4. I wasn't at that one, but my man Leon was.

There were some good fights with Tim Credeur and Nate Quarry slugging the crap out of each other and the main event saw Nate Diaz sub Melvin Guillard. Something funny about this event, a few months earlier when in Germany at UFC 99, I met a guy named Todd Kelley who was vacationing in Europe. He was a baseball coach at the University of Central Oklahoma and he noticed my bag was worn to hell. The zipper was busted, part of it was ripped, the thing was thrashed and it makes sense considering how much I use it.

He told me he was going to get me a bag with the UCO logo on it and give it to me at UFN 19. I told him that'd be great, but was thinking *yeah right.* Sure enough, he showed up at the hotel and had the bag for me, complete with the UCO logo. I've been using it ever since.

The morning after the fights, we all loaded up on two busses. UFC 103 was scheduled for Dallas on Saturday and since it's just a three hour drive they opted for a bus ride down I-35. About halfway we stopped to grab a bite to eat and were told we had one hour then the bus was pulling out. Everybody spread out and I felt like a high school kid on a sports trip.

After the weigh in on Friday I hooked up with an old friend, Gilbert Rodarte. He took me to an old bar in town named Robbie's. It reminded me of the bars in Planada, I mean it was like being thrown back in time. They played the old traditional music, there were big women sitting at the bar, drunks slouched in the corners, and it was best to keep your back against the wall in case of a knife fight. And the whole time I was there I was thinking *shit this is great! It's nice to go back to my roots.*

Surprisingly enough, the owner knew who I was and he had me autograph one of the neon signs and we took some pictures.

UFC 103 saw Frank Trigg return. He was KO'd by Josh Koscheck and being a friend of Trigg's I wish it could have ended a little better for him. Junior Dos Santos stopped Cro Cop and he had requested for me to wrap his hands. I did, and afterward he kept telling me how good the wrap was and that he wanted me to wrap his hands all the time, so I got another customer in Dallas. Paul Daley announced his presence there too. He TKO'd Martin Kampmann in a hurry.

It had been a good few days in Oklahoma and Dallas and I ended up with a new bag and I loved going to the old bar, but it was time to head back to the west coast, and then all the way back home to Planada.

14

BACK TO CALIFORNIA
THE STAPLES CENTER

CHRIS ARREOLA WAS SITTING ON THE STOOL with tears running down his face. I walked over to him. "You know what man, don't cry," I said. "You ought to be proud of what you did. You showed a hundred percent heart."

Chris had just gotten beaten up by Vitali in the Staples Center and of course I was in Vitali's corner, but despite Chris getting whipped, I thought he showed the heart of a Mexican fighter and I wanted him to know it. The weekend was fun because the Klitschko's don't fight in the States too often. The whole family, Charlotte, Carla, Angela, and Daniel, came to the event and we got to spend a lot of time together.

After the fight I was in the back and bumped into Sylvester Stallone. "Stitch, I see you everywhere," he said as he slapped me on the shoulder.

I laughed. "I see you everywhere too Sly." Even though I was in *Rocky Balboa* it's cool to have him talk to me. I mean come on. He's freaking Rocky and Rambo!

A few weeks later I was back at Staples for UFC 104. I didn't see Sly, but I saw some other crazy stuff, including a monster-sized image of myself projected on a building. After a meeting with Isham Harris I was trying to relax when Punkass sent me a text. It read *200 feet tall, bigger than life!* Then there was a photo of me in my Stitch TapouT shirt on a wall. I had to see it in person and it was surreal. I'd seen Kobe Bryant, Manny Ramirez, Michael Jordan, and other famous athletes on the walls in LA, and now I was up there with them. I was fucking ecstatic!

I then headed to the arena and the big fight was between light heavyweight champ Lyoto Machida and Mauricio

Rua. After his loss to Forrest, Mauricio had stopped Mark Coleman and Chuck Liddell. Now he was getting a shot at Lyoto.

I'd mentioned about how all the Brazilians started calling me Santana in Japan at PRIDE while I was doing the seminars. Well Mauricio remembered how I'd wrapped his brother's hands and at UFC 102 in Portland he said, "How come you never wrap my hands Stitch?"

I explained that I work the red corner, but if I could I would wrap his hands next time. That next time was at 104, but I checked and he wasn't on my list. Of course Lyoto was on my list so I headed in to wrap his hands. It was cool because while I was wrapping they were filming a segment and interviewing me about what it takes to wrap hands. I was telling them and my buddy Ian Dixon's WAR tape was all over the shot. I finished the wrap and Lyoto nodded his approval. I wished him luck and left the room.

I was heading down the hall and I thought of Shogun. He'd asked me twice to wrap his hands and I thought *screw it, I'm gonna go wrap him and be a man of my word.*

I entered his room. "Shogun, you want me to wrap your hands?"

"Oh yeah, yeah, you never do. I want you to wrap them," he said.

I got to work on him and the cameras filed in. This time it showed Ian's WAR tape on the pay per view. I knew he was going nuts with joy and I also knew that Lyoto could see us on the closed-circuit TV from his room. I was thinking *I hope he doesn't think I'm a traitor,* and after all I'd be working in his corner anyway. Luckily he didn't and he is one of the most respectful men in the game.

Lyoto and Mauricio fought for five hard rounds in what was a dramatic fight. Each man worked to set their strikes up and each big exchange made me hold my breath. It went to a decision and Lyoto got the nod. A lot of people thought it could've gone to Shogun and all I can say is I'm sure glad I don't have to pick winners because I wouldn't know who to pick on that one.

Immediately after the fight I got a text from Marc Kreiner. The guys from TapouT wanted to treat the cutmen to dinner at a restaurant a couple blocks away. Rudy had already left so Leon, House, and I set out to the restaurant. On the way we got caught up with fans taking photos and signing autographs. Josh Barnett came by and gave me a big hug and took some pictures with fans as well.

There were probably thirty people around us when to my right I noticed two guys messing around. At least I thought they were messing around shoving each other and stuff, too much booze and testosterone after the event. It seemed okay because one was laughing and saying, "He's just drunk."

Then another guy came out of nowhere and shoved the shit out of the drunken guy. He flew to the ground and the side of his face slammed into the concrete. I thought *uh oh, this better not turn into a brawl*. I was literally just a few steps away and I had my bag in my hand so I moved over there like the guy had been KO'd in the Octagon while everyone watched.

He was out for a few seconds and when he came to I noticed he had a cut on his eyebrow. House had some gauze so I unraveled it and tore off a piece. The guy started to come to and kind of sat up, then I helped him to his feet while applying pressure to the cut.

His eyes cleared a bit and then they opened wide. "Stitch!" he said.

I smiled and tried not to laugh as I continued to keep direct pressure on him. "Yep, Stitch is working on you buddy, you're good," I said.

A bunch of the bystanders actually laughed. His breath reeked of alcohol and I looked at his buddy. "Are you with him?" I said.

"Yeah, I'm with him," he replied.

"Just keep an eye on him and keep direct pressure," I said. "He should be okay."

The guy nodded and as I walked away House said, "Hey a bunch of guys were taking pictures of you. Maybe it'll be on You Tube."

We finished up the photos and headed to the dinner with the TapouT guys and I didn't think much about the whole deal.

The next day I saw Mauricio in the hotel lobby. He thanked me again for wrapping his hands and I was glad I decided to do it. Later that day, an interesting post on the popular MMA site Bloody Elbow was brought to my attention. A fan named Tim Wilson posted the story of the guy getting knocked out. I got a kick out of it, and with my image on the building, wrapping both Mauricio's and Lyoto's hands, and helping out some poor drunk guy, seeing the article was a cool way to end an incredible weekend.

The weekend was great because of the above, but even more so because of what I did right before UFC 104.

I went home.

GOING HOME

The drive from Las Vegas to Planada took almost eight hours. I was making it because Le Grand High School was having its one hundred year anniversary. Our graduating classes were so small that we didn't have reunions, so they invited everybody who attended Le Grand to the homecoming football game against our arch rival Mariposa. I decided that even though it was on the Friday before UFC 104 in Los Angeles, I had to be there. I let the UFC know that I wouldn't fly to LA on Friday and instead I rented a car and set out early Friday morning for my old home.

My legs were stiff and my butt hurt from sitting so long, but as I turned off of highway 99 and onto Le Grand road I was waking up and the aching muscles were forgotten. The orchards, the same ones I grew up in, were stretched out before me. I turned off Plainsburg road and before long I was at the little cemetery between the nectarine trees and the corn field. It was where my dad and Tio Miguel were laid to rest.

I stretched my legs and kicked up a little dirt in doing so, then headed to my dad and Uncle's grave. They are buried in the same plot. Tio Miguel was killed when his trailer burned down and his ashes were placed on top of my dad.

I stood there in the sunshine thinking about my youth. I remembered playing in the cotton after a long day of picking, the day my dad finally gave me a grown up sack to fill, the time he and my mom put spider webs on a cut to stop the bleeding, and how I helped him load those last few boxes after having to ride the bus and being left alone on the day we moved to Planada.

After a few minutes I decided I needed to visit Alfred Sanchez's grave. Alfred was my friend the lefty pitcher and he'd passed some time ago. I'd attended his funeral so I knew where his grave was. I said a prayer for him and reminisced about the good old days. I thought of us playing baseball and the times we'd all lay in the muddy fig orchard.

Another childhood friend, Rudy Salcido, had passed as well. I was at an event so I couldn't make it to his funeral. I stood there wishing I knew where he was buried. Then I glanced to my left and couldn't believe it. There was Rudy's grave, right next to his buddy Alfred's. I laughed even as tears formed in my eyes. I wiped them away and laughed some more. I wanted the families to know I visited and that I was thinking of them, so I placed a business card underneath the flowers at each grave.

A few hours later I was standing in the Le Grand locker room waiting to address the football team before the big game. I'd stopped by Noe Trevino's house and visited with his family. Noe was working in Fresno and couldn't come, but I talked to him on the phone. We talked about how his mom used to breast feed my little brother Ernie when my mom wasn't around. We joked about it and later I called Ernie to give him a hard time. Then I picked up Chulo. The last time I was at his house we sat underneath a shade tree on his well-manicured acreage that ran into the canal, and talked about old times. Juni was there. Remember he's the one I kicked at the park after he kept saying, "Show me Duran." After a few beers we came around to that story and we were all laughing about it.

"I still don't know what you hit me with Duran." Juni smiled. "But I was thinking of stabbing you!"

We all busted out laughing and it was just one of many times we laughed on the night.

Now though, I had a serious look as I stood in the locker room and listened to my brother Bennie as he talked to the team. He is one of the true success stories of the town. He went from being a student at Le Grand, to a teacher, to the principal, and now he's the president of Merced College. He'd asked if I would say a few words to the kids and I was excited to do so. My brothers Jimmy and Michael were there too and they'd said a few words. Bennie talked about what it meant to be a Le Grand Bulldog and wrapped it up. He then introduced me and I was standing in front of the team, a bunch of undersized and scrappy Mexicans.

Earlier they surprised me when they all recognized me. Now they stared at me hanging on every word. I considered what to say and then it came to me. "You guys know what I do right. I work with the best fighters in the world."

They nodded their heads and I continued. "One thing I always do is I look at their eyes and see what kind of confidence they have. I can always tell who is going to win just by looking at their eyes."

As I talked I made a point to look each and every kid in the eyes. "I'm looking at you guys and I see nothing but confidence. I know that you're going to do well and represent the school well. And I know that you're going to win."

They got pumped up and after chanting and jumping around they lined up and one by one they shook my hand. Then they all kind of circled up again and started taking pictures with me. Then this one kid, his last name is Martinez and he wore number eleven, came up to me and said he was going to score a touchdown for me. I thought that was cool and it's crazy because he's the grandkid of Johnny Martinez and Johnny married Lucinda Salcido, Rudy's sister.

He went out and he did score a touchdown and the Bulldogs didn't make a liar out of me. They beat Mariposa by the score of 24-14 and I'm proud to say I was there to see it. During the game I saw people I hadn't seen in 35 or 40 years. I gave a lot of hugs and the younger generations kept coming up wanting to take pictures. I did just like I do with the UFC fans and took a photo and visited with every one of them and it was worth it because many of them told me that I inspired them.

I was sitting with Chulo, and Marcial and his brothers Joey and Carlos, and then in the second half I saw Noe's smiling face heading towards me. "I decided screw work and drove the fifty miles to see you," he said.

It was awesome because the old Jacob, Chulo, Marcial, and Noe quartet was together again. Then Alfred Sanchez's sisters came up and gave me hugs and we talked about the old days as well.

It was such an energizing night getting to see all my friends. After the game we had an after party complete with a band. We talked and joked just as we did when we were kids. I had to get up early to make the five-hour drive to Los Angeles so I had just a couple of beers and didn't get to stay near as long as I would've liked. I said my good byes and headed to my room to get a few hours of sleep.

The next morning I woke up to an alarm, not my Tio Miguel stirring. I didn't hear the breathing of my brothers and sisters either, but the sun, just like it was when I was a kid, was too far away to make a line on the Eastern horizon. I got ready and thought of Disneyland. There was a time when I woke up on the migrant camp dreaming of what it would be like to see it. Now I was waking up not far away from where the camp once stood, and I didn't have to dream, I'd seen so much more than I could have ever imagined back then.

I climbed into my car and the sun was just beginning to break the darkness to the east. In an hour I planned on calling my mom to tell her about the reunion. She lives in San Diego now and gets emotional when I tell her about visiting my dad and uncle.

As I left Planada once again, I thought about that time so long ago when the Greyhound bus took me into the unknown. Back then I didn't know what to expect. I was leaving one life to make another. Now as I passed the Fig Orchards, the old canal, and the miles and miles of fruit fields, I knew exactly what to expect. I was driving away from the world that knew me as Jacob Duran, and driving into the one that knew me as Stitch.

I'm proud to say that I've been blessed to be a part of both and I'll continue being a part of both as long as I can. I

hope that I've inspired some, educated others, and kept a few
in the fight.

Acknowledgments

THE GREATEST HONOR BESTOWED ON ME is the writing of this book. I am proud to say that I have experienced a life that nobody else has. To work with the greatest fighters in the world in Boxing, MMA and Kickboxing and to travel to locations many people could never imagine is a dream come true.

The stories in this book are of such moments.

I have had the support of so many people to include you the fans, fighters and trainers. I have met some of the nicest, yet baddest people on the planet. Something we all have in common is that we all want to be the best at what we do and we all have dreams. My friend Mask had a vision and his motto was to "BELIEVE." Believe because "Dreams do come true."

I have to give special thanks to many people who have believed and supported me. The first is my wife Charlotte, who stood by me when times where tough. She knew I had a special talent and encouraged me to follow my dreams and find my destiny. My children, Carla, Angela, Jacob and Daniel, who understand when I miss birthdays, holidays and football games because of my job.

Special thanks to my mother, Maria Inez, and father, Benjamin, who struggled but never complained as we were growing up. We never knew the meaning of being poor! Their work ethic and discipline is what has made me what I am today.

To my friends and family who often say I inspire them, but in reality, they inspire me.

Dana White, Burt Watson and the UFC crew for giving me the opportunity to show my skills.

Martin McNeil for his pictures and helping with the book and Walter McVeigh for his web skills.

Dorothy Duran for creating the book title and Bas Rutten for writing the Foreword—Bas said it came from his heart and I believe it.

My nephew David Duran, who has a vision greater than his age. Through his vision he created the bad ass TapOut Stitch Signature Shirt and also the cover of this book.

Last but definitely not least, my friend and author of *From The Fields To The Garden: The Life Of Stitch Duran*, Zac Robinson. Zac saw a story in my life and contacted me. We met in Germany for the first time and agreed to write a book together. Our agreement was in the form of a handshake. Putting words into a story is an art in itself. Zac Robinson put my life in words for you to enjoy.

Dreams do come true!

Jacob "Stitch" Duran
Las Vegas, Nevada
August 2010

Acknowledgments
(Cont'd)

I SAW STITCH AT UFC 93 IN DUBLIN, Ireland on January 17, 2009. We didn't talk because I didn't know him at the time. A week later I was sitting on my couch watching Affliction's second MMA event. It was in Anaheim, California and there Stitch was, working the corner and taking care of fighters. I got to thinking that he had to have a bunch of great stories and started researching him.

Sure enough, he had a ton of stories and he also had a great life story. I decided to contact him at the end of February and everything fell into place. Now here we are, a year and a half later with his book.

It's been quite a process and I'm proud of the end result. I contacted Stitch out of the blue and he certainly didn't have to give me a chance at helping him put his life on paper. I'm glad he gave me a shot at it and I hope he's as proud as I am with the book. Along the way Stitch and I have become friends. He is truly a class act and I know we'll remain friends for a long time.

A lot of people helped make this possible. Thanks to my wife Heather and kids, Jace and Xin Ai, for allowing me to spend a lot of time in front of the computer. Thanks to Marshall Zelaznik and Burt Watson with the UFC. I was able to watch Stitch work for a few minutes prior to UFC 99 and seeing him in action was very important for the book. Thanks to Walter McVeigh and Martin McNeil for the technical support and photos and for being good friends. Speaking of friends, to Dave Hagander and my dad Bill Robinson, thanks for reading the rough draft and providing feedback. David Duran's cover design captured the essence of the book and I truly appreciate his efforts. Thanks to the guys at Black Mesa Publishing. They believed in this book right from the start and recognized that Stitch's story is one that had to be told.

Finally, thanks to all those who continue to work so hard to help MMA grow and thanks to the fans who eat up every single aspect of the sport. You're going to love reading about Stitch's life.

Zac Robinson
Ramstein AFB, Germany
August 2010

About the Authors

JACOB "STITCH" DURAN is the best cutman in the business. For over three decades he's been involved in all aspects of combat sports. He's competed, coached, promoted, and educated others on the intricacies of wrapping hands and fixing cuts. Now he focuses on continuing to improve the profession of being a cutman. Stitch lives in Las Vegas, Nevada with his wife Charlotte, but on most weekends you'll find him at a boxing or UFC event somewhere around the globe.

ZAC ROBINSON is the author or co-author of five books and counting, including two books in the MMA IQ series and one in the Sports by the Numbers MMA series. He became an MMA fan in 1993, when during college he and his baseball buddies watched UFC 1. For his day job he is an educator for a Department of Defense school in Germany. Zac is married to Heather and has two kids, Jace and Xin Ai.

Black Mesa Publishing
Florida
www.blackmesabooks.com

Made in the USA
Lexington, KY
27 February 2011